The
EXOTIC WOMAN
in Nineteenth-Century
British Fiction and Culture

A RECONSIDERATION

Piya Pal-Lapinski

University of New Hampshire Press
Durham, New Hampshire

PUBLISHED BY UNIVERSITY PRESS OF NEW ENGLAND

HANOVER AND LONDON

University of New Hampshire Press
Published by University Press of New England,
One Court Street, Lebanon, NH 03766
www.upne.com
© 2005 by Piya Pal-Lapinski
Printed in the United States of America

5   4   3   2   1

Library of Congress Cataloging-in-Publication Data

Pal-Lapinski, Piya.
The exotic woman in nineteenth-century British fiction and culture: a reconsideration / Piya Pal-Lapinski.
    p. cm.—(Becoming Modern)
Includes bibliographical references and index.
ISBN 1–58465–428–7 (cloth : alk. paper)—ISBN 1–58465–429–5 (pbk. : alk. paper)
1. English fiction—19th century—History and criticism. 2. Women and literature—Great Britain—History—19th century. 3. Body, Human, in literature. 4. Exoticism in literature. 5. Women in literature. I. Title. II. Series
PR868.W6P355 2004
823'.8093561—dc22   2004019573

The Exotic Woman in Nineteenth-Century British Fiction and Culture

Becoming Modern: New Nineteenth-Century Studies

SERIES EDITORS:

Sarah Sherman
Department of English
University of New Hampshire

Janet Aikins
Department of English
University of New Hampshire

Rohan McWilliam
Anglia Polytechnic University
Cambridge, England

Janet Polasky
Department of History
University of New Hampshire

This book series maps the complexity of historical change and assesses the formation of ideas, movements, and institutions crucial to our own time by publishing books that examine the emergence of modernity in North America and Europe. Set primarily but not exclusively in the nineteenth century, the series shifts attention from modernity's twentieth-century forms to its earlier moments of uncertain and often disputed construction. Seeking books of interest to scholars on both sides of the Atlantic, it thereby encourages the expansion of nineteenth-century studies and the exploration of more global patterns of development.

Stephen Carl Arch, *After Franklin: The Emergence of Autobiography in Post-Revolutionary America, 1780–1830* (2001)

Justin D. Edwards, *Exotic Journeys: Exploring the Erotics of U.S. Travel Literature, 1840–1930* (2001)

Margaret M. Mulrooney, *Black Powder, White Lace: The du Pont Irish and Cultural Identity in Nineteenth-Century America* (2002)

Edward S. Cutler, *Recovering the New: Transatlantic Roots of Modernism* (2002)

William M. Morgan, *Philanthropists in Disguise: Gender, Humanitarianism, and Complicity in U.S. Literary Realism* (2004)

Patrick H. Vincent, *Elegiac Muses: Europe's Romantic Poetess, 1820–1840* (2004)

Piya Pal-Lapinski, *The Exotic Woman in Nineteenth-Century British Fiction and Culture: A Reconsideration* (2004)

For my parents

Contents

Illustrations

Acknowledgments

I began this book several years ago, and without the intellectual and emotional support of Robert Keefe, a brilliant Victorianist, I could not have given it its present shape. My thanks go to him for his insightful comments. Walter Denny drew my attention to the transgressive aspects of Gérôme and other orientalist artists.

My analysis of the trope of "the exotic woman" has benefited immensely from the suggestions provided by several readers at different stages, including Ann Ardis, Deirdre David, and Patrick Brantlinger, Don Cox and Maria Bachman, (the editors of *Reality's Dark Light: The Sensational Wilkie Collins*), Rohan McWilliam, and the two anonymous reviewers of the manuscript. I thank John Paul Riquelme and the participants of the Modernist Studies Association seminar "Orientalism and Modernism" at the University of Pennsylvania in 2000 for sharing their perspectives on the shifting contours of orientalism.

In the English department at Bowling Green State University, my friends Erin Labbie and Simon Morgan-Russell have provided unfailing support, intellectual insights and witty conversation during crucial stages of this project. Tom Wymer was very supportive of my work during his tenure as department chair. The course releases provided by the department, which lightened my teaching load, were very helpful in negotiating a project of this scope.

Thanks to Erin Douglas for her friendship and enthusiasm for female vampires; and to Keith Powell, who did a fabulous job as my research assistant. My cousin, Romita Ray, curator of prints and drawings at the Georgia Museum of Art, helped me to track the location of some of the paintings in this book.

At the University Press of New England, Phyllis Deutsch has supported this project from the start with invaluable suggestions. Both she and Ellen Wicklum have been fantastic editors. I pause here to pay tribute to the memory of Edward Said, whose work has influenced my thinking profoundly, in terms of the complexity and interdisciplinary reach of his understanding of cultural encounters. I would like to thank Rhys, for believing in my ideas more than anyone else and for our amazing talks, without which I could not have finished this book.

To my grandmother, to my parents, and especially to Scott, I owe more thanks than I can ever express for their love and encouragement.

Prélude: Haunting

rushing from my couch, I dart
And clasp her to my desperate heart;
I clasp—what is it that I clasp?
No breathing form within my grasp,
No heart that beats reply to mine
Yet, Leila! Yet the form is thine!
And art thou dearest, changed so much,
As meet my eye, yet mock my touch?

But shape or shade! whate'er thou art,
In mercy ne'er again depart!
　　　　—Byron, *The Giaour* (1812–13)

In June 1813, Byron published his famous orientalist poem *The Giaour,* the first
in his series of "Eastern Tales." Initially 684 lines, the poem continued to grow
as Byron kept adding fragments, mimicking the sinuous form of the odalisque
in the work of his contemporaries Delacroix and Ingres. The poem's serpentine
contortions seemed to have a life of their own, as Byron himself remarked to
his publisher: "I have but with some difficulty not added any more to this snake
of a poem—which has been lengthening its rattles every month—it is now fear-
fully long."[1] Set during the Ottoman domination of Greece, the poem enacts
the interracial love affair between an exiled Venetian (a Byronic persona and
also the "giaour" or "infidel" of the title) and a harem woman, Leila. Guilty of
miscegenation and having transgressed the bounds of the seraglio, Leila is sewn
into a sack and drowned alive. Later, she returns to haunt the Giaour, whose
one remaining desire is to be haunted. Her spectralization further heightens the
elusiveness of her exotic body; we are never informed about her racial origins,
whether she is Greek or Turkish. This defiant odalisque, this hybrid, trangres-
sive "Eastern" ghost slowly takes possession of the Giaour's mind, hovering on
the margins of representation.

By re-presenting herself through a spectral absence, Leila creates a moment of profound sensory dislocation: what the eye "meets," the point of convergence at which it seeks mastery over its own gaze, is precisely the point at which the gaze breaks down, needing confirmation of Leila's (and by extension, its own) presence through "the touch." The split between the gaze/touch at this moment in the poem posits a troubled relationship between Byron's production of Leila as an exotic female body through a reification of the orientalist gaze and the poem's simultaneous spectralization of Leila to expose (or mock) the limits of that gaze. The need of the Giaour's/Byron's gaze to confirm presence (and mastery) seems to be dependent on a concomitant *desire* to have Leila trick the gaze.[2] Moreover, the Giaour himself, as an exile from "the West," must wrestle with the notion of national identity itself as spectral.

This uncanny intrusion of the exotic female body in a work regarded as a seminal orientalist text, marks the beginning of an equivocal trope that developed throughout the nineteenth century and culminated in the fin de siècle.[3] In 1907, the brilliant Colette caused a sensation at the Moulin Rouge when she appeared with her lesbian lover Missy (the marquise de Morny) in a one-act pantomime called *Rêve d'Egypte* (Dream of Egypt). Dressed in a costume that recalled the man-eating Salomes of the German secessionist artist Franz Von Stuck, Colette played a mummy waiting to be "unpacked" by the "male" archaeologist, played by Missy. The performance provoked an audience uproar; as Colette's biographer Judith Thurman asserts, "the stage was immediately bombarded with coins, orange peels, seat cushions, tins of candy, and cloves of garlic, while the catcalls . . . and shouts of 'Down with the dykes' drowned out an orchestra of forty musicians."[4] By converging archaeological narrative with sapphic spectacle, Colette created a moment drawing its frisson from the unsettling potentialities inherent in the figure of the exotic woman/odalisque. This figure had dominated the landscape of European orientalism for two centuries; strategically manipulating its tropological instabilities—and most intriguingly, its hybridity.

In 1903, the Irish novelist Bram Stoker had published *The Jewel of the Seven Stars,* a startling Gothic novel in which the mummy of the vampiric Egyptian queen Tera stages a series of violent attacks on the British Egyptologist who installs her in his "museum." Surrounded by luxurious objects, Tera is veiled, "swathed with many wrappings of linen," apparently waiting to be unveiled/unraveled by European archeologists. The beauty of her arm and hand is repeatedly fetishized: the "slim, tapering fingers" are "perfect" and the "rich creamy" skin is described as "a dusky fair skin which suggested heat, but heat in shadow." This strangely hybrid body is framed by a remarkable history: we learn that Tera was a cross-dresser and a female monarch who had claimed not only "the privileges of kingship and masculinity," but also the "power to compel the Gods."[5] Her violent attacks on the archaeologist's body recapitulate and reverse the repeated violations of her tomb. In *Jewel,* Stoker's obsession with veiling and unveiling the exoticized, hybrid female body interrupts the archaeological impulse instead of merely reinforcing it. In other words, this body is not merely a part of the collection; it also unravels the collection's ideological compulsions. For Byron, Colette, and Stoker, the modernism of the text/performance emerges precisely at the site of their recognition of the uncanny veiled woman who "returns" as an exotic body that contains within itself the potential failure of the colonial/ imperial museum. This failure is simultaneously seductive, terrifying, and inevitable. Furthermore, I argue that this recognition is a product of, and not a departure from, complex constructions of the exotic woman in nineteenth-century British and French culture.

Since the first fabled reports of travelers returning from visits to the Ottoman and Mughal empires in the sixteenth and seventeenth centuries, European culture has been obsessed by the figure of the odalisque, a term initially used to describe a woman living in a Turkish harem or Indian zenana (literally, "woman of the chamber"), but gradually broadening over the course of the nineteenth and early twentieth centuries to include and connect various iconographies of the exotic woman. Visual and verbal representations of the harem as simultaneously a feminine utopia and a prison, a domestic space and a brothel, and an ethnically complex topos where white, black, and brown female bodies became inextricably entangled, point to the multilayered richness of the trope of the female exotic. Like Leila's body, this phantasmatic trope keeps shifting. Moreover, it is important to recognize that although harem odalisques or women "behind the veil" form a large part of this trope, they did not constitute all constructions of the exotic feminine. Many of these constructions, while rooted in the cultural space of the harem odalisque and sharing some of her attributes, at the same time move beyond these and connect with other peripheral and central spaces in European culture. Let me clarify at the outset, therefore, that for the purposes of this project, "odalisque" does not merely designate the inhabitants of a harem. I use "odalisque" interchangeably with "exotic/exoticized woman" as a fluid, shifting category that transforms itself continually. This book attempts to map nineteenth-century Western constructions of the exoticized female body in terms of complicated geographies that fall between, rather than into, polarized categories in which the "other" woman's body is either sexualized or transformed into an embattled domestic body in need of liberation/ unveiling (polarities that tend to persist in Western media coverage of Islamic cultures today). Most important, I am also using "odalisque" as a metaphor. Many of the female figures I discuss in this book are "white" women who have, for some reason or another, been "exoticized." My argument is that the exotic female body has always been inscribed, to a certain extent, by a kind of métissage, a racial elusiveness.

For Edward Said, in *Orientalism* (1978), Gustave Flaubert's Kuchuk Hanem—an Egyptian almeh (dancer/courtesan) encountered by the writer in his travels through Egypt—is the odalisque par excellence whose "dumb and irreducible sexuality" enables Flaubert both to feminize and fetishize the

Orient. Following Said, the odalisque has developed into one of the central tropes of colonial domination.

This development, however, is partly based on the tendency of some post-colonial critics to read the ambivalences in *Orientalism* rather reductively. In a brilliant passage, Said posits the idea that Kuchuk "and the Oriental world she lived in" also provokes a moment in which Flaubert radically questions the "very idea of the subject."[6] Yet the implications of this are not pursued further; on the verge of linking Kuchuk to a historical moment into which modernity might erupt, *Orientalism* backs off.[7]

Twenty-two years after the publication of *Orientalism*, the specter of the exoticized female body continues to haunt the postcolonial project as an immensely overdetermined trope of empire in nineteenth-century Europe. Postcolonial bodies either rewrite, separate themselves from, or attempt to erase the "abject" and "subjected" body of the odalisque. In orientalist discourse, the term *odalisque* usually evokes a seductive nude or clothed woman posed against an elaborately ornamental interior or harem setting. Although it has been customary to read the odalisque as invariably subordinate to the European (male) hegemonic gaze, this figure may, alternatively, be read as occupying an uneasy, or even radical space in terms of representation, positioned as it is on the thresholds of art and ethnography. Instead of merely reifying the ethnographic impulse and intensifying the hierarchic design of the "exhibitionary complex," I intend to show that nineteenth-century aesthetic constructions of exoticism occasionally produce the body of the odalisque via a dissident textuality that resists closure and implodes the imperatives of ethnography, threatening the coherence of "whiteness" as a racial category.

Additionally, by connecting the exotic woman with cultural anxieties circulating around the courtesan's body, I shall argue that, in some ways, these representations are deeply linked to the tensions arising from the encounter between cultures of female libertinism and emerging bourgeois ideologies of domesticity throughout the nineteenth century. Locating the precise intersections of "power" and "pleasure" within the discourses of Victorian sexuality remains a difficult and delicate enterprise. Although recent work on Victorian sexual ideologies by historians such as Jill Matus, Michael Mason, and Matthew Sweet has sought to revolutionize Victorian studies by drawing attention to the ways in which we "invent" the Victorians for our own purposes, we need to be cautious about replacing one totalizing view of Victorian sexuality by another, about replacing "repressive" Victorians by "permissive" ones. In their respective studies, both Mason and Sweet acknowledge, while exploding monolithic constructions of Victorian sexuality, that Victorian sexual experiences as well as gender ideologies, "far from being an unassailable source of power" were "riven with internal contradictions" and "incoherence." For example, in his investigation of Victorian women's sexual pleasure, Mason admits that although progressive gynecologists separated female orgasm from reproductive capacities in their physiological theories, granting women "the right to sexual pleasure for its own sake,"[8] at the same time, their medical practice may have reflected an intensification of clinical power over women's bodies. And while it is true that Victorian doctors such as Michael Ryan discussed women's right to sexual pleasure, such discussions were usually framed via "legitimate" desire; that is, within heterosexual marriage. What these rereadings of the Victorians reveal, very effectively, are the openings, gaps, and rifts that pervade ideologies of desire in the nineteenth century. The recuperation of Victorian desire in such studies, however, must also be positioned against equally unstable constructions of race and exoticism, together with a scrutiny of the way exoticism in particular functioned to produce tenuous cultural moments that interrupted or transformed the constitution of power relations within nineteenth-century culture.

The most sustained critique of Said has come from the historian John Mackenzie who has used his interdisciplinary analysis of orientalism in art, architecture, music, textiles, and theater to point out Said's failure to recognize that orientalist discourses could "modify and even challenge the West" as a "tool of cultural revolution." (10) Although Mackenzie does not focus primarily on gender, his book lays the groundwork for dismantling any totalizing view of exoticism.[9] In the context of women, an earlier work, Lisa Lowe's comparative study of British and French orientalisms, had picked up on Said's elisions. For Lowe, Flaubert's Kuchuk Hanem and Salammbô represent both racial ambiguity and "irreducible ambivalence," manifested in what Lowe defines as the "descending trope" of the oriental woman.[10] As these figures "descend" staircases, they move from inaccessibility to containment. While Lowe's reading provides a starting point for rethinking this trope within the context of specific historical pressures, it also asserts the ultimate control exerted by Flaubert's narrative over the oriental woman's excessiveness, through repetitions of the trope of descent. Similarly, while Meyda Yegenoglu's *Colonial Fantasies* (1998) scrutinizes the ambivalence of the veil, it betrays a tendency to replicate the notion of an initially split, but ultimately coherent Western subject whose identity is reconstituted through contact with the other woman. Reina Lewis' *Gendering Orientalism* (1996) is also problematic in that female depictions of the oriental odalisque are somehow authenticated and privileged over male ones, sometimes at the expense of domesticating/de-eroticizing the exotic woman. In one of the most recent interventions in this debate, Hollis Clayson provides a more finely tuned reading of the French orientalist painter Henri Regnault's odalisques when she highlights a particular representation of a harem scene as "the specific site of Regnault's struggle to . . . uphold the odalisque as the signifier of Orientalism" and his simultaneous "inability to preserve the harem's erotic atmosphere." I shall return to Clayson's argument later, but even here it is worth noting that although she astutely explores Regnault's exoticism as a struggle to negotiate the internal contradictions of masculinity during the disintegration of the Second Empire, her reading of one of his odalisques as a "ghostly cipher" replicates Lewis's impulse to de-eroticize.[11] Therefore, while acknowledging the extremely valuable insights these studies provide into any reconsideration of exoticism/orientalism, I shall simultaneously distance myself from them in certain ways.[12]

By rereading some of these "unstable bodies," I am not claiming that *all* representations of exotic women are disruptive or dissident. Indeed, I identify such a generalized approach as a problem, a critical blind spot. Similarly, by extending the theoretical limits of tropes hitherto designated as marking the exotic woman or the odalisque, I am not suggesting we empty out these terms completely. Instead, I am arguing that these signifiers are more expansive and more unstable than has been acknowledged and their points of intersection with other nineteenth-century discourses of femininity have been ignored or elided. Even Clayson, in her complex articulation of Regnault's orientalism, claims that the "singularity" of his exotic female bodies is dependent partially on a *separation* from "the typical ideological and aesthetic logic of the obliging solitary odalisque" and on the staging of "sensual disempowerment." The implication persists that if exoticism is to be rehabilitated, it must be distanced from the erotic sphere, from seduction. The exotic bodies I have chosen to examine in this book, while tropologically linked with certain "dominant" configurations of the exotic, also radically alter and strategically decenter them, putting seduction to different uses. But I shall go further: I suggest that the figure of the odalisque/exotic female body within the discourse of Western exoticism resists the notion of a coherent, "typical" ideological or aesthetic logic and contains these possibilities of decentering and distortion within itself; it is *already* "haunted" by them. For instance, in a study of the relationship between Ingres's nude odalisques and modernism, Roger Benjamin claims that "Ingres put the body off-balance—a subtle shift in the composure of the *beau idéal*—and opened up a space that could be exploited to produce a realignment."[13]

By locating the dissonances within *oblique* representations of the exotic woman and looking more closely at those that have been neglected, I hope to move toward a more sophisticated analysis of exoticism, one that has already begun to emerge through recent debates within the field of postcolonial and Victorian studies. The first chapter highlights the dialogue between French and British exoticisms, discussing their cross-fertilizations rather than their divergences.

Because orientalism is a vast and inexhaustible topic, I have chosen to focus mainly on the British novel. Some postcolonial critics have read this genre as being aligned with imperialism, as the dominant literary genre in nineteenth-century Britain.[14] By focusing on the way novels negotiated images of exoticized women, I shall argue that this relationship was a very intricate one. On the other hand, the novel centralized women's bodies and subjectivities in unprecedented ways; the critical debate around the novel as a genre tied it to the female body and to female sexuality.[15]

It is also important to consider the interrelationship between British and French odalisques. In many ways, the odalisque was a French visual trope that filtered through to British audiences and influenced British artists considerably. Furthermore, since most postcolonial critiques of orientalism, including Said's, both overtly and tacitly acknowledge the dominance of the French trope in delineating the visual parameters of the exotic female body, it would be impossible to attempt any reconsideration of this phenomenon in British culture without a look at the French context, together with ways in which it was appropriated, varied, and transformed. For the purposes of this book (and to narrow the scope somewhat) I have concentrated on those images of exoticized women within British culture and fiction that have close links with the French tradition.

My focus on the period from 1800 to 1910 also examines the way shifting constructions of the exotic woman parallel altering configurations of colonialism/imperialism throughout the nineteenth century. Again, it has been customary to see a progressive shift toward a hardening of imperialist attitudes throughout the century. While this may be true of certain official discourses, I would like to avoid such a linear approach to aesthetic representations. The "production" of exoticism was not consistently aligned with the production of a national culture; in fact, exoticism often worked to undermine national identity. I am more interested in the ways aesthetic conceptions of the exotic body responded to and refracted the dominant pressures of particular historical moments, instead of merely mirroring them. As I intend to show, in certain instances exoticism often functioned as an uncanny intrusion into discourses of nation, leading to the "splitting" of the national subject envisioned by Homi Bhabha in a famous essay, "DissemiNation."[16] For instance, in the latter half of the nineteenth century, the medicalization of women's bodies generated new, ambiguous iconographies for the exotic woman. These shift further as they begin to intersect with the developing ideology of the New Woman (as explored in chapter 5). Similarly, the development of forensics and toxicology in the 1860s added a new dimension to discourses of racial "poison."

Whereas several recent discussions of the female exotic focus on the veil and the harem, these motifs are not at the center of my analysis. Along with the construction of the odalisque's body as one "haunted" by the white female nude (and vice versa), I take up a range of representations of exotic women: the female poisoner in Wilkie Collins's sensation novel *Armadale* (1866) (chapter 2); the colonial courtesan and professional dancer in an Indian setting (chapter 3); the vampire and New Woman (chapters 1 and 4); archaeological jewelry design and ornamentation in the work of René Lalique and in Bram Stoker's fin de siècle Egyptian fantasy *Jewel of Seven Stars* (1903) (chapter 5); and the positioning of the Italian opera singer within the London operatic arena in Bulwer-Lytton's *Zanoni* (1842) and Vernon Lee's "A Wicked Voice" (1890) set in Naples and Venice respectively (chapter 6).

I demonstrate the way these bodies impinge on and extend the term *odalisque*, creating a "layered" effect. I also investigate the way they are medicalized (chapters 4 and 5). The courtesan's body in particular has been almost completely ignored in contemporary studies of prostitution, probably because it is so difficult to locate. Judith Walkowitz's foundational work on prostitution in England focuses more on middle- and working-class prostitutes. In a later study of transgressive sexuality in London, Walkowitz discusses the public woman as prostitute, ranging from "the courtesans of St. John's Wood to the elegantly attired streetwalkers who perambulated around shopping districts"; yet the courtesan still remains a shadowy figure on the periphery of her discussion.[17]

Moreover, I argue (in chapters dealing with the decorative arts, medicine, and opera) that constructions of exotic femininity in nineteenth-century British culture must be approached through an interdisciplinary perspective in order to understand their complexity. It must also be pointed out that although postcolonial studies have tended to focus largely on the British colonial experience in India, exoticism in British fiction is not defined solely in terms of this experience. While some of my chapters investigate discourses formulated against the background of colonial India, others deal with alternative exotic geographies such as Egypt, or even Italy. Some of the texts negotiate the way cultural locations are hybridized as well, enacting the superimposition of alien spaces onto domestic ones.

Although this book does discuss the crucial motif of the veil—what analysis of exoticism cannot?—I move away from designating it as the primary marker of a feminized racial otherness, toward the concept of an exotic female body that, as it struggles with the limits of its own plurality, its own hybrid textures, eludes ethnographic systems of classification and prefigures a movement toward radical modernity. By shifting the parameters of this trope as a category of analysis, I aim to "unsettle" our understanding of the dialogue between race and sexuality in nineteenth-century literature and culture. To see the exotic woman as a figure that plays a crucial role in the emergence of certain formulations of modernity instead of as a product of a totalizing gaze, to decouple it from imperial hegemony, is to "encounter the past as an anteriority that continually introduces an otherness or alterity within the present"[18] and to recognize the revolutionary otherness of the past.

1

Designing/Desiring the Exoticized Woman

Geographies of Exoticism

How might we begin to approach definitions of nineteenth-century British exoticism? In the mid-eighteenth century, in his Dictionary (1755), Samuel Johnson had defined "exotick" primarily in terms of what it was *not*: as "foreign, not produced in our own country; not domestick." That which was "domestick" was in turn explained as "belonging to the house; not relating to things publick; inhabiting the house; not wild," accompanied from a quotation extrapolated from Richardson's *Clarissa* (1748–49): "The practical knowledge of the domestic duties is the principal glory of a woman." In this way the dictionary authorized the alliance of the domestic with appropriately socialized feminine energy. *Clarissa* was, of course, the great libertine novel of the eighteenth century, a cultural phenomenon. In the novel, Clarissa is split between her virtue and the tormenting allure of the demonic Lovelace and his exotic libertinism. Lovelace removes her from her fanatical, acquisitive upper-middle-class family and installs her in a brothel, a "torrid zone" where his seraglio of prostitutes masquerade as "respectable" women. The seduction of Clarissa transforms her into an exotic being, a "foreigner" who has no place in English society, whose only option is an extravagantly staged death. Johnson's polarization of the exotic and the domestic with reference to *Clarissa* provides a point of departure for a more careful look at the way the exotic/exoticized woman's body interrupted constructions of domesticity within British culture and reorganized the relationship between public and private spheres.

Furthermore, although the term *exoticism* might include the oriental, it was certainly not limited to it. By foregrounding "exotic" rather than "oriental," I play with the idea of intersections between female bodies that inhabited the *near* as well as the *remote* exotic. One of the most fascinating aspects of visual and verbal representations of exoticized women is the way in which these bodies undermine the notion of sharply drawn territorial boundaries between the domestic and the exotic, while appearing to reinforce them. By the late eighteenth century and throughout the nineteenth, for the British Protestant imagination in particular, the *near exotic* could be mapped as Italy, Spain, Greece, and parts of eastern Europe. The *remote exotic* initially designated Turkey and India, and then gradually North Africa and the Far East. In the early 1800s, Italy and Ottoman Greece were especially problematic; their classical past perceived as being in conflict with the more "barbarous" present. In the case of Greece, Turkish domination had forced the classical and the oriental into an uneasy coexistence.

Gothic fiction consistently reimagined Italy and Spain as haunted by wild *banditti*, degenerate monks, claustrophobic convents where female communities became threatening, "savage" landscapes, decaying castles and homeless, wandering young women. (Many of these tropes, which have since been analyzed as symbols of subversion, were being simultaneously reproduced as part of the depiction of the Orient; in fact, the "Oriental gothic" had developed as a subgenre). Both Ann Radcliffe's *The Italian* (1794) and Matthew Lewis's *The Monk* (1795), the two most important novels of the early gothic tradition, are set in Italy and Spain respectively. From about 1830 onward, renewed interest in the Alhambra in Granada highlighted the Moorish elements in Spanish culture. Initial studies of the architecture and ornamentation of the Alhambra culminated in Owen Jones's analysis of geometric patterns in his influential *The Grammar of Ornament* (1856) and his revolutionary designs for the Crystal Palace in 1850. In fact, it could be argued that the entire discourse of ornamentation in the nineteenth century had extensive links with exoticism. Chapter 3 of this book looks at the connections between exotic ornamentation and disruptive femininity against this background.

Moreover, Venice, which seduced, obsessed, and repelled English tourists and expatriates of the nineteenth century, often functioned as a "contact zone"[1] between East and West. Like the Orient, Venice could accommodate moral and sexual exiles from Victorian society, for whom the certainty that Venice would soon be consumed by its waters intensified its decaying oriental splendor. Charlotte Dacre's Gothic novel *Zofloya, or the Moor* (examined later in this chapter) constructs Venice as such an orientalized location. Most significant, the existence of the "near exotic" erodes the viability and legitimacy of a "stable," or "coherent" Occident. In Stoker's *Dracula* (1897), Count Dracula invades England from eastern Europe. This region was inevitably exoticized, not only due to its significance as a transitional point, but also because of its ethnographic complexity. The Ottoman (Turkish) Empire extended over much of the Balkans until the late nineteenth century and, as European travelers often observed, many of the inmates of Middle Eastern harems were of Circassian/Georgian descent. The vampire was both a symbol and product of this racial indeterminacy. Francis Ford Coppola's 1992 film version of *Dracula* picked up on this by presenting the novel as the ultimate fin de siècle harem fantasy, with Jonathan Harker (Keanu Reeves) being menaced by three vampiric odalisques in Transylvania, followed by Dracula's invasion of London and his recruiting of more women for his vampiric seraglio.[2] Another equivocal Victorian monster, J. Sheridan LeFanu's alluring female vampire, Carmilla, Countess Karnstein, also appears in eastern Europe: "You have heard, no doubt," the narrator of *Carmilla* (1872) informs us, "of the apalling superstition that prevails in Upper and Lower Styria, in Moravia, Silesia, in Turkish Serbia, in Poland, even in Russia; the superstition, so we must call it, of the vampire."[3] The near exotic was, in fact, a dangerously seductive, hybrid cultural space inhabited by erotic, transgressive, and infected figures: exiles, vampires, sexual "aberrants," wanderers, prostitutes, gypsies, criminals, and half-castes.

This is not to deny, however, that there were important differences in attitudes to exoticized "European" cultures versus those of the Near East. In a sense the "oriental elements" in the near exotic were more easily susceptible to being consumed, domesticated, and assimilated. Archaeological discoveries in these areas formed the basis of the foundation of European neoclassical aesthetics in the mid-eighteenth century. The rise of Greek and Italian nationalism in the early nineteenth century was opposed in the minds of many British and French visitors to Oriental "despotism." Nonetheless, what I wish to suggest is that despite certain differences, the Orient, both literally and figuratively, continually *impinged* on these places and attempts to recover their "pure" classical past. In Théophile Gautier's 1852 novella *Arria Marcella*, the ruins of Pompeii are haunted by an orientalized female vampire.[4] Both visually and verbally, this shadowy borderland is what the representations of women examined in this book negotiate.

French and British Odalisques: Visual Iconographies

Throughout most of the nineteenth century, the British experience with the "remote" exotic was largely fueled by their growing imperial involvement with India, whereas the French encounter could be said to be dominated by colonial activities in Algeria that began with the blockade of Algiers in 1827. Yet, geographically, there was also a considerable amount of overlap: for instance, Turkey provided some key tropes shared by both the British and French aesthetic traditions of the odalisque. This sharing initiated a kind of "collaboration." Lady Mary Wortley Montagu's celebrated travel narrative *The Turkish*

Embassy Letters (1763) metamorphosed into Ingres's 1862 *Bain Turc* (The Turkish Bath); the painting evolved out of the artist's involvement with Montagu's famous description of the bath in Sofia. Interestingly, Montagu chooses to locate the "Turkish Bath" not in Istanbul, but in the exoticized Occident, Ottoman eastern Europe. Since both Montagu's and Ingres's narratives of the bath have received considerable critical attention, I shall not discuss them in detail. Because of their central place in the iconography of the exotic woman, however, I evoke them here to foreground the intertwining of British and French orientalisms (in this case separated by almost a century).

Recent revaluations of the Ingres painting have tended to undermine the notion of his re-visioning of the Turkish bath as an overheated pornographic fantasy.[5] It is apparent that the painting maintains a peculiar equilibrium between the serenity of the odalisques and an almost baroque maze of swirling, sensual, interlocking forms. In the *Bain Turc,* Ingres presents us with a labyrinth, a maze of exotic female bodies that, while inviting the male gaze, also threaten to engulf it. Just as the *Bain Turc* continues to resist reductive readings, the perception that Montagu's bath is mainly a feminotopia or a women's "coffee house" obscures the fact that it is also an intensely erotic space in which she can flirt with her desire to "possess" the male gaze: "To tell you the truth, I had wickedness enough to wish secretly that Mr. Gervase could have been there invisible."[6] Another famous example of such a collaboration is that between Byron and Delacroix: the artist painted several different versions of Byron's *The Giaour* (1813), along with *The Death of Sardanapalus* based on the verse drama *Sardanapalus* (1821). For both artists, these images serve as masks for a homoerotic, cosmopolitan persona simultaneously dominated by and dominating the seraglio. Because they play on issues of proximity and distance from the oriental male, they also posit a more complicated intervention in the rhetoric of European exoticism. In 1859, the year of publication of Darwin's *Origin of Species,* another English poet, Edward Fitzgerald, created a similar persona. Assuming the mask of a legendary Persian poet, Omar Khayyam, he published his "translation" of *The Rubáiyát of Omar Khayyám.* The illustrations to this work, completed by the Anglo-French artist Edmund Dulac in 1909, centered on the apparitional figure of the fin de siècle odalisque, embodied successively as an intellectual/erotic companion, wine, death, and youth.

I point this overlapping out in order to emphasize that the formulation of a schematic paradigm that aligns French/male exoticism with the blatantly erotic and British/female representations with a more domesticated version can be misleading. Although Lowe has perceptively argued that crucial distinctions between French and British orientalisms must be acknowledged, in doing so, she encourages this sort of binary approach. For Lowe, the major difference lies in the fact that the French orientalist tradition is rooted in a fantasy of displacement, with French colonialism being "buried beneath literary representations of the Orient as temporally remote, or fictions of a distanced and imaginary oriental world." In contrast, British representations include "an important body of writing that explicitly records the contemporary British experience in the colonies." Lowe also argues that whereas French orientalism is structured in terms of a rhetoric of romantic male desire, British narratives are dominated by paternalism.[7] In so doing, Lowe virtually ignores the oriental-gothic tradition of the British novel in the first half of the nineteenth century, which combines elements of erotic/sadomasochistic desire with phantasmagoric qualities. These motifs continued to surface in different forms throughout the British encounter with the exotic.

For instance, the Napoleonic invasion of Egypt in 1798, which marks in many ways the beginning of French imperialism/orientalism, was thoroughly documented in Dominique-Vivant Denon's *Voyage dans la Basse et Haute Egypte* (1802) and the *Description de L'Egypte* (1809–28), an exhaustive study compiled by a team of scholars involved in the Egyptian campaign. A very precise series of observations stemming from this historical moment, therefore, defined the contours of French exoticism. A product of both desire and paternalism, but also moving beyond them toward a new set of concerns, Denon's obsessive documentation of Egypt's imperial buildings associated Egyptian monumentalism with Napoleonic grandeur. Although ostensibly, as Denon stated in his dedication to Bonaparte, the conquest of Egypt would mythologize the narrative of French imperialism, this decaying and buried monumentalism simultaneously threatened to overwhelm and erase that narrative. The "success" of the Egyptian campaign in this case raised seductive phantoms of inevitable decline. As Denon wrote of their arrival in Thebes:

> This forsaken city, which our imagination can only conjure up through the mists of time, so haunted our imagination that, at the sight of those scattered ruins, the army came to a halt of its own volition and spontaneously began to applaud as if occupying the ruins of this capital had been the purpose of this glorious enterprise, thus completing the conquest of Egypt. I made a drawing of this first sight, as if fearing that this image of Thebes would elude me.[8]

Elsewhere, speaking of the Temple at Dendera, which was partially buried in sand, Denon speaks of being more "agitated than satisfied" and the way in which the beauty and taste of the architecture rivaled Doric, Ionic, and Corinthian styles. The facade of the temple leaves him "too overwhelmed to form a judgement" (259). The exotic sublime, therefore, posed an aesthetic problem that resisted Kant's analysis of the sublime in *Critique of the Power of Judgement* (1790). Reflecting on the "dynamically sublime in nature," Kant had maintained that the experience of the sublime, while producing overwhelming feelings of powerlessness, also revealed "a capacity for judging ourselves as independent of it" and an assertion of the faculty of practical reason. Denon's description of the experience of Dendera puts a twist on the Kantian sublime as the second part of the experience; "the feeling that we have pure self-sufficient reason, or a faculty for estimating magnitude" seems to elude him.[9]

One way to grapple with this "gap" in the exotic sublime was somehow to reduce/reproduce the monument. Egyptian monumentalism also threatened the easy assimilation of the East as chinoiserie: delicate, trivial, and pleasant; imagined in terms of miniature porcelain figurines and rococo interiors. Initiated and supervised by Denon in 1805, the "Dessert Service with Egyptian Views" was created by Sèvres in biscuit porcelain. In addition to pieces that included four sugar bowls with Egyptian heads, two jam jars on lion's paws, two "Egyptianizing" ice cream buckets, and a thirty-three–piece tea and coffee service with Egyptian motifs, a huge centerpiece was constructed. This centerpiece contained elements of the temples of Philae, Dendera, and Edfu, four obelisks, four colonnades, two pylons, and two avenues, each lined with nine ram-headed sphinxes on each side.[10] By recasting Egyptian monumentalism as a French table service in fragile porcelain, Denon and Sèvres created a peculiarly hybrid object that symbolized the anxieties engendered by the "discovery of Egypt." Moreover, the dessert service represented the encroachment of fantastic orientalized detail into the fabric of French material existence on an unprecedented scale, in the process changing the texture of materiality—which simultaneously registered the *elusiveness* of exotic monumentality together with the desire to capture and "fix" it, to *reduce* the experience of the exotic sublime, to bring it into aesthetic discourse. It could be argued that the extravagant, hallucinatory details of Flaubert's *Salammbô* are rooted in this disturbing sense of the shifting boundaries of material objects rather than a displaced fantasy of imperialism.

With the expansion of French colonialism, the body of the odalisque became increasingly linked to luxurious, extravagant decorative objects. In several visual representations, such as Alexandre Cabanel's 1887 *Cleopatra Testing Poisons on Condemned Men*, which I discuss in connection with the female poisoner in chapter 2, the odalisque (Cleopatra) is positioned against a monumental background. Cleopatra occupies the representational space of the odalisque as she lounges on silks and furs, gazing at the dead bodies of her male prisoners. The backdrop for the dying men is based on pillars drawn from Denon's plates of Egypt. Cleopatra's body disturbs the internal coherence of monumentalism, which is conflated with emasculation and subordinated to the odalisque's distant and unrelenting gaze. Although the limp male bodies are clearly "infected" with the "softness" of the fabrics on which the queen reclines, the opposition is not quite so simple. Here languor itself is a veil that conceals deliberation and political power, as well as a calculated eroticism. The most disturbing aspect of the painting, however, is the odalisque's *appropriation* of monumentalism. She somehow manages to inhabit the monumental, which is in turn "haunted" by her gaze.

Although this view has recently invited reconsideration, some feminist critics (most notably Linda Nochlin) have argued that the nineteenth-century male artist's preoccupation with languid, nude odalisques who are "veiled" from the

European male gaze and yet blatantly engage in self-display on the canvas, repeatedly feminized and sexualized the Orient in disempowering ways.[11] Recent studies by Alison Smith, Carol Ockman, and Griselda Pollock, however, have demonstrated that the cultural tensions within which the odalisque/nineteenth-century female nude emerged were more complicated.[12] All exoticized female or male bodies were not displayed in the same way. Representations of the exotic female body in the work of artists like Gérôme and Ingres opened up questions relating to the fragile barriers between domestic and public women, the *limitations* of the male gaze, the celebration of the libertine female body and the infiltration of domestic space by the courtesan. Many of these artists had their works regularly exhibited in London as well.

If we look closely at several French works that spanned the nineteenth century—Ingres's *Grande Odalisque* (1814); Henri Regnault's *Salomé* (1870); and two works by Gérôme, *The Almeh* (1878) and *Woman of Cairo* (1882)—the body of the odalisque is layered, revealing tensions and ambiguities. The *Grande Odalisque* was commissioned by a female aristocrat, Caroline Bonaparte Murat—a practice which was common among aristocratic women in the early nineteenth century. Odalisques commissioned *and* modeled by women such as Paolina Borghese and Madame Recamier allowed them access to modes of self-representation outside the range of what was considered "acceptable" and consolidated their socially and politically powerful roles.[13]

In Ingres's painting for Caroline Murat, the odalisque's languid and coolly indifferent gaze, as she looks over her shoulder at the viewer, establishes her self-sufficiency and her control of the exotic space as well, anticipating Manet's shockingly self-contained prostitute, Olympia. At the same time, Ingres's famous distortion of her body, his "serpentine line," undermines the Praxitelean ideals of proportion and symmetry that were to become so crucial to the construction of the perfect Victorian beauty. Here is the nineteenth-century French critic Paul Mantz on *The Grande Odalisque:* "The author of l'Odalisque has made time and time again figures full of air, round, inflated, that, to use a vulgar comparison, make the mistake of resembling those . . . monsters or animals of goldbeater's skin, light air balloons that imprisoned air fills from all sides, without concern for form."[14]

The Grande Odalisque is sexually desirable and beautiful—but also monstrous, disproportionate, indifferent, and inaccessible. She is disconcerting in her *grande*-ness, her strangely imposing monumentality.

Henri Regnault's critically acclaimed *Salomé* was originally modeled by an Italian peasant woman. Nevertheless, the artist's obsession with renaming the painting (he called it successively *Hérodiade, Femme Africaine, Esclave Favorite,* and *Poétesse de Cordoba)* clearly echoed the metamorphic potential of his exotic subject; a potential expressed through Salomé's defiant and enigmatic smile as she balances a sword delicately on her knee. This defiance is intensified in Gérôme's portraits of almehs. The term *almeh* or *almah,* originally indicating a learned woman, had "degenerated" to mean a female entertainer or prostitute. In *The Almeh*, the boldness and directness of the odalisque's gaze is astonishingly powerful. Although her breasts are seductively half-revealed, her arms are crossed over them, marking spatial limits and suggesting inaccessibility. Despite the ethnographic impulse to locate her in terms of class (on the part of the artist and the spectator), her eroticism is tied to a regal physical presence, a fleshy solidity that is simultaneously tangible and remote. Here again we have the female odalisque appropriating (and dislocating) the representational space of monumentalism. These characteristics also mark the bodies of the two almehs in *Dance of the Almeh* (fig. 1) and *Almeh Performing the Sword Dance* (fig. 2); in the latter, the almeh with the swords collapses the dancer and the warrior. The same inaccessibility and cool, bold gaze are apparent in one of Gérôme's numerous Turkish bath paintings: *Women's Bath* (1889), where an androgynous odalisque confronts the viewer with a remarkable sense of self-possession.

In another work, the "Woman of Cairo" poses provocatively with a cigarette in hand, wearing trouserlike garments, both of which would have been perceived as signs of female transgression in nineteenth-century European culture. The famous courtesan Lola Montez was reprimanded for smoking during her North American lecture tour; women who smoked were perceived as masculine, unruly, and immoral. Similarly, Amelia Bloomer's suggestion in 1851 that women should wear tunics over loose trousers aroused ridicule, derision, and fear. In these works, the exoticized feminine does not merely inhabit the level of erotic fetish; instead, it becomes the vehicle through which cultural anxieties generated by the transgressive female body are articulated and explored. Many of the models were white working-class women and/or prostitutes; their location in terms of class added yet another disturbing layer to these works.

British versions of exotic women were in close dialogue with the visual iconography of the French odalisque, particularly from 1850 onward. The influence of the French odalisque was perceived as a threat to the "purity" of the English as well as the classical Greek nude.[15] As stylistic elements of the French nude began to be imported, British versions of the odalisque became fascinatingly hybrid, resulting in works such as George Watts's *Nude with a Peacock Feather* (oriental-Venetian; fig. 3); Lawrence Alma Tadema's *In the Tepidarium* (classical, but suffused with "oriental" languor); Leighton's courtesan Phryne (accused of being too brown); and *The Light of the Harem* (a monumental "white"/grande odalisque enveloped in cold indifference). In addition, transgressiveness was not confined to the nude. Frank Dicksee's dazzling *Leila* (fig. 4), swathed in brilliant red silks, replicates the bold and insolent gaze of Gérôme's almehs. Joseph Kestner has read Dicksee's Leila (based on Byron) as symptomatic of the artist's imperialist sympathies in his *Discourses*, as a "commodified" "object of male gaze/desire, and thus possession." Yet Leila's oblique yet penetrating gaze, together with her complete self-possession resists such reductive readings. If Byron's Leila in *The Giaour* is presented at least for a part

Fig. 1. Jean-Léon Gérôme, *The Dance of the Almeh*, 1863
(Dayton Art Institute, Dayton, Ohio)

Fig. 2. Gérôme, *Almeh Performing the Sword Dance*, 1875
(Herbert F. Johnson Museum, Cornell University, Ithaca, New York)

Fig. 3. G. F. Watts, *A Study with the Peacock's Feathers*, 1862–65
(Pre-Raphaelite Inc. courtesy of Julian Hartnoll)

of the poem as a victim who has lost control over her own fate, Dicksee's representation is that of a female libertine, not easily categorizable in racial terms, a (French?) courtesan whose corporeal presence extends into the luxuriant objects within the space she inhabits, foregrounding her ability, as Marcel Hénaff puts it, to "libidinize the whole economic process . . . showing that the point of work is sexual pleasure, and the point of production is waste."[16] Since Leila has erotic control over both men and commodities, to her they are interchangeable;

Fig. 4. Frank Dicksee, *Leila*, 1892
(The Fine Art Society, London, and The Bridgeman Art Library)

that is, Leila has the power to consume/commodify men for her own pleasure, as the courtesan does. Hence, her amused, ironic gaze directed at the male viewer demonstrates her awareness of her own positioning within the phantasmagoria of luxury that surrounds her and that she partly controls. *Leila* is a perfect example of an aesthetic fracture in Dicksee's imperialist ideology; her exotic body pointing to a deconstructive impulse within the imperial gaze itself. An extension of this impulse can be found in Frank Cadogan Cowper's 1907 work for the Royal Academy, *Vanity* (fig. 5). This painting is a treatment of an exoticized Italian woman or courtesan who is monumental in her terrifying self-absorption. The mirror, the huge orientalized Renaissance turban, along with the black and gold serpentine forms wriggling along her sleeves, and the highly ornate red and gold barrier over which the woman leans—all serve to highlight the artist's anxiety about the space claimed by her erotic power and her gaze, which approaches the mirror obliquely. Yet her self-reflexiveness, as well as what she sees, remains unknowable because the "body in the mirror" cannot be seen by the viewer. Again, at a crucial point, the viewer's gaze fails.

Unlike the French nudes, the lack of immediately identifiable "oriental settings" in some cases reinforced the racial elusiveness of several of these images.

Fig. 5. Frank Cadogan Cowper, *Vanity*, 1907 (Royal Academy of the Arts, London)

Intriguingly, this development paralleled the growth of the empire. Before the emergence of this visual tradition, the combination of eroticism and transgression in the tradition of the French odalisque could be found instead in fictional representations of exoticized women, such as Byron's *The Giaour* and Charlotte Dacre's *Zofloya* (discussed in this chapter).

In the early 1800s, British visions of India in the visual arts were primarily recorded in terms of the picturesque. While the French campaign in Egypt tended to emphasize the monumental and the massive, the British in India were more interested in the scope/range of the colonial gaze and its efficiency as an organizing framework to "manage" the colonial experience. Thomas Daniell and William Daniell's *Oriental Scenery* (1795–1808), which comprised 144 aquatints of Indian architecture, was followed by a spate of other panoramic views that became even more popular with the invention of photography. The panoramas (which often included imperial architecture in Indian cities) produced a sense of panoptical space by means of which the colonizer's gaze could establish control. The ordered delicacy and translucence of the Daniells' picturesque views continually kept the encroaching sublime at bay; *Oriental Scenery* contained a profusion of decaying, dark, and labyrinthine temple interiors, "palaces crumbling into dust, every one of which could tell many tales of royal virtue or tyrannical crime, of desperate ambition or depraved indolence," and "myriads of vast mausoleums" that were domesticated via the enforced tranquillity of the picturesque.[17] Even the violence of the sati (or suttee), the Hindu practice of burning widows, was subordinated to the picturesque. For female viewers in particular, the picturesque was considered "appropriate"; for instance, Englishwomen in colonial India often retreated into the picturesque to diffuse dramatic encounters with otherness.[18]

One area of Indian architectural ornamentation that undermined the stability and severity of the picturesque were the temple nudes. Fragments of sculptures from Indian temples found their way into Charles Townley's collection (eventually given to the British Museum) in the eighteenth century. These sculptures disturbed the picturesque by their profusion of voluptuous curves (challenging the smoothness of the classical line) and blatant eroticism. Many of the nudes were goddesses, and therefore connected explicitly with female power and agency. Although there was no established tradition of the female nude in British culture prior to 1850, colonial travelers were already encountering the exotic female body in these forms. Reactions ranged from disgust and horror to attempts on the part of scholars and artists to connect Indian and Greek eroticism.[19]

French artist Gustave Moreau's surrealistic painting *Salomé Tattooed* (fig. 6), was heavily indebted to Anglo-French archaeological discourses on India and Egypt. The unfinished painting represents Salomé dancing before Herod, with patterns tattooed on her body. The tattoos and background of the painting combine elements of Indian and Ceylonese temple architecture, Greek manuscript

Fig. 6. Gustave Moreau, *Salomé Tatooed (Salomé tatouée)*, 1874
(Musée Gustave Moreau, Paris)

illumination, and Egyptian art. One of the most transgressive moments in Western cultural iconography is mediated through an aggressively hybridized body that displays a bewildering maze of cultural inscriptions. Moreau transforms Salomé into an odalisque-courtesan whose body is impossible to read or place within any framework of cultural signification, a spectral body with slippery contours. Speaking possibly of this painting, Moreau mentioned to a friend that he had developed "a costume for Salomé" out of "mysterious tracings and cabalistic meanderings" that he had "retrieved ... unable to sleep, from the realm of the Invisible (162)."[20]

British constructions of harem women in Egypt and Turkey, even before the exotic nude took off, also punctured the picturesque in interesting ways. John Frederick Lewis's painting *The Hareem* (fig. 7) was exhibited in London in 1850 and attracted considerable critical attention. The superficial "domestic" attributes of Lewis's seraglio interiors have distracted commentators from their more ambivalent qualities. In Lewis's art, domestic spaces are carefully eroticized through the manipulation of the female gaze. Although Lewis tended to emphasize the communal activities of the harem, receiving visitors, feeding animals, intercepting letters, *The Hareem* catches women in the problematic act of looking rather than being looked at. Here, Lewis presents a scene in which a Nubian eunuch shows off a naked female slave to a pasha and the other women of the harem. The complexities of harem politics are captured through the enigmatic and penetrating gazes of the women, directed at each other, at the pasha, at the naked woman, encircling and overpowering that of the "dominant" male figure. Shortly after this painting was exhibited in London, Charlotte Brontë wrote *Villette* (1852), in which the heroine Lucy Snowe is forbidden to look at a French salon painting of an odalisque on the grounds that it is "unsuitable" for a single woman to gaze at an eroticized female body. It is possible that Brontë may have viewed the Lewis painting on an 1850 visit to London. If so, the erotic power of the female gaze that lurks beneath the veneer of domesticity in Lewis's vision of the odalisque may have informed her investigation of the limits set around women's dangerous acts of looking in *Villette*.[21]

Another British nineteenth-century woman novelist and traveler also produced a subtly erotic rather than the "domesticized" version of the harem. In 1835, Julia Pardoe, the daughter of an English army officer, began to travel extensively in Turkey as part of a recuperative process for a medical condition that was believed to be consumption. A travel narrative based on her experiences in Turkey, *The City of the Sultan* (1837), uneasily negotiates the picturesque, which is repeatedly interrupted by the erotic power and striking personalities of the "exotic" women she encounters within the confines of the seraglio. *The City of the Sultan* records Pardoe's ambivalence by alternating a picturesque/ethnographic focus on the accumulation of details related to bodies, ornamentation, domestic interiors, and food with attempts to formulate a rhetoric of rapture: a female erotic gaze that is powerfully drawn to the women Pardoe meets. At first

Fig. 7. John Frederick Lewis, *The Hareem*, 1849 (Private Collection)

she is puzzled by the harem's racial indeterminacy: "The ladies were lying upon cushions, buried up to their necks under the coverings of the tandour; and, as they flung them off to receive us, I was struck with the beauty of the daughter, whose deep blue eyes, and hair of golden brown, were totally different from what I had expected to find in a Turkish harem."

Later, Pardoe, indulging in rapturous detail, describes the "magnificent Sairyn Hanoum," a "dark" twenty-nine-year-old female:

> She was dark, very dark: almost a Bohemian in complexion; but you saw the rich blood coursing along her veins, through the clear skin; her eyes were like the storm-cloud, from which the lightening flashes at intervals . . . and her brow—it was a brow which should have been circled by a diadem, for it was already stamped with Nature's own regality. She was tall, even stately . . . and the proud expression that sat upon her lip . . . dilated her thin delicate nostril. Her costume was as striking as her person; and, had she studied during a century how best to enhance her beauty, she could never have more perfectly succeeded.[22]

Sensing the way in which the exoticized woman focuses her own erotic lens and allows her to experience and indulge erotic/aesthetic sensibilities, Pardoe defends her use of hyberbole in the passage following this description. The "excess" of the harem has infiltrated and shifted the Englishwoman's ways of looking. Another "rapture" involves the Georgian women, whose "intellect and majesty" confuse Pardoe. Throughout the narrative, Pardoe struggles with the complex power dynamics of the harem: how can such beautiful, intellectual, majestic women submit to oppression? It is at these moments that Pardoe's text frustrates its own ethnographic intentions and becomes something other than "a standard guide" to Turkey: "You involuntarily ask yourself if they can indeed ever be slaves; and you have some difficulty in admitting the fact, even to your own reason" (213).

While Pardoe's erotic gaze has to navigate through the onslaught of the picturesque ("appropriate" subjects such as furnishings and domestic rituals), her "organizing" or "totalizing" gaze threatens to be overwhelmed by the almost hallucinatory piling up of detail and dissolved by its immersion in the textures of the material objects she lingers over. One gets a sense that the seductive "luxury and indolence" that these objects represent (and that the picturesque attempts to regulate), continually reproduces itself with a vampiric, inexorable fecundity.

By the latter half of the nineteenth century, designing/desiring the exoticized female body within both the British and French tradition involved the repetition (with variations) of six major tropes not merely restricted to harem interiors: (1) an infectious, erotic atmosphere in which "languor" or "lassitude" predominated; (2) a rhetoric of ornamentation and excess with emphasis on the textures of material objects; (3) a display of racially ambiguous, intertwining female bodies marked by a diversity of skin tones; (4) women (either individually or collectively) lounging, reclining, or performing in public and/or private spaces; (5) an interlocking series of gazes, ranging from the absent/unfocused to the ironic and openly defiant; and (6) women either exhibiting themselves or being exhibited. Ethnographic and fictional discourses quoted and transformed these tropes in various intriguing ways.

Hybridizing the Courtesan

In fact, the kind of luxury that had become a defining feature of the exotic woman echoed the lifestyle of the European courtesan. Jean-Léon Gérôme exhibited his sensational painting *Phryne before the Tribunal* (fig. 8) in London in 1866. As one of the leading Academic orientalist artists of the nineteenth century, Gérôme's work, from the mid-1800s onward, influenced both British and French images of exotic women considerably. Gérôme's paintings on classical subjects, however, are rarely discussed in an "oriental" context, although they frequently reveal shared tropes. In *Phryne*, the famous classical courtesan occupies the same representational space as many of Gérôme's odalisques. The subject matter of the painting involves the courtesan on trial for her disruptive exhibitionism during a religious event. The historical Phryne had impersonated Aphrodite by provocatively bathing in public at the festival of the Eleusinia. At

Fig. 8. Jean-Léon Gérôme, *Phryne Before the Tribunal,* 1861
(Hamburger Kunsthalle)

her trial, she was acquitted after her lawyer exposed her body to the jury. By depicting the moment at which Phryne is dramatically unveiled, the painting assaults the collective male gaze. The facial expressions of the judges (signifying loss of control) were unsettling to viewers when the painting was exhibited in London.[23] If Phryne's unveiled, excessive, unruly body is aligned with Gérôme's odalisques as a classical/oriental hybrid, it can be seen as posing serious challenges to the coherence of the (orientalist) male gaze, as representing that gaze as already fractured and on the point of dissolution. Phryne averts her own eyes, converting her body into a text that both invites and resists "specific" readings. The painting not only elides the classical and oriental in disturbing ways; in its extreme self-consciousness it interrogates the shifting configurations of power within an orientalist aesthetic.

My discussion of Gérôme's *Phryne* foregrounds the alignment of the courtesan or demimondaine and the various manifestations of the exotic woman. The "hybridization" of the courtesan's body had important implications in emerging ethnographic as well as domestic and aesthetic discourses. To a certain extent, the production of the hybridized courtesan was generated by barely articulated anxieties about the fragility of "disciplinary mechanisms" of empire and ethnology; it paradoxically served both to reinforce and dislocate these structures, often within the parameters of the same text. Moreover, the body of the hybrid odalisque-courtesan represented a peculiar threat within the discussions of hybridity and fertility in nineteenth-century ethnographic theory.

I am of course using the term *hybrid* partially in terms of Homi Bhabha's for-mulation. For Bhabha, hybridity is a "problematic of colonial representation" produced by ambivalent encounters between the colonizer and colonized, in which "other 'denied' knowledges enter upon the dominant discourse and estrange the basis of its authority—its rules of recognition."[24] Yet Bhabha does not really investigate the possibility of alliances, affinities between the "colo-nized" and the "estrangements" already present within the colonizing culture. Bhabha's discussion stops short of a rigorous consideration of the effects of hybridity (either literal or figurative) on actual, historicized bodies. It does not pay much attention to how multiple versions of hybridity inscribed on differ-ent bodies may be staged in revolutionary ways. Those occupying peripheral spaces within the colonizing nation might mobilize themselves not only through alliances with the exotic, but also through performances of their own exoticism. I am referring here to Western subjects within the demimonde: a "half-world" made up of "domestic" poisoners, courtesans, prostitutes, bohemi-ans, vagrants, and sexual nomads, whose very identity was constituted through ambiguity as they straddled different worlds. These subjects continually inter-vened in and disrupted the totalizing tendencies of imperialism, nationalism, and ethnography through a series of rebellious gestures. In the novel, they are often presented as possessing exoticized, dissident bodies that radically alter the meaning, effect, and implementation of dominant discourses.

"Hybridity" has become a vexed question in postcolonial studies, following Robert Young's contention in *Colonial Desire* that by privileging hybridity we maintain the idea of "pure" categories and replicate the imperatives of Victo-rian ethnology.[25] Young overlooks the fact that the difference between the deployment of the term by Victorian ethnologists and postcolonial scholars lies in the nature of their political projects and the *uses* to which they put their respective discussions of hybridity. In a recent attempt to wrestle with the apparent impasse posed by Young, R. Radhakrishnan has pointed out that "national sovereignty" and "hybrid 'impurity'" may be "mutually constitutive"; that is, constantly defined against each other, and that we must pay careful attention to the way hybridity can be both "acknowledged and sublated within the higher plenitude of a national consciousness." A way around this might appear if we combine a sense of the nation as already internally dissonant, "het-erogenized from within"[26] with an awareness that "hybridity" is a sliding signi-fier that continually moves between dissidence and assimilation.

To elaborate further on the way the orientalized odalisque and the European courtesan morph into each other, I shall draw on Maurice Merleau-Ponty's idea of "intercorporeities" to rethink the problem of hybridity. In *The Visible and the Invisible*, Merleau-Ponty envisions the reciprocities that pass between bodies through the trope of one of our hands touching the other while it is palpating something else. This creates a kind of reversibility, a shared tactile conscious-ness: "If my left hand can touch my right hand while it palpates the tangibles, can touch it touching, can turn its palpation back upon it, why, when touching the hand of another, would I not touch in it the same power to espouse the things that I have touched in my own?"[27]

Merleau-Ponty extends this reversibility to vision, contending that the "relation of the visible" that constitutes one as "seer" is a field or "circle" that also "forms" the one who gazes. This "coiling over of the visible upon the visible, can traverse, animate other bodies as well as my own (140)." Thus an intertwined corporeal landscape, a "consciousness" that intersects with a "cluster of consciousnesses . . . adherent to its hands, to its eyes" (141) is always emerging. Merleau-Ponty's reconceptualization of the "flesh" as a product of "overlapping and fission, identity and difference" (142) is particularly relevant to the way racially distinct bodies merge and intersect within exotic spaces. For example, courtesans continually flirted with these intercorporeal landscapes, which became a symbol of their libertinism, extravagance, and ability to reinvent themselves. As early as 1724, Daniel Defoe's courtesan Roxana had adopted Turkish dress and the name of one of the most powerful women in Ottoman history to construct her own identity.[28] A contemporary biographical essay on the nineteenth-century British courtesan Lola Montez dwelt at length on her racial origins: "the fountain-head of the blood which courses in the veins of the *erratic* Lola Montez is Irish and Moorish-Spanish—a somewhat combustible compound it must be confessed."[29] The bedroom of the courtesan Marguerite Gautier, in Dumas's *La Dame Aux Camélias,* is done up in Persian style, anticipating the lavish Moorish-style bathroom of the real-life La Paiva.[30] In Balzac's *Splendeurs et misères des courtisanes* (1838), the courtesan Esther is both racially and figuratively a hybrid being. Esther's face reflects her mixed origins, which are "betrayed by the oriental formation of her Turkish lidded eyes." Onto the surface of her exoticized body, Balzac maps his theory of inherited, acquired racial characteristics. Appropriately, she is kept in a house where she is watched over by two servants aptly named Asia and Europe. "Asia" is "a monster," resembling "quaint beings which figure on Chinese screens," but at the same time a shape shifter, "one of those Parisians who were born to belong to whatever country they choose," whereas "Europe" is the quintessential woman of the city, presenting "a face wearied with Parisian corruption . . . at once part-time street girl and stage extra."[31] In different contexts, this intercorporeity/intercorporeality could be voluntarily assumed, appropriated, or even compelled.

To draw attention to the complicated positioning of this hybrid "intercorporeity" between the odalisque and the demimondaine within ethnological texts, I shall examine two key texts of the 1860s: Henry Mayhew and Bracebridge Hemyng's construction of a massive "ethnography of prostitution" in *London Labour and the London Poor* (1861–62); and Paul Broca's influential work, *On the Phenomena of Hybridity in the Genus Homo* (1864). Although these two texts are not usually read in conjunction, I would argue that such a reading is essential in order to engage with the exoticized female body as a multilayered construct of colonial desire instead of a mere symbol of colonial hegemony.

Unlike William Acton's 1851 work, *Prostitution,* which was geographically confined to London and Paris, Mayhew and Hemyng's study of British prostitutes in nineteenth-century London firmly linked prostitution and exoticism by initiating a lengthy anthropological discussion of prostitutes, courtesans, and other "public" women in a wide variety of racial and cultural contexts that included ancient Egypt, Greece, and Rome, the Arab world, and India, along with modern European nations. The study began with an attempt at a general definition of the elusive "prostitute class," which in both Britain and France, could be subdivided into a dizzying series of hierarchical categories dependent on class, motive, and economic status. Striving to come up with an overarching category that would contain different "types" of prostitution, *London Labour and the London Poor* broadened the definition of prostitution to include any expression of excessive female desire outside (or even within) marriage, using the example of "sanctioned" prostitution in Persia: "Prostitution, then, does not consist solely in promiscuous intercourse, for she who confines her favours to one may still be a prostitute; nor does it consist in illicit and unsanctioned intercourse.... In what, then, may it be asked, does prostitution consist? It consists, I answer, in what the word literally expresses—putting a woman's charms to vile uses."[32]

Beginning their anthropological survey with ancient Egypt, Mayhew and Hemyng conclude that female public performers, especially the almehs, although not officially designated as prostitutes by Egyptian culture, must have been so due to their exhibitionism. The Egyptian almehs "played furiously all kinds of music, flung off their garments, challenged the women of the town with gross insulting language and outraged decency by their gestures and postures" (44). Moving onto ancient Greece, the study acknowledges the tenuousness of the line between prostitutes and respectable women (their "mingling" at the baths and the instructions given by courtesans to wives on sexual matters). Yet the authors are also quick to assure the reader that although prostitution was interwoven with Greek civilization at all levels, and many courtesans displayed "brilliancy of intellectual qualities" and considerable learning, they were, at the same time, "common whores." Prostitution is also connected explicitly with the decline of the Roman Empire, when distinctions between the "regular harlot" and the "unrecognized prostitute" became blurred. In the early stages of the empire, chastity was a "peculiar Roman virtue" and prostitutes were usually foreigners, boundaries between them and "reputable women" kept intact (54). The taxonomy of prostitution at this point is mapped onto narratives of the growth and decline of an imperial culture that, in many ways, served as a model for Britain in 1862.

Dividing the work into six sections, "Prostitution in Ancient States," "Prostitution Among the Barbarous Nations," "Among the Semi-Civilized Nations," "Among the Mixed Northern Nations," "In Civilized States," and "Prostitution in London," Mayhew and Hemyng's project attempts to set up a panoptical time scheme; what Anne McClintock has called "an image of global history consumed—at a glance—in a single spectacle from a point of privileged invisibility."[33] The prostitute's body levels some of these cultural distinctions: French prostitutes for instance, exhibit a "lassitude" attributed to Turkish women. Paradoxically, the "hybridized" prostitute body that gradually emerges from this discourse contains within itself the potential failure of this panoptical hierarchy. Claiming that polygamy is practically synonymous with prostitution, Mayhew and Hemyng point out that whereas prostitution is rampant in "barbarous" and "semi-barbarous" nations, at times "systematized" and at others, "loose and scattered," progressive nations are marked by the separation of prostitutes from respectable women into a separate and distinct class. "Progress" is defined by and through these kinds of distinctions. Yet, in their discussions of Britain and France, these distinctions become profoundly unstable as the exoticized prostitute body moves in and out of various social classes. Particularly elusive and dangerous are the "seclusives" or courtesans in London, divided into "kept mistresses" and "prima donnas" who cannot be controlled by the metropolitan police. And then there are those clandestine prostitutes who "eventually become comparatively respectable and merge into the ocean of propriety" (214). The prostitute's relentless capacity for infiltration anticipates the endless circularity of the anthropological project. Moreover, exotic attributes such as "lassitude," appetite," and excess, when grafted onto the European courtesan's body, provide the means for staging such infiltrations.

Furthermore, the hybridization of the prostitute body has important implications when read against the work of Paul Broca, secretary general of the Anthropological Society of Paris and honorary fellow of its counterpart in London. Broca's *On the Phenomena of Hybridity*, published by the London Anthropological Society in 1864, became central to discussions of hybridity and racial theory in the latter half of the century.[34] Broca defined different degrees and *types* of hybridity, beginning his analysis by dismantling the argument put forward by the French racial theorist Gobineau that "the crossing of races constantly produces disastrous effects, and that sooner or later, a physical and moral degeneration is the inevitable result." According to Broca, "certain intermixtures" between "allied" races were perfectly viable, and even desirable. These Broca labeled as instances of "eugenesic" hybridity, whereas "other intermixtures" were notably inferior, tending toward infertility and ultimate extinction. The eugenesic nature of the union, then, depended to a large extent on fertility. Although the level of fecundity in mixtures between allied races may not be "absolutely equal to that of individuals of pure blood," as long as "the relative sterility did not descend beneath the degree when the sterility becomes absolute" hybridity remains eugenesic. Bringing Broca's argument to bear on contamination anxieties about the blurring of boundaries between exoticized courtesans and respectable women, therefore, reveals that there is more at stake.

The lassitude and languor of the odalisque/prostitute, resulting from excessive self indulgence, become the hallmarks of a "seductive" rather than a "productive" body. Not only does this body realign the parameters between "proximate" and "distant" species (being the point of convergence of a variety of racial attributes), sexual desire for this body does not result in eugenesic reproduction. Rather than perpetuate the race, the intercorporeity of the hybridized odalisque/prostitute threatens to reproduce itself endlessly and infectiously.

Excess and Languor

The body of the exotic woman (both visually and verbally) is inevitably marked with languor. This is a key trope that surfaces, in some degree or another in practically every representation of exoticism examined in this book. Instead of reading it as a symptom of passivity, I propose a reading of languor as a symptom of defiance. A languorous body by definition, is one that has given itself over to leisure and excess instead of work, disassociating itself from production. In the late eighteenth century, "languor" was linked to "sensibility," especially in the gothic novel.

G. J. Barker Benfield's analysis of the cult of "nerves" has shown that the conceptualization of sensibility in the mid to late eighteenth century was fundamentally linked with ways of perceiving the body; in particular, the differences between male and female bodies.[35] Sensibility was an emotional, psychological, and intellectual state characterized by an extreme responsiveness arising from a delicate nervous system coupled with an excess of imaginative or cerebral activity, manifesting itself in physical symptoms such as illness, fainting spells, palpitations, and tears. Women's nerves were considered to be more susceptible to attacks of sensibility, which were often used to ward off threatening sexual situations. To illustrate this point, Benfield cites the repeated fainting fits of Richardson's Pamela, which allow her to escape Mr. B's overtures. Sensibility could thus be transformed into a practical weapon of resistance, as a mask to gain control of a situation (as we shall see later in my discussion of Sheridan LeFanu's *Carmilla*).

In Ann Radcliffe's pioneering gothic novel, *The Mysteries of Udolpho* (1794), sensibility is aligned with disease and languor. The heroine's mother dies of a disease marked by "heavy languor" and Emily herself is often subject to fainting spells and languorous depression. Her father also succumbs to the "languor of illness." Rather than associating the languor of sensibility with weakness however, Radcliffe uses this concept to give a fresh twist to a shared trope in the discourses of gothicism and exoticism: the veil. It is possible that Radcliffe might have been familiar with Montagu's *Turkish Embassy Letters*. Montagu comments on the ambiguity of the veil, pointing out the opportunities it offers for masking one's intentions, blurring identity, and making the female body indecipherable. *Veiling* her resilience through sensibility, Emily makes use of both to gain time, manipulate situations, and invent strategies for survival. Assaulted by the despotic Count Morano in her bedroom at Udolpho, she uses the body language and the intertwining discourses of sensibility/languor to confuse his responses; she plays for time. While sinking trembling on a chair, she mentally calculates the distance to the door and the possible effect of an attempted escape on her antagonist. In this case, Emily's manipulation of her "languor" allows her to equivocate.[36]

The "languorous" body is thus a "seductive" body in Jean Baudrillard's sense, in that it can manipulate or reverse signs. Baudrillard defines "seduction" as the infinite play or reversibility of signification, and furthermore, one that offers an escape from or an alternative to the "productive model" of the body within a capitalistic mode of production: "It is capital, that in a single movement gives rise to both the energizing body of labour power" and a "sexual body . . . where everyone is assigned a certain amount of capital to manage."[37] In the nineteenth century, the languor of the exotic body becomes especially significant in interrogating the twin drives of capital and empire and their support structure, the ideal of productive domesticity.

Two years after the exhibition of *Phryne,* in 1868, Eliza Lynn Linton—novelist, journalist, and conservative feminist—published her notorious essay "The Girl of the Period" in the *Saturday Review.* Her subject was the destruction of "ideal womanhood" through female excess, extravagance, and self-display. At the core of this ideal, Linton asserts, lies woman's role as domestic angel, exemplified by a woman who is "neither bold in bearing nor masculine in mind": "a girl who, when she married, would be her husband's friend and companion, but never his rival . . . who would make his house his true home and place of rest, not a mere passage-place for vanity and ostentation to go through; a tender mother, an industrious housekeeper, a judicious mistress."[38] Interestingly, Linton proceeds to use metaphors of race and foreignness to deplore the shift away from this ideal: "Of late years we have . . . given to the world a *race* of women as utterly unlike the old insular ideal as if we had created another *nation* altogether" (my italics). Linton's analogy is telling, as it links transgression of the boundaries of Victorian domesticity with exoticism. What Linton fears is *excess,* especially the excessive indulgence and manipulation of the female body through dress and the cosmetic arts. Through this excess, the girl who "dyes her hair" and "paints her face" sacrifices "cleanliness, decency, modesty, propriety." The body begins to border on the grotesque, creating "monstrosities . . . so soon as she begins to manipulate and improve." Most frightening, for Linton, is the resemblance to exotic beings who inhabit the peripheries of Victorian culture: the black woman, the lunatic, and the courtesan, as the girl of the period "thinks herself all the more beautiful the nearer she approaches in look to a maniac or negress" or imitates the dress of the demimondaine. Linton sees the prospect of respectable women becoming indistinguishable from courtesans as dangerous, precisely because it threatens to collapse categories better kept separate.

That most popular and authoritative manual for Victorian wifehood, Isabella Beeton's *Book of Household Management* (1854), prescribed avoidance of excess in all matters. Beeton stresses the importance of rising early, frugality and economy in personal as well as household expenditures, together with good temper and the absence of self-indulgence. Friendships, dress, and even conversation must be carefully circumscribed, lest women succumb to vanity, gossip, or the urge to express grievances and disappointments. Excess leads to domestic chaos—and languor. If the mistress sleeps late, the servants become "sluggards."[39] When Victorian doctors discussed women's health, they continued to be obsessed by the idea of excess. The word frequently crops up through the works of widely read nineteenth-century physicians like William Acton, Edward Tilt, and Michael Ryan.

Ryan's *Philosophy of Marriage* (1837), which was reprinted several times, dispensed medical and domestic advice for the lay reader. After a fairly sensible warning to pregnant women to avoid "high seasoned foods, and the *excessive* use of wines," Ryan lapses into a diatribe against other types of excess. Public places are to be shunned: "Balls, theatres, crowded assemblies, all public sights, exhibitions, and seeming dangers . . . should be avoided," as should "violent passions. . . . Frights, longings and despondency . . . may retard the growth of certain parts of the infant." Significantly, in Victor Hugo's poem "Phantoms," one of a series of exotic poems, *Les Orientales* (1829), a Spanish woman dies of "the breathless, wild delight" of "balls, dances—dazzling balls." Hugo warns his female readers of the dangers of indulgence: "O maidens, whom such festive fetes decoy!/Ponder the story of the Spanish maid." In addition, according to Ryan, the act of reproduction, from inception to conclusion, is incompatible with "*excessive* exertion of mind" as "*men* of great genius have the fewest children." (my italics). Because the productive body is the prerogative of women; it has to be separated from intellectual production—the happy product of permissible masculine excesses in "imagination, genius and courage."[40]

As I suggest in my references to Ingres and Gérôme, nineteenth-century images of exoticized female bodies could be positioned subversively while simultaneously recapitulating certain fantasies for *both* male and female viewers. For instance, female subjects such as Cleopatra, Judith, Salomé, and the Sphinx, with their startling combination of aggression and sexual power, were considered to be off-limits for female artists, who were expected to restrict themselves to appropriately domestic subjects.[41] In the hypersensual world of orientalist art, women seemed to deliberately flout the advice of Victorian marriage manuals and conduct books. They were often depicted as adorning themselves, dancing, conversing, smoking, bathing, eating, reclining languidly; in other words, celebrating their bodies, luxuriating in shared feminine rituals of excess. What is also remarkable about many of these odalisques is their utter indifference to the gaze of the viewer, a curious awareness of their own impenetrability.

The odalisque-courtesan's taste for languor was also vampiric. In Joseph Sheridan LeFanu's 1872 vampire narrative centering on an eastern European female vampire, Carmilla's languor and illness are her defining characteristics from the beginning. Her victim, Laura, first encounters her as a "a young lady, who appeared to be lifeless . . . apparently stunned, but certainly not dead"(80). Later, she describes Carmilla's movements as "languid—*very* languid." Confused by Carmilla's sexual advances, Laura speculates as to whether she is a man in disguise, but dismisses this notion: "there was always a languor about her, quite incompatible with a masculine system in a state of health" (91). Yet it is a "bodily languor," in no way diminishing her intelligence and capacity for stimulating conversation. Her "exhaustion," is clearly tied to her lesbian sexuality as well as her vampirism; when Laura falls ill as a result of her nightly encounters with Carmilla, the latter's "strange paroxysms of languid adoration" increase.

The text encourages the perception of Carmilla as an exoticized woman through other related motifs. The room that Carmilla occupies contains a tapestry "representing Cleopatra with the asps to her bosom . . . gold carvings . . . rich and varied colour" (85). Visually, Cleopatra was often represented as both languorous and vampiric. Indeed, Carmilla is interchangeable with Cleopatra, in the sense that the inertia of both masks intelligence, strength, and eroticism. For Carmilla, disease and languor not only indicate sexual and intellectual satiation; they also become effective strategic devices to manipulate her observers, lulling them into a sense of false security. Her (apparent) weakness masks her aggression and homosexuality, putting her in control: "People say I am languid; I am incapable of exertion; I can scarcely walk as far as a child of three years old; and every now and then the little strength I have falters, and I become as you have just seen me. But after all I am very easily set up again; in a moment I am perfectly myself. See how I have recovered" (99). Languor, therefore, has its uses. Instead of implying passivity, it could transform itself into a strategy masking aggression, resourcefulness, and erotic defiance.

Before Alexandre Parent-Duchâtelet's immensely influential study of French prostitution, which guided discourses on the subject for the rest of the century, Restif de la Bretonne had advocated seclusion for courtesans. Parent himself supported the idea of the *maison de tolérance*—a similar institution that would effectively keep the courtesan apart from the rest of society, and under surveillance, curtailing her public self-display.[42] Ironically, masquerading as odalisques and harem women, the hybridized *courtesans* of nineteenth-century exoticism confound the very notion of separation. They transform a "domestic" space into an eroticized interior where languid postures signify the consequence of sexual excess and the threat of emasculating disease, to emerge later in the figure of the vampire. Their bodies, while promising fantasies of "private" ownership, are exhibited in salons, travel narratives, and ethnographic fictions before the public gaze. The exoticized courtesan's body, riddling its observers, both reinforces and resists masculine/imperial desire.

Dangerous Pleasures: Italian Vampire-Courtesans and Male Odalisques in British Fiction, 1800–1850

The vampiric female body emerged in the first half of the nineteenth century as another version of the odalisque-courtesan, symptomatic of a female intervention in the male libertine tradition of the seventeenth and eighteenth centuries. Although issues of métissage would crystallize more firmly around this figure with the consolidation of imperialism, these early female vampires conflated hybridized bodies with a type of exotic libertinism that would continue to shift and evolve throughout the nineteenth century. An early nineteenth-century work, Charlotte Dacre's *Zofloya, or The Moor* (a startling example of orientalist gothic) takes the figure of the odalisque in new directions, using exoticism to stage a narrative of female rage and defiance.[43] *Zofloya* is set in Italy, which further emphasizes the uncertainty and difficulty of precisely "mapping" the exotic at this time. The Italian female protagonist in this novel clearly inhabits an orientalist space.

Zofloya (1806) is a remarkable attempt to construct a female libertine who appropriates both violent excess and the allure of métissage to enact her explosively transgressive agenda. A Jewish woman who had adopted the name of the female vampire Matilda in Lewis's notorious gothic novel, *The Monk* as a pseudonym, "Rosa Matilda," Dacre was already aligned with the exotic in her own life, both by birth and in terms of the persona she created for herself. In *Zofloya*, she posits the exoticized vampiric female body as a feminine alternative to the male libertine tradition of the eighteenth century. The novels of Richardson and Laclos had situated women in relation to overpowering male libertines such as Lovelace and Valmont as either targets of seduction through which libertine attacks on bourgeois social institutions could be validated (through the dismantling of their virtue) or clever manipulators working behind tightly constructed personas. *Zofloya* comes closer to Sade's *Juliette* (1797) in the portrayal of the overt ferocity and amorality of its heroine, Victoria. Dacre's focus on Victoria's deliberate self-hybridization (in terms of both race and sexuality) takes the novel even further than *Juliette* in some ways. In a scene of unprecedented violence, the novel culminates in a graphic assault on the "white" female body, perpetrated by Victoria.

Set at the end of the fifteenth century in Venice, *Zofloya* opens with the birthday celebration of the aristocratic Victoria di Loredani. No one can compare with her in either "beauty of person, or splendour of decoration" (3). Yet, at fifteen, Victoria combines ornamentation with aggression and libertine tendencies; "a wild, ardent, and irrepressible spirit, indifferent to reproof, careless of censure" (4) and a "boldly organized mind" (29). Dacre anthropologizes Venice as an orientalist location: governed by the despotic "Council of Ten," the Venetians are predisposed by "nature, climate, habit and education" to violence and torrid passions. When Victoria's virtuous mother Laurina unexpectedly commits adultery with a German libertine, Count Ardolph, she sets into motion a series of events that result in the death of Victoria's father and the subsequent "contamination" of her children, Victoria and her brother Leonardo. The text obsessively circles around the idea of pollution from this point onward. Haunted by this sense of contamination, Victoria determines to become the mistress of a Venetian noble, Berenza. In order to prevent her daughter from plunging into "a vortex of libertinism" induced by "the fatal effects of her own example" (32), Laurina conspires with Ardolph to have Victoria made into a virtual prisoner, guarded by a harshly repressive relative. Victoria uses her intelligence and resourcefulness to escape and return to Venice.

It is from this point that Victoria's transformation into a dissident begins; as the narrative progresses, this dissidence finds its fullest expression in exoticism. In Venice, Victoria meets Berenza again, who makes her his mistress. Because of her contaminated matriarchal heritage, he decides that she cannot be his wife. He beholds her "unembellished," "unornamented," and perceives her "defects": her "stubbornness, her violence, her *fierté*" (69). Here Dacre implies that the surface of Victoria's spectacularly ornamented body had previously functioned as a strategic mask that frustrated attempts at surveillance. Berenza, who is a "refined" libertine, becomes obsessed with "penetrating" Victoria's thoughts so that he can mold her character (71) and convince himself of her purity. Victoria's violence and openly articulated desires connect her with the Venetian courtesan Megalena Strozzi, whom Berenza has cast aside. Strozzi, also a woman of "excessive" passions,' is further linked with Victoria by becoming the lover of her brother, Leonardo. Determined to strip Victoria of her affinities with courtesans, Berenza demands a wife who will willingly submit to being his sole property and a more "respectable object" of his love (129). Realizing that marriage to Berenza is a way of furthering her ambitions, Victoria, a superb actress, decides to assume the "appearance" of a "sincere and honorable" love. The plan succeeds and Berenza exhibits his wife to the Venetians with "a different and far more refined feeling" (128), while Victoria is keenly aware of, and deeply resents, his attempts to domesticate her: "Sometimes she even regretted that, under circumstances so humiliating, she had consented to become his wife, and almost determined to shew her contempt of his fancied condescension, by abandoning him" (128).

Five years later, Berenza's brother Henriquez arrives, accompanied by his Moorish attendant, Zofloya. The subsequent shattering encounter between Zofloya and Victoria unfolds within a bizarre gothic/orientalist mode that completely reverses the process of Victoria's domestication and allows her to reinvent herself as a sort of vampiric odalisque whose aim is the ultimate dismantling of the architectonics of race, class, and gender. Henriquez and Zofloya both become the objects of Victoria's desire; while she experiences a "mad" passion for the master, she begins to see the servant in her dreams. Simultaneously, she develops the "bitterest hate" for Henriquez's fiancée Lilla, who is the embodiment of purity and fragility—and excessively "white" into the bargain: "Pure, innocent, free even from the smallest taint of a corrupt thought, was her mind, delicate, symmetrical, and of fairy-like beauty, her person so small, yet of so just proportion . . . her angelic countenance; slightly suffused with the palest hue of the virgin rose. Long flaxen hair floated over her shoulders" (133). There are repeated references throughout the text to Lilla's "snow-white arms," her "alabastor" skin.

As Zofloya enters her dreams, Victoria has visions of the deaths of Lilla and Berenza, who both are obstacles to the realization of her desires. Dacre describes Zofloya as combining a "noble and majestic" form with the intellectual accomplishments of the Moorish culture of Granada, "beloved by all" (138). Although reduced to the position of Henriquez's servant through unfortunate circumstances, he is connected to one of the oldest Moorish families in Granada, before the expulsion of the Moors from Spain. Irresistibly drawn to the Moor, Victoria notes his "grace and majesty" his face "animated with charms till now unnoticed," all his features displaying "a beauty which delighted and surprised" (145). Zofloya's body allows Victoria (and Dacre) to formulate an aesthetic dominated primarily by the expression of female eroticism. As he begins his seduction of Victoria, her eyes "wandered with admiration over the beauty of his form" (147). At the same time, precisely because of its phantasmic and vampiric qualities, Zofloya's body is irreducible and cannot be *contained* within an orientalist aesthetic. He fills Victoria with sensations "awful and indescribable," as she gradually allows herself to be exoticized. Of course, Victoria's own body in this text is multilayered; she is simultaneously English/Italian/orientalized. As an "English" heroine who is "exoticized," Victoria is able to pursue her libertine identity within a cultural context that primarily validates male libertinism while it attempts to regulate female desire. Her two most radical actions are the seduction/rape of Henriquez and the murder of Lilla.

Having kidnapped and imprisoned Lilla, Zofloya and Victoria throw a sumptuous banquet during which they press "the most delicious viands, the choicest and most intoxicating wines" on Henriquez. Zofloya, "highly skilled in the science of harmony" produces music from his harp that "reduced the soul into the most delicious softness." Overwhelmed by this atmosphere of luxury and orchestrated languor, Henriquez is drugged and is seduced by Victoria masquerading as Lilla. Temporarily inhabiting Lilla's form, Victoria thus "ravishes" Henriquez by turning herself into a hybrid phantasm; the rape is also a vampiric act. Through it, Victoria impinges on Henriquez's consciousness in the same way that Zofloya had entered hers. Yet Henriquez's rejection of both Zofloya and Victoria, his fixation on the "pure" Lilla, leads him to suicide.

Dacre's description of Victoria's subsequent pursuit, murder, and mutilation of Lilla's body pushes the exoticized woman to the limits of transgressiveness. Although it has been customary to read this novel as a "racist" text, I argue instead that it is a deeply schizophrenic one. The violence and libertinism of

Dacre's flamboyantly melodramatic narrative is continually juxtaposed with an exaggerated didactic tone that attempts to keep this violence in check. As a racial outsider in nineteenth-century England, Dacre would have known and experienced the trauma of forced assimilation. In giving us two protagonists who boldly engage in the pursuit of desire and defy racial categorization, the text enacts a form of dissidence that is only available by recasting/rewriting the map of orientalism. When Victoria, in a desperate moment, laments the change in her body as a consequence of her literal and figurative indulgence in métissage, by comparing herself with Lilla ("would that this unwieldy form could be compressed into the fairy delicacy of hers, these bold masculine features assume the likeness of her baby face"), Zofloya counters with, "Beautiful Victoria . . . ; call not that graceful form unwieldy, nor to those noble and commanding features offer such indignity"(213–14). Victoria's final attack on the "fairy delicacy" and "baby face" of Lilla is a release not only for her, but also mirrors the text's urge to dislocate and reassemble the machinery of the uncontaminated body. Every part of Lilla is stabbed relentlessly:

> Victoria, no longer mistress of her actions, nor desiring to be so, seized by her streaming tresses the fragile Lilla, and held her back. With her poignard she stabbed her in the bosom, in the shoulder and other parts, the expiring Lilla sank upon her knees—Victoria pursued her blows—she covered her body with innumerable wounds, then dashed her headlong over the edge of the steep. Her fairy form bounded as it fell against the projecting crags of the mountain. (226)

Unrivaled in British fiction for its depiction of violence perpetrated by a woman on a woman's body, Victoria's symbolic acts of vampiric/sexual penetration represent a destructive and disturbing attempt to "enter"and hybridize Lilla's racially immaculate body. All the orientalist tropes in the novel have been leading up to this moment. Zofloya's seraglio is a dangerous place, symbolizing the specter of Europe's hybrid past (Moorish Spain) returning to assault the "purity" of racial identity.

Confessions of a Thug and the Male Odalisque

Because most critical readings of the exotic woman have been situated within a predominantly heteronormative, or a specifically lesbian context (in the case of the harem) male versions of the female odalisque (which began to emerge as a parallel trope in the early nineteenth century) have been largely ignored. In this section I shall briefly track the figure of the exotic male in an important ethnographic novel from the first half of the nineteenth century to show how the exotic woman's body generated tropes that circulated within an economy of homoerotic colonial desire and produced alternative masculinities.[44] In France, works by orientalist painters of the Egyptian campaign, such as Antoine-Jean Gros's *General Bonaparte Visiting the Pesthouse at Jaffa* (1804) and Anne Louis Girodet-Trioson's *Revolt of Cairo* (1810), repeatedly negotiated exoticized male bodies marked by "luxurious," sensual exhaustion in a variety of settings, often ones that conflated violence, death, and eroticism. British artists like Richard Parkes Bonington, who had studied under Gros, reworked these sources in their images of exotic men. In the late eighteenth century, colonial artists working in India, such as Johan Zoffany, had built up a body of works revolving around Indian male sitters, several of them native princes and political figures. One of Zoffany's portraits of the Nawab of Oudh's minister (1784), shows the sitter with a hookah and a sword, displaying a curious split between an official and a more relaxed identity that, to some extent, mirrored the tensions within the British colonialist.[45] Prominent English male travelers such as Byron and Richard Francis Burton had their portraits painted in Eastern dress. There was more to this conflation of dark and white male bodies than simply the anxiety and allure of "going native." In some ways, official discourses worked to "produce" male bodies that were feminized, hybridized, and eroticized by engaging in the work of empire. Furthermore, this trend was underscored, and even initiated, by the medicalization of the imperial male body in the developing field of colonial medicine during the first half of the nineteenth century.

Published in 1839, the novel *Confessions of a Thug* was probably the most sensational ethnographic fiction to come out of the British Empire in the first half of the nineteenth century, dealing with a subject which was second only to *sati* in the landscape of colonial criminology.[46] This was *thuggee*, an art and a lifestyle practised by those belonging to a cult of stranglers or "deceivers" who waylaid travelers and elegantly strangled them for their money with the infamous "roomal" or handkerchief. Written by a British administrator, Philip Meadows Taylor, who was involved in the control of *thuggee* in colonial India, the novel constructs its "native informant"—the eroticized thug Ameer Ali— as a racially hybrid figure whose body continually registers (and resists) the conflicting demands of colonial desire. Taylor's "ethnographic" novel was an immediate best seller, avidly read by Queen Victoria herself. The thug Ameer Ali is repeatedly feminized in fascinating ways. This exoticization, however, or the transformation of the thug into the "male odalisque" (a site of homoerotic desire) reveals the insecurity of the ethnographic codings it ostensibly attempts to uphold, as it simultaneously stages a radical critique of Victorian domesticity, through a complex series of identifications and disavowals. Moreover, it complicates Spivak's recent contention that the "native informant" is "a figure, who, in ethnography, can only provide data, to be interpreted by the knowing subject for reading . . . a site that can only be read, by definition, for the production of definitive descriptions."[47] In *Confessions,* the identities of both native informant and ethnographer are called into question as each seems to collapse into the other.

The "discovery" and classification of *thuggee* in the criminological archives of colonial India was a process fraught with considerable tensions and ambiguities. Thugs were notoriously elusive and difficult to identify, as they excelled in mimicking respectability, "passing" as "ordinary inoffensive travelers," "traders," and "wealthy merchants."[48] They could not be classified according to religious beliefs, as both Muslim and Hindu thugs were driven by the worship of the Hindu goddess Kali. Protected in many cases by native officials and landowners, thugs embodied a certain form of dissidence, an "infestation" or "contagion" that refused to accommodate itself to the civilizing project. Their violence was directed mainly toward the prosperous merchant class: "women, poets, professors of dancing, musicians, carpenters and sweepers," including the disabled, were spared. In addition, the system ultimately used by colonial administrators to police *thuggee* was itself deeply flawed: because a thug "approver" was used to identify other thugs in exchange for a life sentence instead of death, innocent people were often convicted.

Superficially, Taylor's novel seems to reenact the discursive framework of a thug approver interview, in which the Englishman poses questions and the thug answers. Yet Ameer Ali's "confession" impinges on that framework mainly through the text's problematic construction of the exotic male body. The thug's body encompasses the cold-blooded murderer of great dexterity and strength as well as the object of homoerotic desire, the gorgeous male odalisque whose physical characteristics are repeatedly fetishized and feminized: "his nose is aquiline and elegantly formed, and his mouth small and beautifully chiselled" while his luxuriant beard (another significant marker of Victorian masculinity) hides "a throat and neck which would be a study for a painter or a sculptor" and reveals an hourglass figure, the product of a corset fetish: "a broad and prominent chest" that contrasts with his "small waist" (266). Fairer than most natives, he is the perfect Victorian gentleman, an educated man with a "pure and fluent" knowledge of Persian and Urdu, who has, despite his refinement, "personally engaged" in seven hundred murders.

Ameer Ali's positioning within the harem or zenana is also complex. By turns, he simultaneously accesses and occupies the spaces assigned to the languorous observer of the nautch, the repeated object of female (and male) erotic desire, and the rescuer of harem women (a position iconographically reserved for the British male). He is both inside and outside the harem, at times poised on the threshold, flirting with its liminality as he stages different masquerades. He inserts himself into the narrative of Victorian domesticity as he becomes a devoted husband and father, while continuing with his criminal activities on the side. What starts out as an interrogation develops into a passionate confessional that sets up a peculiar intimacy between the two men. This allows "Ameer Ali" to manipulate the narrative in such a way so as to figuratively assault the limits of the master's body and consciousness. He begins by eroding the boundaries of "civilization" separating the Englishman and the thug: "How many of you

English are passionately devoted to sporting! Your days and months are passed in its excitement. A tiger, a panther, a buffalo, or a hog, rouses your utmost energies for its destruction—you even risk your lives in its pursuit. How much higher game is a Thug's! His is man"(16). As the Englishman surveys the thug's body, his own body gradually succumbs to neurasthenic exhaustion and disorientation; his "nerves require to be composed" (264).

Confessions of a Thug complicates the seductions of languor as well. Within the context of empire-building, languor was considered to be one of the most dreaded effects of the tropical climate on European constitutions—ultimately becoming linked to male neurasthenia and degeneration in the late nineteenth century. The sensual privilege of succumbing to the "lassitude and indifference which comes over the most energetic in tropical heat," indulged in by those on the fringes (such as odalisques, nautch girls, and courtesans), was dangerous for colonial administrators. Through the discourse of climatic degeneration, British medical ethnography in the earlier part of the century produced a male body constantly on the verge of slipping into a seductive state of languor that could ultimately lead to hypochondriasis, making the sufferer unfit to carry out his imperial duties.

James Johnson's pioneering *The Influence of Tropical Climates on European Constitutions* (1821), which set the tone for climatic medical theories in the early period of colonial medicine, maintained that "licentious indulgences" and "intemperance" combined with the effects of a hot climate, predisposed the European male to tropical "derangement" and exhaustion.[49] Most important, bodily surfaces become more permeable, their textures more fluid, due to a condition that Johnson calls "cutaneo-hepatic sympathy": a "consent of parts" between the skin and the liver" in which excessive perspiration has an adverse effect on the liver and induces "torpor." This changes the economy of the male body, undermining its capacity as a "closed" body, vis-à-vis the more open, penetrable, and fluid female body. Johnson connects climatic derangement and languor to sexual commerce with native women and the production of hybrid offspring, citing the mixed-race descendants of the Portuguese as an example.

Two early French orientalist paintings relating to the Egyptian campaign are interesting in this regard. In the first, *General Bonaparte Visiting the Pesthouse at Jaffa*, dark and white male bodies are inextricably entangled through contagion. Similarly, Girodet's *The Revolt of Cairo*, marks a moment of political resistance dominated by the languorous, feminized, hybrid body of the male odalisque (in contradistinction to the darker, more active bodies). This figure embodies the deepest threat to empire and a covert acknowledgment of the allure of anti-imperialist languor. The struggle depicted in the painting between colonizers and colonized suggests a struggle for control over this body.

As in *Confessions of a Thug*, these bodies resist classification. The result is the production of a hybrid male body thath is neither European, nor Indian, neither fully male nor female. Nor has it "gone native." Apart from his association

with women who boldly act out their sexual desires (which Ameer Ali both initiates and satisfies), his aggression and emotional detachment are rooted in his
feminization as they spring from his worship of the active and powerful goddess Kali. Indeed, he explains that all his actions are directed by her. In fact, the
"feminine" in this novel is conceived of as far from passive. In Taylor's Indian
female odalisques or zenana women, Victorian women readers would have been
confronted with female figures who are both sexually emancipated and intelligent. (Thus the whole notion of Ameer Ali's "feminization" is not so simple as
it may appear). As the leader of the thugs, he is at the same time, a superb
administrator and strategist, displaying qualities that Meadows Taylor himself
was noted for in his political negotiations with the rani of Shorpur as well as
his policing of *thuggee*. Not only does he engage in acts of political resistance,
he also throws out the challenge that *thuggee* will somehow never be "contained"
by the English: "Yet Thuggee, capable of exciting the mind so strongly will not,
cannot be annihilated! . . . from every Thug who accepts the alternative of perpetual imprisonment to dying on a gallows, you learn of others whom even I
knew not of" (15).

As ethnographic knowledge seeks closure, it is continually frustrated. The
male odalisque's exoticized body might then be read less as an ethnographic
spectacle than an artifact created by colonial desires that initiate the fragmentation of the white male body. In an attempt to reinforce imperial identities, the
medical discourse of languor paradoxically set the stage for certain orientalist
texts (among them Taylor's) to write exotic bodies with permeable borders that
could potentially throw the imperial archive into disarray. Therefore, to define
the "limits" of the feminized exotic body precisely is an imperial and critical
project I call into question. This book focuses on the idea of permeability, on
the way "limits" between bodies intersect and continually place themselves
under erasure.

Chemical Seductions: Hybridity and Toxicology

The Orientals are not contented, like Mithridates, to make a shield
of poison, but also use it as a dagger. In their hands, this science
becomes not only a defensive weapon but often an offensive one.
The one serves to protect them against physical suffering, the other
against their enemies. With opium, belladonna, strychnine, bois de
couleuvre or cherry-laurel, they put to sleep those who would rouse
them. There is not one of those Egyptian, Turkish or Greek women
whom you call here wise women . . . who does not know enough of
chemistry to astound a doctor. . . . This is how the secret dramas of
the Orient are woven and unwoven.
  —Alexandre Dumas, *The Count of Monte Cristo* (1844–45)

"Armadale" . . . gives us for its heroine a woman fouler than the
refuse of the streets, who has lived to the ripe age of thirty five, and
through the horrors of forgery, murder, theft, bigamy, gaol and
attempted suicide, without any trace being left on her beauty.
  —Review of *Armadale* in *The Spectator*, 1866

What most disturbs the Victorian reviewer of Wilkie Collins's *Armadale* about
Lydia Gwilt's body is its capacity to absorb and transform *traces*. Like the
dilemma of poison itself within Victorian toxicological discourses, the sensational body of this "poisonous" and "poisoning" woman continues to be
haunted by a figurative métissage that enacts (and simultaneously erases) a

similar split between purity and contamination. Lydia's body is an aesthetic/erotic maze, her "beauty" covering the "traces" of the infinite possibilities of her poisonings, "the creative possibilities of impurity."[1] In nineteenth-century Britain and France, toxicology (the study of poisons) was both an emerging discourse in the field of forensic medicine as well as a seductive strategy for women seeking some element of control in their own lives. As Victorian ethnography constructed and debated its classifications (in an attempt to "fix" racial differences that remained elusive) throughout the century the interventions of poisoners, both male and female, baffled forensic toxicologists as they struggled to perfect techniques of poison detection and identification. Almost compulsively, Victorian England exploded with one "sensational" poison trial after another, the most famous being those of Madeleine Smith (1857), Dr. William Palmer (1856), George Lamson (1882), Dr. Thomas Smethurst (1859), and Florence Maybrick (1889); while in France, the case of Marie Lafarge revealed the instability and precariousness of forensic toxicology as a criminological procedure.[2]

The indeterminacy of poison, its ability to camouflage itself, continually evaded and frustrated scientific categories. Readily available, it was used for medicinal, cosmetic, and even aphrodisiac purposes. Its presence in the fabric of everyday life made it simultaneously insidious, attractive, and a useful weapon; poison became a social obsession and an art. As a cultural trope, it signified various kinds of border-crossings—especially racial otherness. Its veiled deceptions and tropical contagions made the Orient (or even locations that signified the near exotic, such as Italy), the ultimate source of the most beguiling and deadly poisons. In Alexandre Dumas's 1844 novel, *The Count of Monte Cristo*, the orientalized hero, Edmond Dantès, discusses the subtleties of the art of toxicology with a female serial poisoner, Madame de Villefort. According to Dantès, the most successful and artistic cases of poisoning are to be found *outside* France, in "Aleppo or Cairo, or even no further than Naples or Rome" where one can see " people walking along the street, upright, fresh-faced and ruddy with health, of whom the devil, were he to touch you with his cloak, could tell you: 'This man has been poisoned for three weeks and he will be completely dead in a month'"(508).[3] Poison and poisoners were repeatedly figured in terms of the exotic: Cleopatra was one of the most compelling prototypes of the female poisoner in the nineteenth-century, particularly in the French orientalist tradition. Representations such as Alexandre Cabanel's painting, *Cleopatra Testing Poisons on Condemned Men* (1887) (discussed in more detail further on in this chapter) and Théophile Gautier's novella *Une Nuit de Cléopâtre* (1838) constructed the Egyptian queen's sexual and political power through her use of exotic poisons. The myth of Indian women who built up a systemic tolerance for poison and then functioned as political/sexual weapons was available to orientalist scholars; ethnological texts imagined that racial mixing resulted in "poisoned" or contaminated blood.

The threat of miscegenation, as the gap between "home" and the colonies narrowed, provided a potent metaphor for the infusion of "poison" in the blood. Yet because of the fluid nature of poison, its propensity to invade, dissolve, and be absorbed without a trace, this otherness was never absolute. Mapped on to discourses of race, toxicological transgressions mimicked the assault of métissage on the formation of racial or national personas. In a recent discussion of hybridity in the Dutch Indies and French Indochina, Ann Stoler argues that racial mixing "called into question the very criteria by which Europeanness could be identified, citizenship should be accorded and nationality assigned."[4] Poison inscribed the bodies of both poisoner and victim with a dangerous sense of receptivity to infiltration; representations of the body of the female poisoner (in fictional, historical and medical/legal discourses) generated a complex exoticism by means of which the very architecture of "pure" ethnological categories was called into question. Toxicological discourses, therefore, make up an underexplored terrain that shapes itself through a continuous and uneasy negotiation with such anxieties, due both to the nature and action of poison itself as well as the hybridized bodies of female poisoners.

Poison was, of course, one of the preoccupations of Victorian sensation fiction. The lesser-known novels of Wilkie Collins in particular reflect a fascination with poison and with women who resort to poison to carry out their transgressive agendas in regard to property, sexuality, and national identity. In Collins's work, the imperatives of criminology and imperialism/exoticism are seamlessly interwoven and foregrounded through the hybrid bodies of his female protagonists. Here, I shall explore the ways in which Collins's sensational fiction reconstitutes (or reclaims) the links between poison and female agency in mid- to late Victorian medical and ethnological discourses by looking at two novels that have received little critical attention so far: *Armadale* (1866) and *The Legacy of Cain* (1888). Although several of Collins's novels link women and poison, such as *Jezebel's Daughter* (1880) and *The Law and the Lady* (1874; based on the Madeleine Smith poison trial), I have chosen here to focus on these two works because of their intense preoccupation with the ways in which the female poisoner's hybrid body insinuates itself within, and challenges discourses of, exoticism, empire, and ethnology.

In the colonies, tropical medicine battled the "poisonous" diseases of the East,[5] while at home, outbreaks of domestic poisonings periodically occurred, as women poisoned their husbands and lovers, slipping through the legal system. Poison lurked on the surface of the female body through its use of "dangerous" cosmetics. The notorious Madeleine Smith, famous among Victorian female poisoners, used the arsenic she regularly purchased for her complexion to finish off her unsuspecting lover. These discourses provide a cultural topography that enables Collins to position female acts of poisoning within a politics of transgression and resistance. *Armadale* introduces us to the beautiful and resourceful Lydia Gwilt, who stages an elaborate poison plot, driven by her desire for property and revenge, while *The Legacy of Cain* uses its dual female protagonists (one of whom, unknown to the reader, is the daughter of a murderess) to investigate issues of heredity and eugenics. In order to grasp the implications of Collins's intervention in Victorian cultural narratives of poison fully, it is necessary to analyze them briefly—especially those toxicological discourses with which Collins would have been familiar, both through reading and other encounters.[6]

Victorian Toxicology: Toward a Theory of Poison

The midcentury's leading toxicologist, Dr. Alfred Swaine Taylor, attempted to define the nature, action, and absorption of poisons in his authoritative *On Poisons in Relation to Medical Jurisprudence and Medicine* (1848). Professor of medical jurisprudence at Guy's Hospital, London, till 1877, Taylor had repeatedly been called in as a forensic expert in many criminal trials, including the high-profile poisoning case of William Palmer. (Copies of Taylor were in Collins's library; he probably thus had access to Taylor's work while he was writing *Armadale* and used it to construct the spectacular poison gas episode at the end of the novel, in which Lydia Gwilt attempts to poison Allan Armadale with carbonic acid.)[7]

Taylor begins by commenting on the difficulty of arriving at a precise definition of the term *poison* or of distinguishing poisonous from nonpoisonous substances. He warns medical witnesses to avoid the "common" definition:

> a poison is commonly defined to be a substance which, when administered in small quantity, is capable of acting deleteriously on the body. It is obvious that this definition is too restricted for the purposes of medical jurisprudence. It would, if admitted, exclude a very large class of substances, the poisonous properties of which cannot be disputed; as, for example, the salts of lead, copper, tin, zinc and antimony, which are only poisonous when administered in very large doses. . . . Each substance must be regarded as a poison, differing from the other only in its degree of activity and perhaps in its mode of operation.[8]

Taylor goes on to cite cases of death by ingestion of common substances such as salt, sulphate of magnesia (Epsom salts), or even cold water "swallowed in a large quantity, and in an excited state of the system" (18). He repeatedly testifies to the elusive nature of the action of poisons on the body; arsenic, for instance, is particularly confusing in this respect. The signs of inflammation of the stomach from arsenic poisoning might be misleading: "we do not find that the degree of inflammation is in proportion to the quantity of the poison taken; sometimes it is extensive under a small dose, and at others scarcely apparent under a large dose" (26). Although arsenic sometimes does not produce any *local* action (a change in the part of the body with which the poison comes into contact), it operates stealthily by *remote* action ("the power which most poisons possess of affecting an organ remote from the part to which they are applied"). This is also the case with poisons such as "large doses of hydrocyanic acid or strychnia," which "kill with great rapidity, without producing any perceptible local changes " (27). Another subversive effect of poison on the body is absorption into the bloodstream: Taylor infers that "most, if not all poisons can, sooner or later, enter into, and circulate with the blood" (32). Yet the *operation* of the poison after absorption by the system mystified toxicologists:

> Admitting that every poison entered into the blood, and could be chemically detected in this fluid, it would yet remain to be explained how it operated when there, to destroy life. At present there is no satisfactory theory to account for the fatal effect . . . it may be expected that in the progress of microscopical research, the precise effect produced by poisons on the blood will hereafter become a subject of demonstration; but, at present, the modus operandi is a perfect mystery. We trace the poison to the circulation, and we observe that death is the result, but neither the chemist nor the microscopist can throw the least light upon the changes produced by poisons on the blood or in the organs necessary to life. (36)

The action of poison therefore remained invisible, covert and resistant to easy classification.

Ian Burney's exhaustive research on poisoning trials in Victorian England, especially the William Palmer trial, has compellingly demonstrated how the medico-legal discourses of the day, including that of "expert witnesses" like Taylor, sought to convert "contingency into axiomatic truth" to make the "invisible and ephemeral weapon (poison) insinuated into the civilized social body" visible and transparent through chemical analysis. Burney asserts that textual authority on poison was achieved at the cost of erasing the uncertainties at the heart of the complicated debates around the "invisibility" of the poison in the bodies of the victims and the constitution of legal proof of poisoning. Similarly, the evasiveness of poison muddied the "purity" of the boundaries between "sensational" public discourses and "official" scientific ones.[9]

Arsenic, for instance, turned up everywhere. Because traces of arsenic were found in the bodies of those who had died of natural causes, the foremost toxicologist in France, Matthew Orfila, became concerned that if the earth contained arsenic as well, graveyard seepage would make the testing of exhumed bodies for arsenic poisoning extremely problematic. The landmark French trial of Marie Lafarge in 1840[10] intensified the opacity at the heart of these forensic controversies. Marie was accused of systematically and ruthlessly poisoning her husband Charles Lafarge by administering arsenic to cakes and food. The complex ramifications of the case relating to class and sexuality emerge in her own memoir, which was published and translated into English in 1841.[11]

Matthew Orfila was called in to prove the presence of arsenic in the body of Lafarge. By using the new apparatus developed by the English chemist James Marsh, Orfila demonstrated the existence of an arsenic deposit. Orfila also claimed, however, that the sensitivity of the apparatus could produce conflicting results. In other cases in England, the Marsh test was not always reliable in detecting arsenic in suspicious circumstances.[12] The new Reinsch test for arsenic, published in 1841, proved to be equally contradictory. Testifying at the trial of Thomas Smethurst for the poisoning of his wife by arsenic in 1859, Alfred Taylor admitted that his tests (by the Reinsch method) might have been contaminated.[13] Smethurst was at first convicted, and then ultimately pardoned owing to a lack of conclusive evidence. Despite advances, poison continued to elude the clinical gaze, allowing the poisoner powers of infiltration, invasion, and inscription that remained perpetually opaque. The poisoned body recapitulated the riddle of hybridity: once inside, the "exoticism" of poison became diffuse, indeterminate, its radical otherness held in tension with its ability to unsettle toxicological categorizations. According to Taylor, the power of poison was (hidden) in the amount absorbed, and not in that which was clearly visible in the organs: "It has been truly remarked by Orfila, in regard to arsenic, and it equally applies to all poisons, that that portion which is found in the stomach *is not that which has caused death;* but the *surplus* of the quantity which has produced fatal effects by its absorption into the system." (*On Poisons,* 117)

Poisonous Exoticism

Between 1837 and 1838, there were 540 poison deaths in England and Wales, with opium and arsenic topping the list. Between 1863 and 1867 (the period during which Collins wrote and published *Armadale*), there were almost three thousand deaths from poison, with opium and its various derivatives accounting for 482.[14] According to Taylor, "there is no form of poisoning so frequent as that by opium and its frequent preparations" (466). Opium was a pervasive and subtle "poison" masquerading as medicine and recreation; an indisputable part of the fabric of daily life in Victorian England, widely available before the Pharmacy Act of 1868,[15] despite the fact that Robert Christison's pioneering treatise on toxicology in 1829 had classified opium as a "narcotic poison."[16] Christison described opium as "the poison most generally resorted to by the timid to accomplish self-destruction. . . . It has likewise been long very improperly employed to create amusement. And in recent times it has been made use of to commit murder" (530). In 1837–38, opium and its derivatives headed the statistics on poison deaths in *The Lancet* and the *Medical Gazette.*[17] Increasing doses of laudanum (an opium derivative) caused children to become "pale and wan, with a peculiar sharpness of feature" and eventually to "waste away." Habitual opium use or "chronic poisoning by opium" could cause not only death, but also "numbness of the limbs, coldness of the feet, inability to walk far without aching pains . . . and a general sense of lassitude" (*On Poisons,* 475). Yet of all poisons, the status of opium was the most ambivalent, the most hybrid. Its sensual uses combined pleasure, languor, and death.

Besides, opium also signified a kind of racial or cultural "poisoning." Opium smoking was invariably associated—visually and architecturally—with the orientalized space surrounding the exotic woman. Gérôme's numerous portraits of the Turkish bath depicted racially indeterminate odalisques overcome by the luxurious languor produced by smoking opium or tobacco through the narghile or hookah (a smoking device that passed narcotic fumes through water).[18] This indeterminacy was also apparent in Delacroix's famous *Women of Algiers* (1834), where pale and dark bodies seemed to blend and merge, encroaching on each other's bodily presence. The haze of the narghile here accompanied "the bitter gaze" of the odalisque, an alienating and distancing returned look that somehow obstructed the viewer's desire to master that space—but also an interlocking series of gazes *within* the painting, as the women exchanged looks with each other.[19] These interlocking gazes create an intercorporeality that somehow *excludes* the gazer. In British exotic and Pre-Raphaelite art this sense of languor is much more intense; in fact, it could be argued that "languor" was central to the Pre-Raphaelite aesthetic. Leighton's *Odalisque* (1862), Watts's *Nude with Peacock Feathers* (1865) and Dicksee's *Leila* (1892) are suffused with a heightened sense of languor that outstrips their French counterparts. In these representations, the women are not smoking hookahs; the languor is entirely *internalized,* an integral part of their bodies. Another British painting from the second half of the nineteenth century, John Atkinson Grimshaw's *Dulce Domum* (fig. 9, 1876–85) combines languor and exoticism in interesting ways. In *Dulce Domum* (Sweet Home) the central female figure reclines languidly on a chair in a living room crammed with exotic objects. Her gaze shares the indifference of Delacroix's odalisques. The overwhelming green hue of the exotica that surrounds her is juxtaposed with the paleness of her dress, which it threatens to swallow up at any moment. In his paintings of Gothicized landscapes, Grimshaw uses these shades of green to create a sense of the uncanny, of a landscape alienated from itself. Here, this color has invaded the home and suffuses the exotic furnishings. The representation raises the question of whether the woman can stabilize the "home" or whether the exotic might in turn consume/destablize her body. In Grimshaw's uncanny combination of languor and exoticism, the "home" becomes a "foreign" place in which the woman as center is off-balance.

Once under the influence of languor or sensual self-indulgence, women's bodies were no longer "productive"; they could not be easily co-opted into a mechanics of reproduction that served as the domestic backbone of empire. Languor could also be contagious; once European women in the tropics succumbed to it,

Fig. 9. John Atkinson Grimshaw, *Dulce Domum*,1876–85 (Private Collection)

they became unfit for the task of empire-building. Aptly, Taylor noted that the initial symptoms of large doses of opium or its tincture included "giddiness, drowsiness and stupor" (468). The development of "Arab" smoking rooms in private houses (such as the billiard room at Newhouse Park in Hertfordshire) in the later part of the century also drew on the connection between opium and the East. Such interiors themselves were often "hybrid," like the breathtaking Arab Hall at the home of the artist Frederick Leighton, built between 1877–79, composed of motifs from Sicily, Persia, Syria, and Turkey.[20]

Collins himself gradually became a laudanum addict through taking it on a regular basis for his agonizing attacks of gout.[21] In an August 1884 letter to Charles Kent, he described the action of laudanum as having a "twofold action on the brain and nervous system—a stimulating and sedative action" (472).[22] Earlier, in 1869 he had written to Elizabeth Benzon: "My doctor is trying to break me of the habit of drinking laudanum. I am stabbed every night at ten with a sharp-pointed syringe which injects morphia under my skin—and gets me a night's rest without any of the drawbacks of taking opium internally" (2:319). Ingesting "poisons" such as arsenic and opium—and in the process building up a systemic tolerance—was evocative not only of the East, but also of places on the border between the Orient and the Occident, such as eastern Europe (parts of which were under the Ottoman (Turkish) regime until the late nineteenth century. In an 1875 edition of *On Poisons,* Taylor referred to the legendary practice of arsenic eating in that region:

It is stated that in certain parts of Styria and Hungary, there are human beings who have so accustomed themselves to the use of arsenic, as to be able to take this substance not only without the usual symptoms of poisoning, but with actual benefit to health. This subject would hardly require serious notice . . . but that it has already formed part of the medical evidence in some criminal trials for poisoning. (68)

Despite Taylor's assertion that "there is no reason to believe that arsenic-eating is practiced in this country," there were at least two celebrated poison trials in which the slow, voluntary ingestion of arsenic was cited as evidence for the defense. Madeleine Smith, tried for poisoning her lover Emile L'Angelier in 1857, claimed that she had applied arsenic, diluted with water, to her face, neck, and arms, to beautify her complexion. Significantly, she mentioned that she "had been advised to the use of arsenic" by "the daughter of an actress." Similarly, when Florence Maybrick was accused of the murder of her husband, in 1889, the defense attempted to provide evidence of James Maybrick's "arsenic habit." The testimony of the druggist at the Maybrick trial suggested that "arsenic-laced tonics" were popular with gentlemen for their supposed ability to improve sexual performance—sort of a Victorian Viagra.[23]

The Female Poisoner in Victorian Historiography

Victorian historiography often associated female poisoners with political power, which in turn was conflated with their sexuality and appetite. Gaetano Donizetti's popular opera *Lucrezia Borgia* (based on Victor Hugo's play *Lucrèce Borgia,* was performed in London between 1839 and 1888. As an opera fan, Collins knew the work; in *The Woman in White,* Walter Hartright spots the Italian criminal Count Fosco at the opera house during a performance of *Lucrezia Borgia.*[24] Initially, the opera attempts to "normalize" Lucrezia by focusing on her relationship with her son, Gennaro, although their exchanges are charged with erotic overtones. In the final act of the opera, Lucrezia poisons her enemies (including her son) at a sumptuous banquet. The German historian Ferdinand Gregorovius, in the preface to his book on her in 1874, announced his intention of "rehabilitating" Lucrezia, and "clearing up" her myth. Accusing Hugo and Donizetti of having transformed Lucrezia into "the type of all feminine depravity," Gregorovius set out to present her as "amiable, gentle, thoughtless and unfortunate"; that is, a victim, lacking agency.[25] Yet, for some Victorian women writers, it was Lucrezia's poisonous pervasiveness that had an emasculating effect: George Eliot drew on this in her portrayal of her enigmatic, cryptic female poisoner, Bertha, in *The Lifted Veil* (1859). In Eliot's text, the feminized hero is mesmerized by Lucrezia Borgia's portrait: "This morning I had been looking at Giorgione's picture of the cruel eyed woman, said to be a likeness of Lucrezia Borgia. I had stood long before it, fascinated by the terrible reality of that cunning, relentless face, till I felt a strange poisoned sensation, as if I had long been inhaling a fatal odour, and was just beginning to be conscious of its effects."[26]

The other two legendary women poisoners who dominated the landscape of Victorian historiography were the marquise of Brinvilliers, convicted of poisoning in the France of Louis XIV, and Cleopatra. Marie Brinvilliers's glamorous, although nefarious, poisonings, her eventual torture and forced public confession at the scaffold became a historical fetish, generating biographies, novels, and visual representations, both in the seventeenth century and after. Witnessing her execution, the sympathetic Madame de Sévigné sensed the "infectiousness" of her crimes, which pervaded the very air of Paris: "Well, it's all over and done with, Brinvilliers is in the air. Her poor little body was thrown after the execution into a very big fire and the ashes to the winds, so that we shall breathe her, and through the communication of the subtle spirits we shall develop some poisoning urge which will astonish us all."[27]

Here, both Eliot and Sévigné imagine the *fluidity* of the female poisoner's body, which cannot be contained by torture or execution, or the frame of a portrait; a fluidity that "never closes up into a volume" and becomes the poison itself.[28] Among the most shocking features of the Brinvilliers case was Marie's strategy of subverting her domestic role by masquerading as a "nurse"; she would visit hospitals in order to test out her poisons on the sick. Marie's erotic appetite, together with her desire for economic independence and power were emphasized in the mid-Victorian novel by Albert Smith, based on her life, entitled *The Marchioness of Brinvilliers* (1846). The Brinvilliers case was also noted as having set off a "poison epidemic" or the "Affair of the Poisons" in seventeenth-century France, in which various women, such as Catherine Deshayes (otherwise known as La Voisin) regularly resorted to poison and witchcraft. Several of these women, perceived as a threat to the state, were imprisoned and/or executed. The king's mistress, Athenais De Montespan, who "surrounded herself with a brilliant luxury" and was noted for her extravagance, was also involved, as was the dramatist Jean Racine.[29]

Exoticism, luxury, political authority, erotic power, and poison—all these converged in the body of Cleopatra. Cabanel's *Cleopatra Testing Poisons on Condemned Men* (fig. 10; discussed in chapter 1) imagined the Egyptian queen as both languorous odalisque and in supreme control. Clinical and detached, Cleopatra uses men for her toxicological experiments. Her languid posture serves as a facade that offsets a deliberate and absolute power. The spectacle-within-a-spectacle, of the queen dispassionately observing male bodies on the brink of dissolution, confounds all attempts to stabilize the queen's body as object of a totalizing gaze. In a way, the painting can be seen as an extension of Theophile Gautier's 1838 novella *Une Nuit de Cléopâtre* (*Cleopatra's Night*), which casts the queen as imaginatively staging her own spectacles of excess, but never being consumed by them herself. In Gautier's text, she offers herself to

Fig. 10. Alexander Cabanel, *Cleopatra Testing Poisons on Condemned Men,* 1887
(Koninklijk Museum Voor Schone Kunsten-Antwerpen)

the slave Meiamoun, who must pay for his erotic encounter by submitting to death by poison. As in the Lucrezia Borgia narrative, he is poisoned in the course of a voluptuous banquet, whose feverish orientalism is visualized in hyberbolic detail by Gautier. This moment, however (in which the queen's body becomes ambivalently encoded as the perfect receptacle of imperial desire/erotic male fantasy and the signifier of absolute female power over the male body), also looks forward to her suicide, a powerful anti-imperialistic gesture that preserves her political and personal sovereignty. In response to the question, "What signifies this corpse upon the pavement?" Cleopatra replies, "only a poison I was testing with the idea of using it upon myself should Augustus take me prisoner."[30] If we position the figure of the Victorian female poisoner in Collins's fiction against the background of these cultural narratives of exoticism, we can begin to probe the power and sense of agency, along with the intercorporeality, created by her alliance with poison.

Armadale's "Sensational" Female Poisoner and the Politics of Hybridity

Topical and exciting, *Armadale* burst upon the Victorian literary scene in 1866. Collins had been "obsessed" with the novel for sometime, as he mentioned in a letter: "the characters themselves were all marshaled in their places, before a line of 'Armadale' was written. And I knew the end two years ago in Rome, when I was recovering from a long illness" (2:259). The Victorian "sensations" and excessive pleasures/terrors of *Armadale* offer some of Collins's most sophisticated insights into the inextricable tangle of race, sexuality, power, and criminality that dominated the cultural life of the British Empire at home and in the colonies. While *Armadale*'s heightened awareness of the complexity of the exotic subject allows for a subtler engagement with issues of race than does *The Moonstone*, at the same time its multilayered approach to these concerns must necessarily problematize any straightforward postcolonial reading of the text. Inhabiting the core of the narrative is the female poisoner Lydia Gwilt; one of Collins' most revolutionary women, she horrified some contemporary critics.[31]

Occupying the center with her, is the figure of the biracial, feminized male hysteric, Ozias Midwinter, whose relationship with the Anglo-Saxon, property-tied Allan Armadale is mediated through the connection of both men with Lydia. (This connection is further complicated by the fact that both men bear the name Armadale, a symptom of Collins's literal and symbolic use of métissage throughout the novel.) Lydia's sexual/intellectual desire for Midwinter coexists with her hatred of Allan Armadale. Her repeated attempts to poison him are assaults not only on his power of ownership (which Lydia hopes to claim, through a complicated masquerade and play on names) but also on his Englishness, a national identity that aggressively homogenizes disparate elements. I read Lydia as a figuratively hybrid woman, an exoticized criminal who, through her use of poison and her existence on the margins of Victorian society, is driven by her urge to dislocate imperial and domestic authority radically. Exoticism and poison in *Armadale*, far from working to bolster ethnological stereotypes, become here an integral part of Lydia's experience of hybridity and effective strategies through which she can stage her resistance.[32]

Armadale begins in the German spa town of Wildbad, with the deathbed confession of Ozias Midwinter's father, Matthew Wrentmore (later named Armadale), a West Indian proprietor. In it, the dying Armadale/Wrentmore reveals a fiendishly complicated history that threatens to haunt his son and future generations of Armadales.[33] By a twist of fate, Wrentmore had become possessor of the name and colonial estates of the disinherited Allan Armadale. In retaliation, the "real Armadale" had destroyed the prospects of a marriage between Wrentmore and Miss Blanchard, daughter of another West Indian colonial. While Wrentmore languished from an illness caused by "negro-poison," Ingleby/Armadale had assumed his identity, gained the affections of Miss Blanchard, and assisted by the "wicked dexterity" of her "precocious" maid (Lydia Gwilt, in an earlier incarnation), had married her. Deprived of the ideal colonial wife as well as an addition to his colonial property, Wrentmore had murdered Armadale while investigating a shipwreck, passing on his legacy of guilt to his biracial son, Ozias Midwinter (also named Allan Armadale, as Collins's frenzied doubling continues). Meanwhile, the murdered Armadale's widow has given birth to yet another "Allan Armadale."

The text enacts the exigencies of mixed racial identities from the beginning, recognizing their precariousness together with their alluring "contagion" or "poison." Midwinter is nervous, dark, and succumbs frequently to both languor and hysteria. He inherits his exotic qualities from his mother, the "other" Mrs. Armadale, whose marginalized presence hovers over Wrentmore's confession of loss and murder. Shut out from his narrative, yet inescapably implicated in the burden of "contamination" it carries, handed down from father to son, she represents that which he has fallen into through his failure to make a suitable colonial marriage with the "fair" Miss Blanchard. Yet her exoticism surfaces on her body in complex ways. Both her sexuality and her gaze are unsettling precisely *because* of their rejection of ethnological categories:

> A woman of the mixed blood of the European and African race, with the northern delicacy in the shape of her face, and the southern richness in its colour—a woman in the prime of her beauty, who moved with an inbred grace, who looked with an inbred fascination, whose large languid black eyes rested on him.... For the first time in his life, the Scotchman was taken by surprise. (21)

Armadale continues to be haunted by the ghost of the biracial woman. Her "contagion" is passed on to her feminized son, Midwinter, with his "tawny complexion, his large bright brown eyes," his "dusky hands," and "foreign look" (60). A homeless wanderer, he suddenly invades the "stable" existences of the propertied Norfolk Armadales, making their Anglo-Saxon flesh "creep." His "savage" otherness is apparent to the rector, Mr. Brock, from the start as he recovers from "brain-fever":

> his tawny, haggard cheeks ... his tangled black beard; his long, supple, sinewy fingers, wasted by suffering, till they looked like claws ... a nervous restlessness in his organization which appeared to pervade every fibre in his lean, lithe body. The rector's healthy Anglo-Saxon flesh crept responsively at every casual movement of the ... supple brown fingers, and every passing distortion of the ... haggard yellow face. (64)

Fascinated by his exoticism and subsequent lack of "healthy muscularity," Allan Armadale befriends Midwinter. In contrast, Allan himself is blond, muscular, "noisy, rosy, good-tempered" (284), with all the attributes of the man of property and "perfect" English squire. As such, he is able to patronize his namesake and alien double, deriving entertainment from his attempts to domesticate the exotic object of his attention. In his relationship with Allan, Midwinter finds himself increasingly caught up in this process of domestication, driven by a relentless urge to homogenize and manage his nomadic identity, distancing him from his mixed heritage and his mother's "negro blood." It is this pattern of assimilation, initiated by the homosocial bonding between Allan and Midwinter, that is interrupted by the appearance of the strangely hybrid Lydia Gwilt, who appropriates the exotic uses of poison for her own ends.

Exoticizing Lydia

Collins reveals Lydia's affinities with exoticism gradually and subtly in ways that heighten her sense of agency and relate directly to her pursuit of power. As a poisoner, she is in a unique position to introduce impurity into the "English" social and legal body (represented in the novel by Allan Armadale) and to throw discourses of law and property into disarray. What makes her remarkable among Collins's heroines is not so much the successive masquerades and manipulations of her body (Magdalen Vanstone in *No Name* and Valeria Macallan in *The Law and the Lady* also use disguise to further their own ends), but rather a strange awareness of the seductiveness of hybridity—surfacing through her desire to poison, her opium addiction, and her erotic connections with men who are racially other. Her immersion of herself in hybridity's irresistible pull is in direct contradistinction to Midwinter's guilt. Both realize that they present threats to Allan Armadale's Englishness, but Lydia succumbs to it while Midwinter resists.

Lydia's frequent lapses into exotic languor are tied to her love of music and laudanum. Both bring her "delicious oblivion." In moments of crisis, she soothes herself alternately with her "darling drops" of opium and Beethoven's "Moonlight Sonata." She admits to being a laudanum addict: "Who was the man who invented laudanum? I thank him from the bottom of my heart. . . . I have had six delicious hours of oblivion"(426–27). Such bodily engagements with laudanum intensify Lydia's intercorporeal connections with the exotic Orient. Travelers and orientalist historians emphasized the tenacious hold that opium had on oriental bodies. Colonial historian James Tod, in his well-known work on northern India, *Annals and Antiquities of Rajasthan* (1829), gave several examples of this: from the use of poisoned shirts or robes as strategic weapons by the warrior classes of India to their eventual degeneration due to excessive opium use.[34] Others claimed that Indian children were given opium at an early age for its soothing properties, and female infanticide was effected by smearing the mother's nipple with "a fatal dose of opium"(35).[35] Another facet of the oriental poison myth, existing in a fascinating and unique relation to the female body, was the "poison-damsel," located in the shadowy contact zone between history and fantasy.

Orientalist scholarship invariably located poison-women within narratives of political violence and intrigue. Fed on poison from childhood, these women built up a tolerance and thus became immune to poison themselves. Used as weapons of war, they apparently were able to poison their victims through sexual intercourse, or simply by mixing their bodily secretions, such as perspiration or saliva, together with those of their victims. Although her own agency was limited, the poison-woman was able to penetrate and dissolve the permeable boundaries of the male body while remaining impenetrable herself.[36]

In complete control of her own sexuality, Lydia manages to construct it as simultaneously languid and aggressive. In a telling scene with Midwinter, Lydia

Fig. 11. Illustration to *Armadale* (Cornhill Magazine)

inserts herself into the Victorian cult of domesticity by adapting herself to the "civilized" ritual of tea drinking, which he proceeds to fetishize.[37] The original *Cornhill* illustration of this scene (fig. 11) communicates this tension very effectively through its depiction of Lydia's hauntingly languid detachment, anticipating Cabanel's Cleopatra. In the illustration, her Pre-Raphaelite mass of hair is also tightly braided and "domesticated." Midwinter senses the distance between Lydia's unnameable, restless desires and the stifling domesticity of the space within which she is forced to contain herself. Indeed, Lydia's dangerousness consists partly in the way her body rehearses respectability only to discard it:

> Her hands moved about among the tea things with a smooth, noiseless activity. Her magnificent hair flashed crimson ... as she turned her head hither and thither, searching, with an easy grace, for the things she wanted in the tray. Exercise had heightened the brilliancy of her complexion and had quickened the rapid alternations of expression in her eyes—the delicious languor that stole over them when she was listening or thinking, the bright intelligence that flashed from them softly when she spoke. . . . Perfectly modest in her manner, possessed to perfection of the

graceful restraints and refinements of a lady, she had all the allurements that feast the eye . . . a subtle suggestiveness in her silence, and a sexual sorcery in her smile. (383)

In terms of both race and class, Lydia's origins are uncertain. James Bashwood, the detective employed to trace her history, discovers the impenetrability of certain areas of her past: "She may be the daughter of a Duke, or the daughter of a costermonger. . . . Fancy anything you like—there's nothing to stop you" (522). As a child with "beautiful hair" she is adopted by a quack doctor and his wife, the Oldershaws, who exploit her hair as an advertisement for their perfumery business. Entering the Blanchard family as a maid and "Miss Blanchard's new plaything," she uses the ensuing events involving the confusion between Wrentmore and Ingleby to consolidate her position and blackmail the family into providing her with a Continental education. After being involved in a sexual scandal, Lydia opts for a convent, where one of the priests fears she is "possessed by the devil" (523). Leaving the convent, she supports herself by "playing the pianoforte at a low concert room in Brussels" (524), adamantly resisting all male sexual advances. Ultimately falling in with a Russian baroness, a cardsharp whose "name is unpronounceable by English lips" (524), she wanders all over Europe with her new companion. Her nomadism as well as her constant association with the "foreign," articulate a rejection of stable national or sexual identities. Every attempt to convert her body into property, to fix or contain it, is met with resistance.

Nineteen years after the publication of *Armadale*, the Italian ethnocriminologist Cesare Lombroso published *The Female Offender* (1895), the culmination of his research into the psychology and physiology of female criminals. Professor of forensic medicine at the University of Turin from 1876 onward, Lombroso laid the cornerstones of criminal anthropology/anthropometry when he published *The Criminal Man* (1876). His views continued to be influential well into the first half of the twentieth century. Lombroso's measurements of the skulls and brains of a wide range of women, from different ethnic backgrounds (mainly Italian), convicted of crimes as diverse as murder, theft, infanticide, and complicity in rape and poisoning, led him to formulate the concept of the inherent "atavism" of the female criminal; an atavism that was an inevitable symptom of racial degeneration. He concluded, for instance, that "female poisoners, thieves and assassins are most remarkable for cranial asymmetry and strabismus; while the female assassin has most often a virile and Mongolian type of face" (86).[38] In chapter 12 of *The Female Offender*, "The Born Criminal," Lombroso catalogued the attributes of women in whom the degenerative process had taken hold more firmly than men. While other women (whom Lombroso called "occasional criminals") may have been "led into crime either by the suggestion of a third person or by irresistible temptation," the women in whom "the complete type" of degeneration appears have criminal propensities that "are more intense and more perverse than those of their male prototypes"(147).

Among other qualities, these women display cruelty, "want of maternal affection," vengeance, "intense erotic tendencies," greed, religiosity, contradictions, sentimentalism, and intelligence. Discussing several well-known female poisoners in the course of his work, such as Marie Brinvilliers and Marie Lafarge, Lombroso praised their superior cranial capacities, acute minds, and ability to write "extremely well" (171). At the same time, he observed that "naturally poisoners are not wanting amongst hysterical criminals" (234). Lydia Gwilt's and Helena Gracedieu's diaries, in *Armadale* and *The Legacy of Cain* provide evidence of their ability to construct their own narratives, manipulate events, and reimagine their bodies. "Virility" was another marker of the "reversion" to the "primitive type": looking at portraits of "Red Indian and Negro beauties," Lombroso argues that it is difficult to "recognize them as women, so huge are their jaws and cheekbones, so hard and coarse their features" (112). *The Female Offender* brings together images of the poisoner, the hysteric, and the exotic woman in order to subject their bodies to the relentless discipline of criminal anthropology. Yet their bodies are never fully contained by the text; female criminals are more evasive, more *hybrid* than male ones, ambiguously positioned along the spectrum of civilization and savagery. They occasionally display "Darwinian traits" of beauty and feminine softness; they use makeup to disguise their atavistic features. Everywhere, the body of the exoticized female criminal eludes Lombroso. *Armadale* both challenges and anticipates Lombroso's discourse through its focus on Lydia Gwilt's complex negotiation with hybridity.

Lydia first uses poison as a weapon against domestic violence. Obsessed by jealousy and his fear of her sexuality, her first husband Waldron asserts his claims to absolute ownership of her body by imprisoning her in an isolated mansion in Yorkshire. His physical abuse of her is precipitated by her "clandestine" sexual liaison with a Cuban officer, Captain Manuel. When Waldron strikes Lydia with his whip, she feigns submission before turning to poison as a way out of her intolerable marital situation:

> From that moment, the lady submitted as she had never submitted before. For a fortnight afterwards, he did what he liked; and she never thwarted him—he said what she liked; and she never uttered a word of protest. Some men might have suspected this sudden reformation of hiding something dangerous under the surface. . . . All that is known is, that before the mark of the whip was off his wife's face, he fell ill, and that in two days afterwards, he was a dead man. . . . The evidence of the doctors and the evidence of the servants pointed irresistibly in one and the same direction; and Mrs. Waldron was committed for trial, on the charge of murdering her husband by poison. (527)

Like other famous "best-selling" female poisoners of the period, among them Marie Lafarge, Madeleine Smith, and Florence Maybrick, Lydia manages to escape the death penalty due to the contradictions in the forensic evidence at her trial. Her affair with the Cuban is thought to have provided her with access to the poison: "unless she contrived, guarded and watched as she was, to get the poison for herself, the poison must have come to her in one of the captain's letters" (529). The letter containing poison is itself a hybridized document; written by Manuel, it yet mimics "Englishness," for Manuel writes English "perfectly." For Lydia, both the letter and the poison, superimposed on each other, open the way to freedom and renewed control over her own body.

Exotic men such as Manuel and Midwinter, therefore, are crucial to the driving force of Lydia's desire. Her sexual desire for them is underscored by a deep sympathy for their "otherness," an otherness she continually senses in herself. Unlike Midwinter, Manuel has no desire to "assimilate." He reappears in Lydia's life after her marriage to Midwinter, just before her second attempt to poison Allan Armadale, during a performance of Bellini's *Norma* in Naples. The opera is significant here, as the plot involves political rebellion; in occupied Gaul, the Druid priestess Norma resists colonization by the Romans, even as she is simultaneously caught up in a sexual relationship with the colonizer. (Interestingly, Manuel is costumed as one of the Druids). Located in an intermediate space between colonizer and colonized, Norma's dilemmas parallel those of Lydia Gwilt. Furthermore, like Norma, whose suicide by fire symbolizes both resistance to colonialism and capitulation to her erotic attachment, Lydia is destined to die by voluntarily gassing herself with poisonous carbonic acid as she attempts to "rescue" her lover, Midwinter. By the end of the nineteenth century, *Norma* was translated into sixteen languages and had gone on to be performed in thirty-five different countries.[39] In *Armadale* Lydia's visit to the opera at a critical narrative juncture reinforces the problematic position of the exotic woman within a dissident discourse—especially if we consider Catherine Clément's view that even though the exotic heroines of nineteenth-century European opera often self-destruct, their revolutionary insurgence simultaneously constitutes an interruption of colonial discourses. In a brilliantly lyrical analysis of this moment, Clément writes:

> These furies, these goddesses, these women with fearsome arms and inspired eyes, these Turandots and Normas collected the witch's inheritance in the nineteenth century. . . . Look at these foreign women . . . these recalcitrant women, bent on their own destruction, determined to leave their lives behind. Turandot resists the Mongol rapist, Norma resists Rome . . . Carmen the Gypsy resists all men. These woman are all exotic. . . . Resistant women, burned women: that was the fate of the Sorceress, and it is Norma's.[40]

Equipped with her knowledge of toxicology, Lydia becomes obsessed with the murder of Allan Armadale. Superficially, her motive appears to be the possession of Armadale's Thorpe-Ambrose property; by going through a marriage ceremony with Midwinter (whose name is also Armadale), and manipulating events cleverly, she will be able to pose as "Mrs. Armadale" and inherit the property on Allan's death. Beneath the surface, however, Lydia's desperate, multiple attempts to poison Allan signify an attack on everything he stands for: the hierarchies of class and imperial identity, which refuse to acknowledge their own ideological fissures.

For Lydia, Allan's response to *Norma* in Naples betrays an "Englishness" that is confident in the sense of its own hegemony: "Armadale said—with an Englishman's exasperating pride in his own stupidity, wherever a matter of Art is concerned—that he couldn't make head or tail of the performance" (557). Lydia's frantic desire to separate Midwinter from Allan, to "decolonize" the former— are based on a recognition of Englishness itself as fraught, unstable, incoherent. Another *Cornhill* illustration shows Lydia mediating between the "fair" and "dark" Armadales; from the beginning, in Wrentmore's confession, it was she who had initiated the confusion between them. In the illustration, her dress is literally split, in terms of light and shadow, complicating the very notion of "whiteness." Because both Allan and Midwinter desire Lydia sexually, her body becomes the embattled site upon which their racial and cultural anxieties are played out. Adept at the art of poisoning, she herself becomes the "poison" that once absorbed, induces vulnerability and dissolution.

"Becoming" Poison

Lydia is also allied with two other figures who constantly move back and forth between center and periphery in Victorian society. The first is Mother Oldershaw of the "Ladies' Toilette Repository": Lydia's foster mother, correspondent and business partner, based on the notorious beauty expert, Madame Rachel Levison. The sensational trials of Rachel Levison for fraud, which took place in London during the period that Collins was writing *Armadale,* stirred up Victorian England's deepest fears about ambitious and resourceful female tricksters.[41] An "exotic" outsider herself, the Jewish Madame Rachel had opened a cosmetics shop in Bond Street in the mid-1860s that converted the Victorian fascination with exoticism into a wildly successful business enterprise. Her business was built upon creating and marketing exotic bodies that remained essentially inaccessible and unattainable. Here, she promised to use her Eastern cosmetics, "preparations made up of the purest, rarest and most fragrant productions of the East," such as "the Magnetic Dew of the Sahara," "Jordan Water," "Favourite of the Harem's Pearl White," "the Royal Arabian Toilet of Beauty as arranged by Madame Rachel for the Sultana of Turkey," "Arab Bloom Powder," and the "Arabian baths" to "remove all personal defects, put a bloom on old visages . . . and thus manufacture antiquated belles into charming juveniles" (5–6). By trading on "colonial desires," Rachel was able to invade the bastions of the wealthy bourgeoisie, even getting herself a box at the opera. At her second trial in 1868, she was convicted for massive fraud and even accused of dabbling in prostitution. For Victorians, the most horrifying aspect of the trial was the existence of female criminals like Rachel at the heart of respectable society, women who could construct their own master narratives. The newspapers compared Rachel to women authors of sensation fiction such as Mary Elizabeth Braddon: "For here is sensation and plot quite as thrilling as *Lady Audley's Secret,* with morals nearly as offensive as those which the purveyors, foreign and domestic of fornicating literature commonly venture upon. . . . Mrs. Levison, we are asked to believe, could invent this plot and is master of this language, and yet Mrs. Levison cannot write and probably can hardly read" (122).

Cosmetics and poison, were of course, aligned in Victorian discourses on the female body. "Arsenic Complexion Wafers" were in use till the beginning of the twentieth century, and beauty guides claimed that cosmetics for the skin contained "the most deadly poisons in the whole catalogue for chemical products" such as corrosive sublimate, prussic acid, and arsenic.[42] The idea of sculpting an artificial body with the use of poisonous cosmetics could also make one's body fade into that of the racial other. As one American doctor commented, the use of lip salve was necessitated by a "life of dissipation" that affected the blood, "impoverishing" and "decolorizing it." Frequent use "thickened" the lips giving a "peculiar tint to the mouth," likening it to the "shriveled, purplish one of a sick negress" (350). The *Cornhill Magazine* cautioned its female readers against the dangerous effects of rouge and pearl powder, pointing out that pearl powder was mainly used by "foreign actresses," and that Englishwomen should not attempt to "pass" by altering "obstinately brown complexions" by such means (344).[43] The alliance between Lydia and Mother Oldershaw (Rachel) heightens the poison-maquillage connection in *Armadale;* both women are involved with "poisons" that threaten to corrode/destroy stable cultural identities.

Lydia's other associate is the abortionist and quack psychiatrist, Dr. Downward, who helps her to initiate her plan to murder Allan Armadale with poison gas in his newly designed sanatorium. The madhouse becomes the final fixed yet inchoate space in which Lydia passionately tries to "reclaim" Midwinter and force him to negotiate his own "otherness" or hybridity; an acknowledgment that would also find expression through his renewed desire for her. By now, her hatred for Allan Armadale and the kind of normalization he represents has reached fever pitch; as she reveals in her Italian diary: "If some women bring such men into the world, ought other women to allow them to live? It is a matter of opinion. *I* think not. What maddens me, is to see, as I do plainly, that Midwinter finds in Armadale's company, and in Armadale's new yacht, a refuge from *me*" (553). On a tour of the madhouse, Dr. Downward explains the architectural features of certain rooms, which contain hidden "fumigation apparatuses," so that asthmatic nervous patients can be "noiselessly" provided with oxygen. For Lydia, this signifies a kind of panoptical reversal, where she can observe Allan Armadale without being seen, as she floods the room with poisonous carbonic acid. The ingeniously constructed madhouse gas chamber allows her simultaneously to envision regaining control of the gaze and compelling Armadale to experience profound alienation. Downward explains the action of the poison, contained in a "purple flask": "Quantities of little bubbles . . . will kill him slowly, without his seeing anything, without his smelling anything, without his feeling anything but sleepiness. Will kill him, and tell the whole College of Surgeons nothing, if they examine him after death, but that he died of apoplexy or congestion of the lungs! What do you think of that, my dear lady . . . ?" (642).

Yet Lydia ultimately turns her elaborately conceived poisoning device on her own body. When Midwinter, suspicious of her actions, changes places with Allan, Lydia drags him out and then enters the poison chamber herself. Her suicide, far from being the sacrificial act that enthralled Dickens and Forster,[44] can be read as a frantic gesture of defiance. In this way she evades a criminal trial, her body resisting reappropriation and reinscription by the legal/criminological system. If, in *Armadale,* we read hybridity and "poison" as interchangeable, then Lydia's final exhibition of agency is to allow the poison (carbonic acid) to envelop her body completely. Like Cleopatra, she stages the spectacle of her own death. To succumb to poison is to embrace her own nomadism, exoticism, and sense of estrangement *within* herself, to experience herself as a "foreign body."[45] The embrace of poison is also an escape, from a body continuously subject to the pressures of normalization and surveillance. Choosing Allan over Lydia, assimilation over his own hybridity, Midwinter resists this embrace to the very end. Lydia's final gesture dramatizes a self-hybridization that is also a moment of deliberate, flamboyant excess. Ultimately, as Lydia *stages* her hybridity, she simultaneously acknowledges that its disruptive power and ability to grant agency is limited and must be realized elsewhere, through death. As Bellini's colonized Norma claims before her contemplated suicide through fire:

Ma tosto . . . adesso consumar potrei l'ecesso.
[But soon—now—I shall commit the fearful excess.][46]

The Legacy of Cain and Hereditary Poison

In his last completed novel, *The Legacy of Cain* (1888), Collins uses the figure of the female poisoner to intervene in contemporary discussions of heredity and degeneration. Lombroso had already laid out the fundamental concepts of his theory of criminal atavism in *The Criminal Man.* The other major post-Darwinian investigator of issues relating to heredity was the British ethnologist Sir Francis Galton, who, like Lombroso, helped to revolutionize criminology by pioneering the development of fingerprinting techniques. Regarded as the founder of the eugenics movement, Galton published *Hereditary Genius: An*

Inquiry into its Laws and Consequences in 1869.[47] In his introduction, Galton clearly set forth his agenda, emphasizing the importance of "natural inheritance" and advocating the necessity of selective breeding:

> I propose to show in this book that a man's natural abilities are derived by inheritance, under exactly the same limitations as are the form and physical features of the whole organic world. Consequently, as it is easy, notwithstanding these limitations, to obtain by careful selection a permanent breed of dogs or horses gifted with peculiar powers of running, or of doing anything else, so it would be quite practicable to produce a highly-gifted race of men by judicious marriages during several consecutive generations.[48]

The Legacy of Cain investigates the discursive fragility of degeneration theory through the intertwining bodies of its two heroines, Helena and Eunice. Like Lydia Gwilt, they narrate their own version of events through their diaries. Eunice is the daughter of a murderess, convicted and hanged for her crime. Although the text does not explicitly name the crime, it hints at poisoning, as the evidence at the trial reveals "deliberate and merciless premeditation" (2).[49] Her daughter is adopted by a minister, Mr. Gracedieu (the name a peculiar echo of the wrecked ship in *Armadale*), who brings her up with his own daughter without allowing either of them to know their real ages, so that Eunice's heritage with its "poisonous" maternal taint may be suppressed, if not erased. The doctor at the prison, a Galtonian, predicts a disaster:

> When I think of the growth of that poisonous hereditary taint, which may come with time—when I think of passions let loose and temptations lying in ambush—I see the smooth surface of the Minister's domestic life with dangers lurking under it which make me shake in my shoes. . . . I should come down to breakfast with suspicions in my cup of tea, if I discovered that my adopted daughter had poured it out. (21)

Collins deliberately confuses the bodies of the two sisters, so that it becomes impossible to classify them or trace either one to the murderess. Eunice has odalisque-like qualities: she is dark and indolent, with a pale complexion. Helena is fairer, with grey eyes and light brown hair. However, Helena finds Eunice's languor contagious: "I noticed the old easy indolent movements again . . . which I can never contemplate without feeling a stupefying influence that has helped me to many a delicious night's sleep" (42).

Both women acknowledge and are ready to act on their sexual desires, focusing on the same man, the weak and vacillating Philip Dunboyne, who cannot decide between the sisters. Collins reverses the gaze so that Philip's sexual attractions are repeatedly the subject of female erotic fantasies in the novel; as Eunice comments: "His hair curls naturally. In colour, it is something between my hair and Helena's. He wears his beard. How manly! It curls naturally, like his hair; it smells deliciously of some perfume which is new to me" (53). Helena voyeuristically consumes Eunice's articulation of her desire while reading the latter's diary: "If I had not seen the familiar handwriting, nothing would have induced me to believe that a girl brought up in a pious household . . . could have written that shameless record of passions unknown to young ladies in respectable English life" (100). For Philip, the object of their desires, the two sisters' bodies are constantly encroaching on each other as he moves back and forth between them.

While Eunice has a near pyschotic episode in which her mother's spirit exhorts her to murder Helena, it is Helena in the end who resorts to poison. When Philip lies ill in their house, Helena begins to poison him gradually. She confesses in her diary that she is motivated by his sexual rejection of her: "I had made my poor offering to a man who secretly loathed me. I wonder that I survived my sense of my own degradation" (276). As Eunice wrestles with her "hereditary taint," Helena embraces poison to gain absolute power over the male body. Like the Italian opera and French novels, access to which had been denied by the harsh regime of her fanatically religious father, poison is seductive and "foreign." It also provides a way for Helena to articulate her overwhelming rage: "Rage—furious, overpowering, deadly rage" (275).

In her diary, Helena records her experience of reading about "a strange case of intended poisoning" in which a married woman seeks revenge for some "unendurable wrong at the hands of her husband's mother." When caught in the act, this young woman "of strong passions" had cleverly disguised her guilt by implicating her maid. The contemplation of poison as a way out eventually leads to a legal separation, freeing the wife from her oppressive marriage. Helena comments on the impact of the poisoner's "extraordinary courage and resolution": "A remarkable story, which has made such an impression on me that I have written it in my Journal" (262). She returns to it repeatedly as she contemplates the art of toxicology and its place in her own life: "I went back to my bedroom, and opened my Diary, and read the story again. . . . Would it be running too great a risk to show the story to the doctor, and try to get a little valuable information in that way? It would be useless. He would make some feeble joke; he would say, girls and poisons are not fit company for each other" (283).

Through her reading of this poisoning case, Helena recognizes the female poisoner as a transgressive woman struggling to recover agency in a world that consistently encourages her to discipline her desires. As she begins to live this narrative, she constantly flirts with the desire to flaunt her knowledge of it as a signature of her rebellion and agency. The governor notes that Helena's "insolence" and "audacity" springs from "a secret course of reading" (183). (Her father, the Reverend Gracedieu, is a harsh and repressive parent who forbids his daughters to read novels and newspapers.) Yet Helena's engagement with poison is more complex than this: by taking on Eunice's poisoned maternal "inheritance," she exoticizes herself and triggers the collapse of classification systems based on theories of inherited criminality. Helena is convicted, goes to prison, and escapes to America, where, as "the Reverend Miss Gracedieu" she carries on her masquerades by becoming the "distinguished leader of a new community" (326). Like Madeleine Smith, who wrote passionate love letters to her lover Emile before poisoning him, Helena will not allow her sexuality to be silenced or denied.

In *The Legacy of Cain* the male body is more vulnerable to infiltration by various types of poison. The prison governor speculates that Eunice's upbringing in the minister's household, together with "the better qualities in her father's nature" will counteract her mother's poisonous blood. Yet the minister himself "degenerates" into imbecility and madness, his collapse supposedly brought on by fanaticism and overwork. Consumed by sexual jealousy, he savagely attacks the picture of his "virtuous" dead wife (who had rejected the murderess's daughter and attempted to prevent her entry into the household). The threat of degeneration seems to be contained *within* the Gracedieu family as Collins shifts the source of poison from the maternal body to that of the father. As their father degenerates, Eunice and Helena both experience varying degrees of freedom/agency. Meanwhile, Philip Dunboyne, initially seduced by Eunice's "poisonous" exoticism, is literally poisoned by Helena.

Collins's *empoisonneuses* use poison to textualize bodies (their own and that of others), investing them with a dangerous hybridity that dismantles the formulation of fixed national/imperial identities. The crime of poisoning opens up for them "the point of departure" through which, muses Hélène Cixous, "we suddenly become the stranger, the foreigner in ourselves. We separate ourselves from ourselves."[50] They consistently throw attempts to fix their bodies through the lens of Victorian ethnocriminology into disorder. In both novels the connections among women, poison, and exoticism allow a disturbing polyvalence to erupt into the articulation of whiteness/Englishness, disabling the self-legitimations of colonial discourse from within. Seduced by poison's exotic femininity, Collins's female poisoners are able to evade/defy hegemonic domestic and imperial narratives of race, sexuality, and desire.

✿ 3 ✿

Infection as Resistance

Exoticized Memsahibs and
Native Courtesans in Colonial India

In this chapter and the next, I consider the transgressive space(s) occupied by hybridized female bodies both in relation to "contagion" and the disciplinary procedures instituted to control it. Foucault's dissection of the emergence of the "clinical gaze" in the eighteenth and nineteenth centuries provides a useful framework for theorizing the location of disease within imperial discourse. In *The Birth of the Clinic: An Archeology of Medical Perception*, Foucault notes the centrality of the clinical gaze to ways of "scientific" seeing and outlines the shift at the end of the eighteenth century from clinical methodologies focused primarily on restoring *health* ("qualities of vigor, suppleness and fluidity which were lost in illness" [35]) to forms of medicalized knowledge that structured themselves around the idea of *pathology*.[1]

Prior to this moment, the disease always hovered between visibility and invisibility. Between the disease and the symptom was a "distance" that often manifested itself "obliquely and unexpectedly" (90), creating the recognition that the disease contained impenetrable, hidden layers that marked the limits of medical perception: its ability to penetrate and classify. This distance was replaced by the evolution of a totalizing clinical gaze in which the symptoms themselves became identified with pathology, and the pathological body entirely transparent.

Foucault does not extend his analysis to the rise of colonial medicine, which accompanied colonialism and quickly established itself as one of the most important branches of medical knowledge in the nineteenth century. Neither does he discuss the way clinically pathologized bodies (in colonial medicine, especially, disease was usually configured in terms of the exotic other) might interrupt this gaze or how contagious bodies might generate a different kind of knowledge, intervening in this clinical trajectory. There are also limitations to Foucault's generalized approach to medical discourse and historical shifts. As we saw in chapter 2, forensic medicine acknowledged and continued to struggle with the opacity and inaccessibility of poison well into the nineteenth century.

Moreover, diseased female bodies were subjected to a different type of medical gaze than male ones; this is another blind spot in Foucault's attempt to situate the clinical gaze. There is no doubt however, that *The Birth of The Clinic* sets up a powerful paradigm for characterizing the *drive* toward complete knowledge of the pathological other, especially in the context of imperial medicine. In this chapter, I intend to complicate this Foucauldian idea by focusing on British colonial writer Flora Annie Steel's fictionalization of "contagious" exchanges between "memsahibs" and courtesans in colonial India and the subtle seduction of Englishwomen's bodies by the latter.

During the mid-nineteenth century, successive epidemics of "Asiatic cholera" swept Europe. Death by this "Indian Plague," which reached Britain in October 1831 (resurfacing in 1848 and 1854), was dramatic, sudden, and swift. Healthy and alive in the morning, a cholera victim could be dead by the evening, having passed through the agonies of cramps, vomiting, and diarrhea. The expansion of British colonialism, marked by the spectacular displays of the Great Exhibition of London in 1851, had ironically provided the very circumstances by means of which the disease had traveled westward from India in 1817.[2] For Charlotte Brontë, in *Shirley* (1849), cholera was intensely racialized: "The future sometimes seems . . . like some gathering though yet remote storm . . . commissioned to bring in fog the yellow taint of pestilence, covering white Western Isles with the poisoned exhalations of the East, dimming the lattices of English homes with the breath of Indian Plague."[3]

Thomas Mann's 1912 novella, *Death in Venice*, casts cholera-racked Venice as one of the points of entry through which contagion creeps into Europe. "The poisoned exhalations of the East," which the colonial medical establishment was struggling to control throughout most of the nineteenth century, could stage a reverse invasion, dissolving the boundaries between "home" and the colonies. Brontë's conception of an "infected" fog owes much to the theory of miasmatism, which prevailed in the early Victorian period; those who subscribed to this believed that diseases such as fever and cholera traveled through and flourished in foul air, or "miasma." Before the etiologies of specific diseases were discovered and debated, it was literally the breath of the infected "other," whether constructed in terms of race or class, that was imagined as invasive and threatening.[4]

The association of severe and debilitating infections with the climate and environment of the tropics led to the proliferation of medical treatises and practical-advice books on the subject; among them works such as John Clark's *Observations on the Diseases in Long Voyages to Hot Countries* (1773), Johnson's influential study (discussed in chapter 1), and British obstetrician Edward Tilt's *Health in India for British Women* (1875).[5] Controlling the spread of disease was essential for the survival of empire; by insidiously emasculating the representatives of the imperial administration and assaulting their bodies, disease itself could become a site of resistance to colonial authority. Flora Steel slyly described capitulation to North Indian "fever" amid the rigidly inscribed social rituals of Anglo-India in her autobiography, *The Garden of Fidelity:*

> In Lahore we were put up by Henry (afterwards Sir Henry) Cunningham. . . . Here I had my first experience of Panjab fever. As bride, I was of course taken into dinner by my host. Just at dessert time he surprised me by saying in an undertone—"I'm getting fever—speak to your other neighbour and take no notice; I shall get through." He did; but before the ladies left I saw tears running down his cheeks. He was shivering all over.[6]

Colonials did not always "get through." According to reports provided by doctors in the British Indian Medical Service, around 8,500 British soldiers succumbed to cholera between 1818 and 1854. Malaria (known as "intermittent fever") smallpox, enteric fever, and venereal disease were among the other leading causes of sickness and death. Along with the shift from earlier climatic and miasmic theories to the germ theory of disease in the later nineteenth century, colonial medicine also registered a corresponding shift from concern with the effects of hot weather to fears of contagious oriental bodies, chief among which were Indian prostitutes and courtesans.[7] The controversy over "lock hospitals" (where prostitutes were detained until cured of VD) and licensed prostitution was symptomatic of the high prevalence of VD amongst British troops, presumably contracted through their encounters with native women.[8] As the century progressed, Victorian colonial medicine became inevitably preoccupied not only with preserving the "health" of the colonizers, but also with regulating the bodies and medical discourses of the colonized.

European and British women were considered by the imperial medical establishment to be particularly susceptible to the rigors and infections of the tropics.[9] Numerous advice books warned women of repeated assaults by the tropical environment on their bodies. An 1864 domestic manual entitled *The Englishwoman in India: Containing Information for the use of Ladies . . . on the subject of their Outfit, Furniture . . .* , cautioned that footstools should always be used "as they keep the feet out of the way of scorpions. . . . In the sleeping rooms there should be little besides the actual cot, above all, no water, nor any clothes hanging up, as they attract mosquitoes" (37–38). Writing from the Agra Fort in North India in 1857, one memsahib described the intolerable heat: "The heat now began to be overpowering: I was awakened one morning by the most stifling sensation in the air and felt quite ill. The ayah and the bearer said the hot winds had commenced . . . it made your brain feel on fire, and all the blood in your body throb and burn like liquid fire."[10]

While Flora Steel and Grace Gardiner in *The Complete Indian Housekeeper and Cook* (1909) advised that colonial Englishwomen should adapt their dress to the climate, at the same time they warned against succumbing to "oriental" sloppiness and languor: "There is really no reason why the Englishwoman in India should burden herself with the same number of petticoats, shifts and bodices and what not, that her great grandmother wore in temperate climes. We do not advocate any sloppiness of dress, on the contrary, we would inveigh against any yielding to the lassitude and indifference which comes over the most energetic in tropical heat, but we would have people be as comfortable as they can be under the circumstances."[11]

On her initial arrival in India, Steel battled against indigestion caused by eating mangoes: "this disability to keep even a spoonful of mango down remained to the last day of my life in India. . . . I have tried again and again; always with the same despairing result" (*Garden of Fidelity*, 29).

The vicereine, Lady Mary Curzon wrote despairingly to her mother in 1899: "it is a very worrying time for me—what with Nannie ill, and my wet nurse with gastric fever and Cynthia vaccinated and my second nurse ill, and I have toothache till I cry. I am never out of sickrooms though the house is full of guests."[12] Miscarriages were common as women traveled with their husbands to different parts of India, where proper medical help and assistance were not always easily available. As increasing numbers of women began shipping out to the colonies during the mid- to late Victorian period, the management of their bodies became the business of empire. These bodies were encoded simultaneously as fragile, "spotless," and particularly vulnerable to the threat of climatic degeneration/ racial pollution.

Disease and Female Degeneration

In 1875, Edward Tilt, member of the Royal College of Physicians and fellow of the Obstetrical Society of London, published a medical manual entitled *Health in India for British Women* (which I discuss more fully in chapter 4) in which he traced the connections among specifically feminine diseases, reproduction, tropical climates, and colonization. Chapter 4 of this manual, "Diseases of European Women in India," concerns itself with the ominous failure of women's reproductive capacity in the tropics due to the predominance of uterine disease. Besides being the author of numerous books on gynecology that went into several editions—including *On Diseases of Menstruation and Ovarian Inflammation* (1850), *A Handbook of Uterine Therapeutics* (1863), and *Health in India for British Women* (1875)—Tilt was one of the original fellows of the Obstetrical Society of London, eventually became its president, and held various important appointments throughout his medical career, which ended in 1893. While pushing the innovative use of the speculum and challenging certain contemporary gynecological practices, such as the excessive use of surgery, he also clung to others, including recommending clitoridectomy as a cure for masturbation and the application of leeches to the vagina.

Tilt agrees with previous practitioners of colonial medicine that "during their stay in India our countrywomen are unusually prone to disturbed action of the reproductive organs, and particularly to ovario-uterine disease (55)."[13] He then sets out to explain the probable causes; most of which center around "excitement" and a fast, fashionable, public lifestyle that resembles that of the demimondaine:

> Thus placed in circumstances adverse to health, women find themselves the more sought after because they are few in number, and they naturally enough give themselves up to the pursuit of pleasure, and set at defiance the laws of hygiene . . . before long the colourless lips and the sallow cheeks denote that climate has intensified the effects of neglected hygienic rules. There is an effort made to continue fashionable life at one of our Eastern capitals, but the effort induces abdominal pains, nervousness, depression of spirits and perhaps hysteria. . . . Suppose . . . the lady be married; if bent on pleasure she seldom takes more care of herself during pregnancy than during menstruation, and a miscarriage is a likely event. (56)

Vanity, pleasure, excess, and indolence interfere with the incorporation of the colonial wife into the ideological web of reproduction and motherhood, severely damaging her "female" functions, reducing the womb to a "morbid" state. This deformation of the uterus begins with the effect of climatic change on menstruation: "when women are transplanted from temperate regions to tropical countries, frequent perturbations of the menstrual function may be expected" (58). Miscarriages are brought on by "fever, diarrhea, or the continued heat of the hot season" (59). According to Tilt, the "too early resumption" of exercise, social and marital obligations, and a refusal to confine herself to her bed and room caused the unnatural enlargement of a woman's uterus—and in India it was often "beyond the scope of the womb's recuperative power to reduce itself." Consequently, it became "a permanent menace of disease," continually "congested, irritated, ulcerated."

Disease and deformity usurped and dismantled the memsahib's reproductive role. This state of disease was aggravated by "tropical anaemia," caused by "habitually intense heat" and malaria, along with "a complete change of habits which too often impart a certain amount of oriental indolence to the once hardy Englishwoman." By producing "orientalized" female bodies, infection threatened to unravel the domestic threads that held the imperial fabric together. Tilt concluded that "the reproductive power of our countrywomen suffers diminution and that their children must return to England or degenerate" (98). His question: "Can the Anglo-Saxon race colonize India?" points to the crucial importance of women's bodies within the ideological narratives of empire. *Health in India for British Women* clearly constructs uterine infections and deformity as symptomatic of the female body's revolt against both domesticity and imperialism.

The Infectious and Transgressive Zenana

Apart from the colonial brothel, the other significant space that aligned infection, femininity, and the threat of resistance was the zenana or women's secluded, inner quarters. The contagion of both had to be contained in order to ensure the health of the empire. Feminist historians have referred to the zenana as the "uncolonized space,"[14] as here women could be more easily isolated from the influence of the "civilizing mission," which would include the intervention of colonial medicine. Although this definition is problematic, as it proposes the idea of the zenana as hermetically sealed off from the outside world, in the latter half of the nineteenth century European women doctors, reformers, and missionaries became intensely preoccupied with "opening up" the zenana, bringing "light" into the "darkness" of the harem.[15] They encountered considerable resistance from the zenana women, however, as their narratives testify. In 1856, one reformer complained that "the obstacles to the conversion of females living in the higher circles of society are very great. They have no opportunity whatever of listening to the Missionary when he preaches in the streets and bazaars. He cannot visit their apartments, nor can they go to him."[16] Even if female missionaries managed to penetrate the interior of the zenana, they were confronted with opposition, as the women held obstinately to their own religious beliefs. Mrs. Weitbrecht, in *The Women of India and Christian Work in the Zenana* (1875) admitted her failure to convince Hindu women to give up their goddess worship in favor of the Christian male god: "I told them that she was only a stone, and had no virtue in her, and that there is only one true god, who has created us all . . . they were staunch in their belief of this goddess."[17]

Moreover, the zenana was marked as a site of infection, as European doctors did not have easy access. In her novel *The Potter's Thumb*, Steel called the zenana the "plague-spot" of India; she in fact believed that the introduction of female doctors into the zenana was a mistake, as it would prevent women from discarding the veil in order to procure proper medical assistance (*Garden of Fidelity*, 177). Weitbrecht also mentioned the "collection of dirty courtyards, dark corners, break-neck staircases, filthy outhouses" in the zenana.[18] Toward the end of the century, the Dufferin Fund was set up to bring imperial medicine into this gendered "inner" space. Mary Frances Billington, praising the work of the Dufferin Fund in *Woman in India* (1885), quoted a contemporary

British journalist on the absolute necessity of invading the zenana if imperialism was to achieve its "greatest" mission:

> what is it at present that hinders all real progress in the country but the overpowering influence of the zenana. Once break down that, or shed light into it and give it a *healthy* and upward direction, and I believe that progress and enlightenment will make such bounds in this country that the regeneration of India will be a living reality. . . . *Get at the women then.* . . . Show them the beauties of Christianity, appeal to their hearts by wisdom and the personal example of beautiful lives, and you will see such an era of progress set in that the regeneration of India will be a reality, and the conversion of its people an accomplished fact. When that is done, England's great mission in India will have been accomplished. (111; my italics)[19]

As an overdetermined cultural space that could produce instability/insurgence in the face of progress and "civilization," the zenana, like the brothel, had to be reinvented, reconfigured, reinscribed. The question I raise here is whether a vulnerability or receptivity to contagion, languor, and sickness constitutes an interruption of colonial imperatives. If it is possible to conceptualize contagion in the imperial context as both racialized and feminized, then in what ways can engagement with disease be implicated as part of a discourse of resistance and rupture, a masking of the "transparency of the symptom" particularly for the colonial British female novelist writing about Indian women?[20]

Flora Steel and *Voices in the Night:* Plague Regulations and the Courtesan's Intervention

The daughter of a Jamaican sugar plantation heiress, Flora Steel had accompanied her husband to India immediately after their marriage, in 1868. She became known later as the "female Kipling," an epithet she probably would not have welcomed.[21] In 1870, Steel lost her first child in a life-threatening pregnancy, due to inadequate medical attention. Though this experience obviously took an emotional and psychological toll, she described herself as having the "recuperative power of an animal" (*Garden of Fidelity*, 45). From 1889 onward, she traveled between India and England, researching her novels; the most famous of which was her best-selling Mutiny romance, *On the Face of the Waters* (1897), written after she was allowed access to the archives of the Indian Mutiny of 1857.

In 1887, she also authored the most popular and definitive domestic guidebook for memsahibs, *The Complete Indian Housekeeper and Cook,* which went into several editions. Here, Steel maintained that ill health was the result of lifestyle (the habit of darkening rooms) rather than climate or environment: "the forced inertia caused by living without light is responsible for many moral and physical evils among European ladies in the tropics."[22] This view was somewhat different from the prevalent nineteenth-century belief that exposure to the tropical sun caused degeneration, and that second- or third-generation Europeans inevitably deteriorated under such conditions, becoming "pallid, weedy and unhealthy looking" (221), a view expressed by members of the Society for Tropical Medicine and Hygiene (later the Royal Society) as late as 1907.[23]

Recent analysis of Steel's work has mostly centered around *On The Face of the Waters.* While commentators such as Jenny Sharpe and Benita Parry have acknowledged the contradictory attitudes toward imperialism in her writing, drawing attention to the figure of the memsahib as a site of uneasy articulations, Steel's Indian women tend to be read as passive racial stereotypes.[24] Here, by looking at some of her lesser-known, (but no less remarkable) fiction, which has so far been largely ignored, I offer a more problematic reading of her odalisque-courtesans, and *their* interventions in the memsahib's "vulnerable"[25] sexual and domestic identities.

Steel's late Victorian novel *Voices in the Night: A Chromatic Fantasia* (1900),[26] which deals with the onset of bubonic plague in the fictional town of Nushapore in imperial India, engages with some of the central dilemmas of colonial medicine and its attempts to control the exotic female subject. *Voices in the Night* is remarkable for the way in which its narrative enacts the tension between resistance to disease and disease-as-resistance, while simultaneously investigating the problem of female intervention. Steel interweaves the stories of two British women, Grace Arbuthnot, the governor's wife, and her son's governess Lesley Drummond, with those of several Indian women, among them an impoverished but aristocratic Muslim wife, Noormahal, and a princess turned courtesan, Sobrai Begum. A characteristic feature of Steel's fiction is her fascination with fiercely independent and rebellious Indian courtesans. The landscape of the novel is split into the two halves of a colonial cantonment town, with its British section, and the native quarters, or "bazaar areas," which, in colonial iconography, became the locus of contamination as well as political resistance.[27] Many cantonments also contained areas known as "regimental bazaars," where prostitution could be regulated. Described in terms of filth and clutter with its "cavernous shadows" and "squalid shops," Steel's bazaar is dominated by the courtesan, Dilaram, "yawning, blowsy, ill kempt," with an "indescribable grace" and a sharp wit. Spatially, the novel maps the areas of bazaar, brothel, hospital, zenana, and the interior of the Arbuthnot's residence, Government House (Nushapore's center of imperial power), continually negotiating anxieties about boundaries that threaten to shift and unfix themselves through the spread of plague.

The action of *Voices in the Night* unfolds against the background of the colonial administration's attempts to check the spread of plague in the bazaars and cantonments of Nushapore. Steel's novel is extremely topical; in the 1890s, due to major plague epidemics, the British government in India had implemented stringent anti-plague measures, which included compulsory segregation and hospitalization, the right of forced entry into Indian houses (even if it implied violating the seclusion of women), along with a massive campaign to cleanse or flush out the bazaars with disinfectants. Before the transmission of plague became clear, the bodies of the colonized were regarded as the source of infection. Though few Europeans came down with the disease, they were haunted by anxiety; an 1899 address in *The Lancet* blamed the encroachment of the disease on trade and expressed the fear that it would travel from India through Egypt into Europe.[28] For the colonized, resistance to plague regulations that treated their bodies as "state property," became linked with political dissent, and it is this situation that Steel so compellingly dramatizes in her novel.[29]

In *Voices in the Night,* while the local governor, Sir George Arbuthnot, vacillates as to whether he should institute such measures, his wife Grace has meanwhile hidden a secret letter from her father outlining the British government's official intentions, in her jewel box. When the box is stolen and the letter is believed to have disappeared into the depths of the bazaar; Grace's indiscretion prompts the "natives" to strategize their resistance and begin planning countermeasures against the plague regulations. Throughout the novel, Grace, delicate, languid, elegant, and unhappily married, is uncomfortably positioned, as she conceals her unconscious collusion with the "natives" from her husband, desperately trying to recover the letter. While struggling with her guilty secret, she senses a strange connection or affinity with the courtesans or dancing girls in the bazaar; an affinity that interrupts her regulated life as imperial wife and mother: "As she passed up the wide stairs . . . the open window let in a sound. . . . The most restless sound in the world . . . it came faintly, indefinitely from the distance and darkness of the city. She could see through the murk and shadow, the light of flicker and flare on the circling faces round the shrilling voice or posturing figure of a woman" (142). The "insistent throbbing" from the bazaar produces a "passion of unrest" in Grace that can only be suppressed by watching her sleeping son who, as yet uncontaminated, embodies the "spirit of the (conquering) race" (142–43).

Grace's antithesis is the ideal colonial governess Lesley Drummond: practical, "lacking sentiment," "an ordinary woman," who assists the novel's hero, Jack Raymond, to foil the Indian insurgents protesting the anti-plague measures, in the process proving herself an efficient guardian of empire. Earlier, both Grace and Leslie find themselves hosting a tea party in what had formerly been a courtesan's pleasure garden: "It was a quaint place, tucked away between two angles of the city wall for greater convenience in secret comings and goings to secret pleasures; and it was all the quainter now because of the Englishwomen sipping tea on the steps of the gilded summer house, the Englishmen calling tennis scores in what had been the rose water tank, in which kings' favourites had bathed, and on which they had floated in silver barges" (235). As the courtesans' sensual yet spectral presences invade the atmosphere of the garden, they also assault the "civilizing impulse" of the English tea party, overwhelming and disturbing Leslie: "What was she, Lesley Drummond, doing there in that garden whose suggestiveness seemed to stifle her?" While Leslie struggles against the garden's unsettling seductiveness, Grace, enjoying an adulterous flirtation, seems to welcome its dangerous sensuality: "the scent of the garden drifted in unchecked, and mixed with the faint scent of heliotrope from Grace Arbuthnot's dress" (243).

It is the Indian women in the novel, however, whose bodies not only become the location of the threat of disease; but also vehicles through which the discourse of infection is translated into that of insurgence. The British colonials in *Voices in the Night* are haunted by echoes of the Indian Mutiny of 1857, in which courtesans and bazaar prostitutes were supposed to have played a crucial role by disseminating rumors and urging the mutineers on by taunting their masculinity. Veena Oldenburg's perceptive research on nineteenth-century Indian courtesans has shown that in many cases, they supported the rebellion financially as well.[30] Besides, they could weaken the British military substantially by transmitting venereal disease and other infections; a problem the imperial government sought to control with the Indian Contagious Diseases Acts of 1864, which established a system of licensed prostitution where the women were periodically examined.[31] In *Voices in the Night,* the courtesan Dilaram, refusing to submit to the licensing system, instead actively stirs up unrest by spreading rumors that the British are using the plague to "search respectable houses" to kidnap young women for licensed brothels. Phillipa Levine's study of the licensing of prostitution in colonial India points to the labyrinthine complexity of this debate. Even after the imperial CD Acts were repealed, forms of licensing continued in India; the subject of a fierce controversy between regulationists and antiregulationists, between social purity activists, feminists and imperial administrators.[32]

Most Indian courtesans received training in classical music and dance; actively shaping/producing culture in the process. Steel's courtesans are always dancers or "nautch" girls. Emma Roberts, author of *Scenes and Characteristics of Hindustan* (1835), observed that it could be a lucrative career for some: "Many of the nautch girls are extremely rich, those most in esteem being very highly paid for their performances: the celebrated Calcutta heroine already mentioned receives 1000 rupees nightly, whenever she is engaged" (348). Several travel narratives claimed that the girls were asked to sanitize their dancing in front of an audience composed of European women. Writing in 1777, Jemima Kindersley commented that "it is their languishing glances, wanton smiles, and attitudes not quite consistent with decency, which are so much admired" (336). Despite this, female observers of the nautch (with some notable exceptions) expressed a level of discomfort with the public display of the female body. Although these accounts agree that the nautches are not "indecent," they nevertheless condemn the performances as meaningless and grotesque.[33]

Gérôme's painting of an Egyptian dancer, *Dance of the Almeh* (1863), is an interesting example of how the exoticized woman's body could be liberating for women viewers, despite its superficial trappings of erotic fantasy. In ethnographic travel literature, the Eastern dancing girl, known as almeh/ghazeeyeh (plural ghawazee) in the Middle East and nautch girl in India, was marked by her visible, public body (as distinct from the invisible, private body of the harem inmate).[34] Gérôme's almeh publicly displays her flamboyant, uncorseted body with considerable self-assurance. She refuses to be domesticated. When the painting was exhibited in the Salon of 1864, it was viewed as "immoral" by some critics.[35]

According to Edward Lane, in his *Manners and Customs of the Modern Egyptians,* the dancer's display of her body negotiated the realm of the *unspeakable:* "Some of them, when they exhibit before a private party of men, wear nothing but the shintiyan (or trousers) . . . or semi transparent coloured gauze, open nearly halfway down the front. To extinguish the least spark of modesty which they may yet sometimes affect to retain, they are plentifully supplied with brandy or some other intoxicating liquor. The scenes which ensue *cannot be described"* (my italics).

Indescribable, unrepresentable, dressed in clothes that dislocate gender specificity, the almeh ultimately repudiates Lane's ethnographic/clinical gaze. Lane also pointed out that "these women are the most abandoned of the courtesans of Egypt" and that "women, as well as men take delight in witnessing their performances" (386).[36] Neither did the dancer always stay within the bounds of pleasurable or acceptable entertainment. British observers of the "nautch" in India often commented that the nautch woman's movements often crossed the line between desire and repulsion, "if thrown off their guard by applause, there is some danger of their carrying the suppleness of their body and limbs quite beyond the graceful, and even bordering on the disgusting," producing a sense of unease in the male viewer: "the situation of the gentleman in this case is irksome and uncomfortable." European women could not be exposed to such exhibitions; as Emma Roberts wryly remarked, the girls had to regulate their dancing in front of a female audience: "In the presence of European ladies the dancing of the nautch girls is dull and decorous." Both Flaubert and Lucy Duff Gordon, however, commented on the Egyptian dancer's reluctance to dance in the nude.[37]

In colonial India, performed in the "bazaar" areas as well as in private homes, the nautches constantly crossed borders. They sometimes involved cross-dressing as well. Consider, for example, Burton's version of the nautch, in which the principal dancer resists the male gaze and the girls perform a "melodrama" in male dress, "confusing" the sexes: "You feel that there is something in her look which spurns rather than courts ardent eyes. . . . Now for the ballet, or melodrama, the favourite piece of the evening. The ladies all equip themselves in manly and martial dresses" (354).[38] At the core of Steel's narrative are two spectacular performances that mark the exotic female body as not only excessive and infected, but also as a site where revolt is articulated and reformulated *through* the threat of infection. The first is the erotic self-display of the courtesan/dancer Sobrai Begum. In Sobrai, Steel presents an amazingly emancipated woman who is able to shrug off the sexual restrictions of both Indian and British culture. A former princess who has escaped a respectable but dull life of genteel poverty to enter a licensed brothel, Sobrai constructs a spectacle of herself as a public woman, dancing before the British soldiers "with a fierce exultation" and an unrestrained yet dignified sensuality (162). As an upper-class woman turned prostitute, her body challenges social hierarchies because of its extraordinary mobility. During the dance, she comes face to face with Grace Arbuthnot, who happens to be passing by. Despite her husband's attempts to distract her from this display, Grace sees "in the flesh" what she had earlier envisioned "in her mind's eye" (162), as the courtesan's spectacular body claims visibility.

For Grace, Sobrai's revolutionary exhibitionism intensifies and actualizes the allure of the unsanitized space, providing a momentary glimpse of an unregulated female body drawing its energy from the "contamination" of the overcrowded bazaar. Here, Sobrai deliberately constructs herself as a seductive body that undermines the coherence of the manageable, productive female bodies that are essential for the proper functioning of empire.[39] Sobrai's act is particularly significant in the light of the newly passed legislation of 1895, under which prostitutes were prohibited from residence in regimental bazaars.[40] The discovery of Grace's stolen pearls in Sobrai's room further destabilizes the boundaries between their bodies; creating an uneasy sense of physical/emotional/moral exchange and shared culpability that reinforces Grace's feelings of guilt, collusion, and contamination.

The second performance takes place in the household or zenana of another economically disadvantaged Muslim aristocrat, Noormahal, whose space is violated as two British men force themselves in to search for plague victims. After years of struggling with her abusive husband to claim an inheritance for herself and her child, Noormahal stages her resistance to both patriarchy and imperialism through suicide: "With one cry of 'Liars,' . . . the slender white figure leaped into the air; and the Nawabin Noormahal, the Light-of-Palaces, went down as she had stood, mocking, defiant, into the depth of the well" (290).

Noormahal's defiant suicide is also connected with a tremendous act of domestic insurgence: refusing her husband entry. There are smaller, quieter acts of rebellion as well; Noormahal and her aging aunt secretly bury the body of a female relative who dies of plague to prevent it from being desecrated by the clinical gaze of inspection. In this novel, the other woman's body signifies the burden and consequences of defiance; the "contagion" that "fallen" memsahibs have to struggle to avoid is not only that of disease, but also of female disorder, communicated insidiously through the native woman's attempts to intervene in the imperial narrative of her body-as-spectacle.

The Exoticized Adventuress in *The Potter's Thumb*

An earlier novel, *The Potter's Thumb*, considered by some of Steel's contemporaries to be her finest work,[41] compulsively redraws the boundaries of harem, bazaar, and the colonial boudoir by probing the tensions and "contagious" affinities that exist between two women—the courtesan Chandni and the memsahib Gwen Boynton. The action of the novel unfolds against the initiation of a British irrigation scheme in the town of Hodinuggar; as in Steel's other fiction, *The Potter's Thumb* positions the colonial administration against an impoverished and decaying Indian aristocracy, whose resistance takes shape through women's involvement in intrigue. This involvement is facilitated, rather than hampered by seclusion; like Lady Mary Wortley Montagu and Julia Pardoe before her, Steel is fully aware of the flexibility of the veil: "For the custom of seclusion renders intrigue absolutely safe, since none dare put the identity of a white robed figure to the test, or pry into the privacy of a place claimed by a *purdahnishin*."[42]

Recasting intrigue to reflect defiance, Chandni initiates an ingeniously convoluted plot to steal the key of the sluice gate so that the native inhabitants of the town can divert the water for their own purposes. In this sense, the courtesan's insurgence drives the narrative and constructs the plot. Prostitute, dancer, and bazaar woman, Steel imagines Chandni in terms of massiveness and authority—a modern Medea haunted by a consciousness of her own power; a mysterious, imposing, hybrid figure in "her trailing white Delhi draperies and massive garlands, a figure which might have stood for some of those strange solemn-eyed statues, half Greek, half Indian" (258). She arranges her own spectacles of subversion through mimicry, giving "a spirited imitation of the way the memsahibs waltzed with the sahib logue" (36). As a courtesan, she negotiates inner and outer worlds with ease, rejecting marriage with vehemence: "She was not going to marry a fool in order to wear a veil and live with a lot of women" (254).

While Chandni presides over the bazaar, the colonial ballroom serves as a backdrop for the elegant professional adventuress, Gwen Boynton, who, like the courtesan must use her sexual power and intelligence to ensure her own survival. Widowed and in debt, Gwen is a perfect example of Tilt's "fast," "fashionable" memsahib on the brink of uterine degeneration, manipulating the surface of her body to entrap men: "her evening dresses always had a seamless look, and the lace about her fair shoulders always seemed pinned on with cunning little diamond brooches glittering and sparkling" (28). Gwen's "seamless" appearance brings her closer to the flowing, uncorseted, languid body of the odalisque; as Steel comments earlier, "the burka is of all disguises the most complete" (27). Flirting with her suitor, Dan Fitzgerald, as she assesses his financial worth, she decides that "if he did not get his promotion, she could not possibly marry him" (27). Because of her debts, which Steel implies arise from her love of luxury, Gwen becomes entangled in Chandni's web of blackmail and deception, the ultimate goal of which is to disrupt the British irrigation project.

Between them, they drive the young imperialist, the naive and earnest George Keene, to suicide when he realizes that Gwen has tricked him in order to obtain the key to the gate of the canal. Significantly, this occurs while he is recuperating from fever in the hills. Gwen Boynton's connection and complicity with the courtesan is underscored when the former dresses up as an Indian woman, growing uneasily aware of a seductive contagion that reproduces her body as alien, hybrid, indefinable: "It seemed scarcely a minute ago since she had passed swiftly into the solitude of her own room in order to think. She, Gwen Boynton, in native dress, with a white, scared face. . . . Now she had to pass out of that room again as an Englishwoman, and the transition left her oddly undecided" (102). Here, Gwen senses her Englishness only as a "partial presence," one that interrogates itself through mimicry.[43] Thefts and feverish exchanges dominate the narrative; as in *Voices in the Night,* the text obsessively enacts the fraught, shared guilt between courtesans and memsahibs. Keys and stolen jewels pass back and forth, mapping covert, barely articulated strategies of resistance to imperial rule.

Steel punctuates the narrative with a song of the bazaar sung by a mad potter, the theme of which is female desire and restlessness:

It was a woman seeking something
Over hill and dale, through night and day, she sought for something (95)

On hearing the potter's song, the other Englishwoman in the novel, the practical, efficient Rose Tweedie feels a "stress, a strain, a desire such as she had never felt before" (96). In the end Rose, like Lesley Drummond in *Voices in the Night,* surrenders to the dictates of domesticity in the service of empire, allowing herself to be transformed into the ideal colonial wife. Rose plans her "pretty" garden and drawing room to the strains of "Rule Britannia" (329), while Chandni contemplates the power and pleasure of intrigue: "Every atom of her blood came from the veins of those who for centuries had woven a still finer net of woman's wit around the intrigues of their protectors" (291).

Ultimately, Gwen and Chandni's transgressive actions go unpunished, while the representatives of imperial duty and moral rectitude in the novel, Dan Fitzgerald and George Keene, both perish. Even though her plans to sabotage the colonial infrastructure eventually backfire, Chandni ends up with three thousand rupees, priceless stolen pearls and a position of power in the world of bazaar and court intrigue; Gwen Boynton is conveniently "left free to marry for position without remorse" (350). The contaminated bazaar, with its courtesan's houses and zenanas, continues to haunt the margins of the colonial boudoir as the text reveals its surreptitious pleasure in, and desire for, tacit rebellions.

Although she became involved in the suffragette movement later in life, Steel clearly saw herself as contributing to the "civilizing" impulse of empire, both through her efforts to "educate" Indian women and as an imperial wife. In

The Complete Indian Housekeeper and Cook, she reminded her readers of the analogy between effective household management and a benevolent imperialism: "an Indian household can no more be governed peacefully, without dignity and prestige, than an Indian empire"(9). For Steel, domestic roles were subsumed within, and served to buttress the overarching agendas of empire. As a result, Rebecca Saunders has interpreted the death of Alice Gissing, the unconventional, "fallen" memsahib in *On the Face of the Waters,* as punishment: "Steel here is as much the tool of imperialism as any memsahib. Alice is sacrificed to women's larger role of helping Englishmen control Indians."[44] However, in the two novels I have discussed here (and particularly in *The Potter's Thumb*), Steel seems to avoid such acts of closure. Steel's construction of both British and Indian women's bodies in these novels as battlegrounds where the conflicting drives of infection, resistance, and empire compete for mastery allow her to indulge her own clandestine fantasies of contagion. Not surprisingly, then, it is her *exoticized* female bodies that claim their right to agency. The affinities that take shape as the bodies of memsahibs and native courtesans intersect, reveal the colonial female novelist grappling with her own specter of the hybridized odalisque—which in turn, reveals the profoundly disturbing implications of her place within imperial history.

🍀 4 🍀

Tropical Ovaries

Gynecological Degeneration and Lady Arabella's "Female Difficulties" in Bram Stoker's *The Lair of the White Worm*

As the British empire reached its zenith in the 1870s, the clinical gaze of colonial medicine became increasingly centered on the management of English-women's reproductive capacities. Although the effects of tropical climates on European constitutions had been investigated in earlier medical texts, toward the fin de siècle anxieties about gynecological decay in the "torrid zones" easily lent themselves to mainstream discourses of racial degeneration.[1] In this chapter, I look more closely at Edward Tilt's treatise *Health in India For British Women* (1875), which argues that the "morbid womb" was a major threat to the imperial vision and that Englishwomen returned "home" from the colonies with their "tropical" ovaries in dangerous states of debility and decay: "For it must be borne in mind, that whether in India or in our other tropical possessions, European women are generally young. They leave Great Britain at about twenty, and seldom remain in India after forty" (55).

Tilt repeatedly invokes the views of other important practitioners of tropical medicine such as Sir James Ranald Martin, presidency surgeon of Bengal, and Sir Joseph Fayrer, president of the India Office medical board, to support his thesis. He foregrounds the alarming statistics provided by his friend and colleague Duncan Stewart, professor of midwifery in the Medical College of Calcutta and physician to the Hospital for Native Women: "eight out of ten of the European female residents are habitually subject to deranged menstruation, leucorrhea, or to cervical inflammation" (Tilt, *Health in India,* 55). With her defective and monstrous womb harboring its "hideous progeny"[2]—the potential failure of empire—the memsahib returns home to England, in an effort to recuperate and re-anglicize her exoticized body. The links among climate, racial decline, and reproductive chaos became a significant feature of debates within colonial medicine at this time; the proper functioning of the reproductive organs was central to the preservation of the Raj.[3]

Recent studies of feminism and early modernism have reconstructed the "New Woman" as a complex social and political being. According to Ann Ardis, for example, the New Woman's revolutionary sexuality, together with her ideological distances from various other feminist and socialist reformers hybridized her political presence, allowing her to resist/evade categorization to a certain extent.[4] Sally Ledger and Lisa Hamilton have also explored the deployment of this figure in conservative as well as radical discourses of sexuality, while Nancy Paxton's work on Anglo-Indian rape narratives calls attention to the ways in which the New Woman's disruptive erotic potential inhabits and reconfigures colonial spaces.[5] I would like to extend these discussions by suggesting that the often overlooked "contact zone"[6] among the discourses of ethnology, empire, and gynecology are crucial to our readings of the phenomenon of the monstrous New Woman in British fiction and culture in the late nineteenth century. Tilt's work provides fresh points of entry into the ways in which popular literary representations of the vampiric female body appropriate his notion of the "tropicalized uterus" and are themselves situated within the intersections of colonial gynecology and ethnographic discourses of racial hybridity. Focusing specifically on Bram Stoker's nightmare of the morbid womb, *The Lair of the White Worm* (1911), I shall argue that the serpentine Lady Arabella March dismantles biological and colonial imperatives by aggressively pursuing the pleasures of uterine "devolution."

Stoker's last novel presents us with his most sustained and compelling images of the terrifying spaces opened up within the female body when the reproductive process has gone awry. Critics have tended to dismiss this work as a product of psychosis brought on by tertiary syphilis; in doing so, have encouraged rather narrow readings of the text's horrific representations of female genitalia.[7] In fact, however, there is considerable doubt as to whether Stoker was actually suffering from syphilis toward the end of his life. In her recent biography of Stoker, Barbara Belford suggests, for example, that there is simply not enough evidence to prove this diagnosis conclusively, indicating instead that he may have died of a stroke.[8] I would go still further: resisting reading *The Lair of the White Worm* as a syphilitic/psychotic text allows for a more complex interpretation of the novel's racialized sexual dynamics. What is far more fascinating than the purely autobiographical resonances of this text are the cultural ones, which reveal the connections between fictional treatments of the female body and gynecological "science" at the end of the nineteenth century. Stoker's narrative in *Lair* obsessively probes the relation between the deformed womb and questions of racial survival through miscegenation, a concern that resonates not only through Tilt's work but also the leading ethnological debates of his time.[9]

Two of Stoker's brothers were part of the medical establishment: his elder brother William was appointed president of Ireland's Royal College of Surgeons and of the Royal Academy of Medicine, while George Stoker worked as a surgeon in South Africa.[10] Given Tilt's prominence, it is highly probable that they would both have been acquainted with Tilt's work. Stoker's library, auctioned off after his death, reveals his considerable interest in both ethnography and colonial medicine.[11]

Although Stoker's novel was published more than thirty years after *Health in India*, the debate over the effects of tropical "exhaustion" was at its height shortly before and after the publication of *Lair*. Addresses by prominent medical men on this subject appeared frequently in the *Transactions of the Royal Society of Tropical Medicine* between 1907 and 1913.[12] Tilt's *Health in India* was one of the texts that expanded the terms of this debate through his explanation of the probable causes of uterine degeneration. From the beginning, he reveals his preoccupation with ethnological categories; "amongst races little restrained by social position or the dictates of morality," uterine diseases in native women can be linked to their excessive sexuality, whether sanctioned by religion, poor hygiene, or the "first impulse of passion" (53). This insidious contagion, which marks the body of the other woman, assaults the young memsahib who, arriving in India, is attracted to excessive behaviors that ultimately cause a "morbid" and diseased uterus (57). Tilt finds the permeability of European women's bodies particularly disquieting. As their boundaries are gradually loosened by contact with the tropical climate and with native women, these bodies endlessly "reproduce" uterine monstrosities instead of good imperialists. According to historian Anna Davin, a "powerful ideology of motherhood" emerged in the late nineteenth and early twentieth centuries in response to the need for "the maintenance of empire" as well as "production under the changing conditions made necessary by imperialist competition." Motherhood became a national duty rather than a moral one; journals such as the *Eugenics Review* in 1911 questioned whether the "new woman" was capable of producing "a stronger and more virile race."[13]

The Lair of the White Worm opens with the imperialist Adam Salton's return home from the colonies to confront the horror of tropical ovaries at home. Stephen Arata, in a recent reading of *Dracula* as a reverse colonization narrative, sees Dracula as possessing a "vampiric fecundity . . . that threatens to overwhelm the far less prolific British men," paralyzed by fears of degeneration."[14] In *Lair*, however, it is the monstrous Englishwoman's *lack* of fecundity that transforms her body into a site of fear and resistance. The deepest threat does not arise here primarily from either reverse colonization by the racial other (though the novel does agonize over the problem of miscegenation as a solution to degeneration), or from fears of male sexual impotence. Rather, it arises from within Englishness or "whiteness" itself: an Englishness transformed and depleted through its imperial activities, fascinated by its own "original" hybridity and lack of internal coherence.[15]

Exotic Abjection: Gynecological Degeneration and the Serpentine Body

In search of the origins of British civilization, Salton returns from Australia to claim his inheritance in Mercia, the heart of "Roman Britain," which is also the subject of his anthropological research. On his arrival, he is greeted by his granduncle, who informs him that he is the last of his race and that by returning home, he is about to penetrate the "real heart of the old Kingdom of Mercia, where there are traces of all the various nationalities which made up the conglomerate which became Britain."[16] In a journey that formulates itself as the reverse of Marlowe's in Conrad's *Heart of Darkness*, Adam moves toward the racial chaos and mongrelization at the heart of "whiteness." His uncle narrates the history of Castra Regis, the great estate that dominates the landscape and is the family seat of the aristocratic but degenerate Caswall family. They are described as a "strange race" (17) characterized by certain stigmata: mesmeric and demoniac powers that are "partly racial and partly individual," and "thick black hair growing low down on the neck" signifying "vast physical strength and endurance" (16–17).[17]

Arriving in Mercia, Adam encounters three women: the enigmatic Lady Arabella March, the Eurasian (half-Burmese) Mimi Watford, and her anemic half-sister, the dovelike Lilla. Stoker presents us initially with an entire spectrum of racial types. On one end stands Edgar Caswall, the last scion of the Caswall family: the tropicalized European, a "cultured savage" whose physiognomy displays "traces of the softening civilization of ages" (27), and who returns from Africa, accompanied by Oolanga, his African servant, a "pure, pristine, unreformed, unsoftened savage" (28). On the other end is Lady Arabella, who is classified as belonging to "the Caucasian type, beautiful, Saxon blonde, with a complexion of milk and roses, high-bred, clever, serene of nature" (28). Interestingly, however, the text proceeds to interrupt and dislocate these ethnological categories as it begins to articulate its anxieties: Arabella's perfect Caucasian physiognomy conceals her monstrously "deranged" womb.

Adam first sees Arabella "glide" into a mound of black snakes, "clad in some kind of soft white stuff, which clung close to her form, showing to the full every movement of her sinuous figure" (25). Georges Clairin's 1876 painting of the actress Sarah Bernhardt's serpentine body, wrapped in white satin, closely resembles Stoker's visualization of Arabella; both articulate anxieties about the public woman's body. Indeed Bernhardt, with her "satin-lined coffin, menagerie of wild beasts, interest in executions and necklace of petrified human eyes" deliberately manipulated these anxieties in order to cultivate her public image.[18] Racialized images of snake-odalisques proliferated in late nineteenth-century European culture.[19] Jewelers such as René Lalique (whose work is discussed in chapter 5) crafted necklaces in elaborate serpentine designs. In 1895, for Bernhardt's performance in *Theodora,* Lalique designed a snake diadem.[20] Perhaps the most notorious conflation of the exotic and the serpentine occurs in

Flaubert's *Salammbô* (1862), where the Carthaginian Salammbô's rituals of goddess worship involve a seductive encounter with a python.[21]

In 1892, Sir Joseph Fayrer (also an expert on serpent poison) read a paper to the Victoria Institute in London on ophiolatry (serpent worship) in India, referring to a tribe called the Nagas who take "the serpent as their emblem or cognizance." In the process, he simplified the implications of serpent iconography in the Hindu religion, using it as an example of the "primitive" customs and superstitions of the colonized, and stating categorically: "As regards Europe, there are next to no traces of its prevalence among the Germans . . . nor among the Gauls nor Britons." Contradicting Fayrer, others in the audience pointed out the prevalence of serpent mounds and worship in Europe's past: "in the British Isles, in America, Spain, France" lurking under sites which had been "Christianised" with a church or a cross.[22]

Stoker's novel seeks to uncover such sites in its search for Britain's "perverse" and racially tainted history. Adam takes to keeping pet mongooses, which attack Arabella viciously and are torn to pieces by her as a result. She inhabits "Diana's Grove," which, as Adam is informed by his archaeologist friend and mentor Nathaniel Salis (a Van Helsing–like figure), in the native Mercian language originally meant "the lair of the white worm." The actual lair, as Adam discovers later, is a well hole in Arabella's house, which is, of course, a striking enactment and figuration of Tilt's discourse of gynecological abjection:[23] "The open well hole was almost under his nose, sending up such a stench as almost made Adam sick, though Lady Arabella seemed not to mind it at all. It was like nothing Adam had ever met with. He compared it with all the noxious experiences he had ever had—the drainage of war hospitals, of slaughterhouses, the refuse of dissecting rooms" (172).

Here Stoker's language mirrors Tilt's invocation of the acute inflammation of the womb in the tropics, the change in the cervix: "the mucous membrane covering it is red, and the mouth of the womb is more or less ulcerated and patulous. Generally the lining membrane of the cervix is in a similar state, and from it there flows a yellow discharge" (Tilt, *Health in India*, 62). In the "second and most frequent variety of uterine disease," the diseased cervix is enlarged (which he also refers to as defective involution), characterized by "the softness of the uterine walls," "the watery or bloody uterine discharges" (63).[24] In *A Handbook of Uterine Therapeutics* (1863) Tilt recommends ways in which women could prevent their wombs from becoming abject, stressing "a right understanding and performances of the duties of married life," and the "careful management" of pregnancy, menstruation, and lactation. Women are accustomed to commit "imprudences" during menstruation, which results in uterine disease. Although Tilt, unlike his contemporary William Acton, admits that women are capable of "strong passions" that need to be satisfied, the only legitimate means of satisfying these desires is through marriage. Nevertheless, doctors should regulate women's desire to marry, as it is undesirable in some cases. For a menopausal woman, it is "imprudent" to marry "without the sanction of a medical opinion." Marriage is, however, the perfect solution for young widows with a tendency toward "ovarian congestion" and "uterine ulceration."[25]

In *Health in India,* Tilt refers to lactation as an important means of prevention of female diseases. "The greater inability to nurse in India than in England" owing to the "debility" caused by the heat and other tropical diseases "helps to explain the frequency of uterine disease in India." He believes that "the act of suckling promotes the return of the womb to its proper size . . . except in some cases of extensive cervical ulceration" (*Health in India,* 61). Many colonial women rarely breast-fed their infants, employing native wet nurses in several cases—a practice charged with ambivalence and the threat of contamination.[26] Lactation, both biologically and in terms of its iconic significance, was an important strategic device for maintaining the purity of the race and bolstering the memsahib's reproductive functions. The native wet nurse was yet another contagious body on whom both the mother and child might develop a dangerous dependency. The actions of sucking/giving suck is of course, also a sign of vampiric propensities (a nexus Stoker had already explored in the famous "breast-feeding" scene in *Dracula,* in which Mina Harker is "suckled" by the Count).[27] Colonial narratives sometimes constructed the wet nurse, or *ayah,* as a vampiric figure. In Alice Perrin's short story "The Centipede," an ayah accidentally releases a centipede into a white child's bed while trying to cure the "babba" of an earache. The memsahib awakes screaming to see the centipede fasten "its poison feet" into the child's neck.[28] Joan Copjec has connected vampirism to the experience of breast-feeding.[29] After the breast has been drained, anxiety sets in for the infant and the breast becomes "extimate"; on one level the infant "internalizes" the breast as familiar, while on another it becomes alien, other. In Perrin's story, the connection between the ayah and the vampire works in two ways. The ayah's milk, absorbed by the child, might "poison" the blood. The ayah functions as "mother" and yet is racially other. The centipede is the symbolic extension of a breast that after the act of nourishment, has become vampiric, penetrating the colonial child as an extimate object. Therefore, for the colonial Englishwoman, both pregnancy and breast-feeding were desirable for a variety of ideological reasons. In order to maintain their reproductive potential and protect imperial children from vampiric contagion, women were continually encouraged to reproduce *themselves* as mothers.

Lady Arabella's vampiric project is, of course, predicated on a rejection of this imperative. In a later revised and truncated version of the novel, by sucking and contaminating the blood of young children, she "decolonizes the breast," unraveling the iconography of lactation, which from the late eighteenth century onward had occupied a preeminent position in the European cultural imaginary, and which served not only to dichotomize the maternal and the sexual, but also to highlight the importance of women's reproductive role in nationalistic enterprises.[30] In *Lair,* Adam comes across the body of a female child with

teeth marks on her neck; this discovery prompts Sir Nathaniel to reveal something of Lady Arabella's history. As a child, she had "wandered into a small
wood near her home" where she was found "unconscious and in a high fever,"
having "received a poisonous bite." From that moment, she had developed a
"terrible craving for cruelty" (61), an appetite that resulted in the presumed
killing of her husband, Captain March, years later. As Sir Nathaniel surmises,
Lady Arabella has been both raped *and* suckled by the White Worm: "God
alone knows what poor Captain March discovered—it must have been too
ghastly for human endurance, if my theory is correct that the once beautiful
human body of Lady Arabella is under the control of this ghastly White Worm"
(62). Both versions of the novel compare her to a "cocotte" or a courtesan. Adam
reflects: "I never thought this fighting an antediluvian monster was such a complicated job. This one is a woman, with all a woman's wisdom and wit, combined with the heartlessness of a *cocotte* and the want of principle of a
suffragette" (140).

Cocottes and Suffragettes

In chapters 1 and 3, I theorized the courtesan as the most elusive, threatening,
and fascinating public female body to consistently resist domestication, whether
at home or abroad. The courtesan's power to undermine and unsettle social
hierarchies lay in her insidiousness and her adeptness at camouflaging her body
(a characteristic shared by Lady Arabella), which could erupt at any moment
into excessive exhibitionism, infecting respectable women. These women
undermined the doctrine of the separation of spheres by eroticizing and fem-
inizing public spaces. Experts at manipulating their visibility *and* invisibility,
wealthy courtesans and clandestine prostitutes claimed public space cleverly
and boldly (in contradistinction to the street prostitute, who was easily identifiable). Parent-Duchâtelet, in *De la Prostitution dans la Ville de Paris* (1836),
had divided kept women into several categories, including *femmes galantes,
femmes à parties,* and *femmes de spectacles et de théâtres.* Women in the first category "are indistinguishable from respectable women . . . but allow themselves
to be accosted, pursued and escorted." To this chameleonlike quality, women
in the second category bring "the grace and charms of a cultivated intelligence,"
presiding over private circles and salons where they drain men of their "fortune
and their health."[31]

Parent-Duchâtelet's fairly loose definition of women in the second and third
groups would have included female writers, artists, actresses, dancers, opera
singers, and revolutionaries, who displayed their intellectual and erotic excesses
outside the domestic sphere, and who seized the unique opportunities that the
growth of urban centers offered them to be public women—among them Cora
Pearl, Sarah Bernhardt, George Sand, Maria Malibran, Lola Montez, Rachel

Felix, and Louise Colet.[32] The courtesan La Païva, for instance, not only filled a lavish house with ostentatious furniture, including a Moorish-style bathroom; she also presided over salons frequented by leading intellectuals. On seeing her with one of her lovers, a contemporary male poet described her as a vampire.[33] In his *Studies in the Psychology of Sex* (1899–1910), Havelock Ellis called for the recognition of the prostitute/courtesan as an independent woman and a professional who deserved respect.[34]

Reading Sade's *Juliette*, Marcel Hénaff has distinguished between "a prostitution of poverty" and a "prostitution of libertinism," arguing that the latter allows for an " attack on the economic order" through the "complete perversion of capital."[35] In the nineteenth century, the two were not always so easily separable; in many cases, economic necessity coexisted with (or may have preceded) the courtesan's libertine sexual politics. Hénaff does not engage with the extremely complicated stratifications that "layered" the demimonde—both in England and in France. He does, however, zero in on an important aspect of the courtesan's power: her ability to "demonstrate the dissolution of the family's system of coerced, controlled exchange" (274). No longer following the "imposed limited routes of exchange which establish families and trace the boundaries of cultural and symbolic endogeny. . . . She *herself* exchanges herself, and with everyone. She causes wealth to circulate, but only so it can be wasted (in luxury and sexual pleasure). She makes speech circulate, but only so it can be made public and infinite" (275).

Like Tilt's "native women," the European courtesan's body was also ultimately a diseased one, as she succumbed to the "hectic pleasures" of her lifestyle—Dumas's consumptive Marguerite Gautier being the most famous example. In Verdi's opera, *La Traviata* (1853) based on the Dumas novel, the courtesan Violetta attempts to keep her disease at bay by hurrying from "pleasure to pleasure," perishing in the "vortex of desire." The 1856 premiere of the opera in London aroused considerable controversy and anxiety because of its valorization of the courtesan.[36] Signifying both the French courtesan and the Italian opera singer, the spectacle of Violetta's body threatened to contaminate conservative British national and sexual agendas. Toward the end of the century, the demimondaine's frenetic exhibitionism and self-indulgence became yet another symptom of degeneration. For Max Nordau, writing in *Degeneration* in 1895, the wealthy woman's propensity for extravagant and luxurious clothing was a symptom of her devolution; he excoriated the "oblique lines, incomprehensible swellings . . . expansions and contractions, folds with irrational beginning and aimless ending, in which all the outlines of the human figure are lost, and which cause women's bodies to resemble . . . a beast of the Apocalypse."[37] In contrast to Nordau, Lombroso and Ferrero in *The Female Offender* commented on the prostitute's ability to disguise her atavistic stigmata (shared with other criminals and "primitives") through the cosmetic arts. Listing off famous historical/mythical courtesans such as Ninon de Lenclos,

Phryne, and Thaïs, they marveled at the ability of these women to maintain their beauty and seductive power well into their seventies and eighties.[38]

We know from *Dracula* that Stoker was familiar with both Nordau and Lombroso.[39] My contextualization of *Lair* through reference to artistic as well as "scientific" representations of female sexual and social "aberration" at the end of the century is designed to foreground the following: Lady Arabella's vampiric/serpentine body simultaneously undergoes a series of *becomings* that play on a range of fin de siècle anxieties: she is the native wet nurse, who, by suckling colonial children, contaminates their blood; she is the hybridized libertine-courtesan who, as depicted in a series of contemporary etchings by French artist Albert Besnard entitled *La Femme,* degenerates from experiencing the bliss of "properly managed" lactation into a vampire bending over the emaciated corpse of her illegitimate infant;[40] and she is the colonial Englishwoman with an enlarged, deranged uterus "of abnormal growth" that, in its most terrifying incarnation, eventually threatens to become phallic. As Adam and Sir Nathaniel pursue Lady Arabella after her metamorphosis into the worm, they see "a tall white shaft . . . an immense towering mass . . . tall and wonderfully thin" (151). Such transformations echo Lombroso and Ferrero's fears regarding the fluctuating surfaces of the courtesan's body—the inevitable exposure of the cocotte's innate "masculinity" through aging, a process that would make her stigmata more visible: "when youth vanishes, the face grows virile . . . and exhibits the full degenerate type which early grace had concealed."[41]

Arabella is also the menopausal woman, who, according to Tilt, became capable of succumbing to demonomania or "belief in Satanic influence" upon losing her reproductive viability. *The Change of Life in Health and Disease* lists "demonomania," "erotomania," and "homicidal mania" as possible consequences of menopause.[42] Above all, though, she is dangerous because she possesses qualities associated with both the "cocotte" and the "suffragette." The suffragette's body was pathologized and racialized in the British press.[43] Antisuffragists compared the danger of women's entry into the political sphere to that of miscegenation, while a popular gynecological textbook published as late as 1917 speculated that suffragism arose from sexual frustration.[44]

At the same time, however, suffragists such as Christabel Pankhurst propelled their denunciation of the double standard of sexual morality by distancing themselves both from the prostitute and the racial other. In *The Great Scourge and How to End It* (1913), an exposé of venereal disease, Pankhurst condemned prostitution as a moral and sexual disease, the cause of "physical, mental and moral degeneracy and race suicide."[45] Here Pankhurst parallels Tilt closely through her repeated invocation of anxieties about racial survival and constant references to the falling birth rate; the primary reason for which, she argues, is the sterility of married women infected by their husbands with gonorrhea (*Great Scourge,* 17). The system of licensed prostitution in India contaminates the sexual innocence of white women: "Many soldiers return from India diseased, and they infect their unhappy wife and offspring" (*Great Scourge,* 150). By folding the bodies of both the courtesan and the suffragette into each other, therefore, Arabella mutates into that which is truly baffling, "monstrous," and unclassifiable.

Why White? Domestic Métissage

The worm's "whiteness" eventually comes up for discussion: "why white?" asks Sir Nathaniel, before proceeding to give a geological explanation (171–72). Aside from its anxieties about degeneration, the novel also envisions "whiteness" and "Englishness" as a problematic and deeply fissured ethnological category, rather than merely a mask or "veneer" that slips off to reveal the essential blackness beneath, as Jennifer DeVere Brody has recently suggested.[46] Lady Arabella never leaves England; her "tropical ovaries" are insidiously domestic, not foreign. Although *The Lair of the White Worm* may appear to valorize the late nineteenth-century imposition of racial hierarchies, particularly in its representation of Caswall's African valet, it repeatedly equivocates on the issues of their stability, coherence, and logic. While Arabella repels the sexual advances of Oolanga, on the grounds of his racial inferiority, she later "sucks" him into her well hole in a ferocious encounter, with Adam as a traumatized, voyeuristic witness. The transformation of the perfect Caucasian beauty into a white worm that manifests its physical presence through images of uterine devolution, provides an important point of intersection between Tilt's medical discourse on the memsahib's lack of fertility and Nordau's definition of degeneration. In a chapter entitled "Diagnosis," Nordau defines degeneration as "a morbid deviation from an original type." He goes on to describe the actual process: "When under any kind of noxious influences an organism becomes debilitated, its successors will not resemble the healthy, normal type of the species, but will form a new sub-species; which like all others possesses the capacity of transmitting to its offspring in a continuously increasing degree, its peculiarities (*Degeneration,* 16). In *Lair,* with the white woman's body under threat, mutating into another "species," the only solution (threatening in itself) seems to be miscegenation.

The covert desire for miscegenation, and the proposition of racial mixing as a way to diffuse the threat of the degenerate womb, is articulated through the figure of the half-Burmese Mimi Watford. Mimi is "almost as dark as the darkest of her mother's race," but repeatedly described as stronger and healthier than her white half-sister, Lilla, "sprung from old Saxon stock," who suffers from physical weakness as well as nervous disorders (33). The mere touch of Mimi's hand can momentarily infuse Lilla, "dead to sensibility and intention" with "youth and strength" (69). Importantly, Stoker pits Mimi's hybridity against the "monstrous whiteness" of Edgar Caswall and Lady Arabella; she continually battles them down with the power of her gaze in mesmeric struggles over Lilla.

The latter eventually succumbs and dies after Mimi leaves her to marry Adam Salton. By co-opting and regulating Mimi's hybridity through marriage, Adam can experiment with racial regeneration. The marriage effectively separates Mimi from Lilla and Arabella, the "degenerate" white women in the narrative. In order for Adam (and Stoker) to reinscribe Mimi's hybridity for their own purposes, the "contagion" passing between black and white female bodies must be arrested. When Arabella invites Mimi to a tea party, she is narrowly prevented from slipping into the "black orifice," well lubricated by her hostess (157). At the same time, Mimi's body, being both "black" and "white," cracks these categories open.

Fin de siècle orientalist paintings of odalisques continually depicted dark and white women's bodies engaged in seductive encounters. The suggestive overtones of representations such as Gérôme's *The Great Bath at Bursa* (1885), in which a white bather's body is intertwined with that of her black female slave, and Fernand Cormon's *Jalousie au Sérail* (1874), where a darker, serpentine rival leans over a murdered white woman's body, point to moments of lesbian desire, charged with considerable disruptive potential.[47] By hinting at deeper collaborations, rather than mere sexual encounters, these moments are not fully contained by male sapphic fantasies. The hierarchy between these bodies is also at times unclear: although ostensibly that of "slave" and "mistress," the darker woman often supports her languid, pale companion, and seems to have more authority and presence.

These juxtapositions also surface in British paintings of exotic women, especially with regard to classical subjects such as Alma-Tadema's *Antony and Cleopatra* (1883), in which Cleopatra glances obliquely at the viewer with a black female slave whispering in her ear. Late Victorian art critics were also troubled by Frederic Leighton's 1882 painting of suntanned Greek courtesan Phryne: "Sir Frederic Leighton's 'Phryne' is a brown woman—a colour for which we do not understand the reason, as Phryne was a Greek, and therefore a white woman."[48] The erotic fantasy of collapsing the two bodies into one coexists with the nightmare of a degenerative contagion that threatens to erode the reproductive base of the imperial fabric.

Tilt's *Health in India* turns to miscegenation as a solution to the problem of reproductive failure and continued colonization. From recommending "a dash of Hindoo blood" in colonial wives, Tilt moves on to considering "colonization by intermarriage" (99). "The Company's servants frequently had matrimonial relations with Hindoo women of a better caste . . . if we find that we cross badly with the mild and inoffensive Hindoo, why not go northward for strength and stamina, why not seek more efficient mates in the Punjab?" (108–10). This view was consistent with Broca's speculations concerning the viability of different degrees of racial intermixture. In addition to advocating the view that sexual relations between "proximate" or related races produced "eugenesic" hybridity measured by prolific fertility, while miscegenation with "distant" races resulted in infertility and degeneration, Broca went further, suggesting that the racial composition of the French nation had evolved out of eugenesic hybridity: "The population of France . . . presents everywhere the character of mixed races . . . nevertheless, this hybrid nation, so far from decaying . . . far from presenting a decreasing fecundity . . . grows every day in intelligence, prosperity and numbers."[49] Because hybridity, racial survival and fertility were inextricably linked, the female body occupied center stage in theories of racial regeneration.

Even earlier in the century, American ethnologists Josiah Nott and George Gliddon had promoted their theory of "plurality of origin" or polygenesis, "together with the recognition that there exist *remote, allied,* and *proximate* 'species,' as well of mankind as of lower animals."[50] Nott and Gliddon maintained that the crossing of remote species produced hybrids often doomed to extinction, whereas that between proximate species reproduced not mixtures, but "pure" or "primitive" types (94–95). At the same time, they admitted that "every race, at the present time, is more or less mixed" (95) and therefore, distinct racial origins even among the Caucasian group had to be recognized/differentiated in order to anatomize the purity and vigor of the "blond" race (105–9). The original "commingling" between the "blond" and "brown" European races in Spain and Britain, for instance, had not produced a "complete fusion"; instead, "the types of each" remained "clearly traceable" particularly in the "dark-haired, dark-eyed and dark-skinned Irish" (109). At the heart of this ethnological dilemma was the slippery nature of "whiteness" itself—a racial category that, despite efforts, continued to resist clear delineation and definition. Nott and Gliddon develop the division of "blond" and "brown" Caucasians from the French surgeon-ethnologist Bodichon. The blond race is marked by "tall stature, fair skin, natural chastity, inclination to sentiment rather than sensuality" and "elevated reason" producing men like "Bacon, Luther, Descartes, Cuvier, Washington, and Franklin," while the characteristics of the brown race include "short stature, brown skin, sensuality" producing orators, artists, poets—Cicero, Michelangelo, Napoleon (106–7).

Stoker agonizes over this issue through the figure of the half-Burmese Mimi Watford. The union of Mimi Watford's parents is clearly a coupling between races that would not have been regarded as "proximate," as her father is British and her mother Burmese. (According to a chart provided in Nott and Gliddon's *Types of Mankind,* Mimi's mother would have belonged to the Malay group, the midpoint on the racial hierarchy between Caucasian and Negro).[51] Yet Mimi is presented as someone who clearly possesses intelligence, health, and stamina. If Adam's sexual pursuit of the Eurasian woman can be read as a desperate attempt to regenerate a national/imperial identity faced with the threat of decay through its overproduction of morbid wombs, Mimi nevertheless, has, through her Burmese mother, inherited her "tropical ovaries." Despite Adam's attempts to co-opt her hybridity, she is always on the verge of slipping into Arabella's "lair," which, in true vampiric fashion, if not capable of reproducing the colonizing race, is always capable of reproducing *itself* as other: after being blown up with dynamite, the worm's dismembered fragments attract "every natural organism which was in itself obnoxious" (219).

Arabella's whiteness undermines and assaults notions of racial proximity and distance. The destruction of her body reveals "a shining mass of white"—"the vast bed of china clay through which the Worm originally found its way down to its lair" (220). In the heart of the English countryside, the cradle of English civilization, that which is most "proximate" becomes the most monstrously alien. As I have shown, the articulation (and control) of the contagion flowing between dark and white female bodies is shared by several discourses that seek to organize relations between European and native women, including those of medical ethnography, orientalist art, and the suffrage movement. By expressing hesitation or doubt as to whether this contagion arises from within, or from the other, and embodying it through the specter of gynecological insurrection/ degeneration, *The Lair of the White Worm* constructs the female body as the site of the most powerful resistance to any coherent sense of racial identity, uneasily acknowledging its capacity to lay bare the incoherence and inherent contradictions within the discourses of empire and ethnology.

❦ 5 ❧

"Exotic and Rare Beauty"

Archaeology, Ornamentation, and Vampiric Bodies

> Every fashion couples the living body to the inorganic world. To the
> living, fashion defends the rights of the corpse.
> —Walter Benjamin, *The Arcades Project*

In 1900, the French jeweler René Lalique exhibited his art nouveau jewelry at
the Exposition Universelle in Paris, creating a sensation with his unprecedented
combinations of the inorganic and organic, the "natural" and the artificial. Prior
to that, some of his work had already been displayed at Agnew's galleries in
London. From 1878 to 1880, Lalique had also spent time training in London at
the art school attached to the Crystal Palace in Sydenham, visiting and observing the collections of the major museums. Lalique's pieces, ranging from combs
to corsage ornaments), were rooted in his reinvention of monstrous natural
forms: scarabs, bats, insects, and snakes. As his art developed, these forms mor-
phed into the contours of vampires, androgynes, courtesans, and exotic women.
Dominated by the hybrid forms of "decadent" women, Lalique's art brought a
new edge, a fresh uneasiness and instability both to fin de siècle fashions and to
the surface of the white woman's body.

Lalique used exoticism to create an unsettling aesthetic that had its basis in
the breakdown of distinctions between the natural and unnatural, between the
perception of jewelry as art and as the product of a consumer culture propped
up by the aggressiveness of female extravagance. Commenting on Lalique's
debut exhibit at the 1895 Salon, the curator of the Musée du Luxembourg drew
attention to the revolutionary innovativeness of his work, which had "profoundly altered the basic condition and appearance of modern jewellery . . . from

what was merely a brilliant industry to the status of an art."[1] Additionally, in laying the foundations of the "ultimate modern *bijou*," Lalique's creations, (grounded in late nineteenth-century exoticism), also extended the boundaries of the odalisque's body.

In this chapter, I link Lalique and Stoker through their preoccupation with the "metaphysics" of jewelry and its relationship to the exoticized fin de siècle female body. In 1903, Stoker published what could be considered his most enigmatic and radical novel, *The Jewel of Seven Stars*, centering around the archaeological excavation of the body of a powerful Egyptian queen. The book inaugurated the cult of the Egyptian gothic, undergoing successive filmic and literary transformations. In this case, twentieth-century appropriations of the book have tended to soften, obscure, or simplify its sophisticated and puzzling approach to England's "Egyptological" past and the rise of a museum culture that gained its momentum from displays of exotic artifacts. Having provoked a "profound sense of unease . . . hard to exorcize," the original ending of the novel was significantly revised. As critics have pointed out, the novel still attempts to "resist interpretation."[2] More significant, although the publication of Stoker's *Jewel* in 1903 coincided with the exhibition of more than three hundred drawings of Lalique's jewelry in London's Grafton Gallery, the connections between the two have never been explored. By investigating this shared cultural moment, I shall engage with the ways in which both Lalique and Stoker use jewels/jewelry to generate versions of exotic bodies that defy the axiomatics of absorption into imperial collections, or refuse to inhabit the exhibitionary spaces assigned to them.

Anyone for Diamond Omelettes? Women and the Sexual Politics of Victorian Jewelry

While the above mentioned fin de siècle interventions configure a new kind of "odalisque," they also come out of a complicated cultural topography that evolved as the century progressed. Since the middle of the nineteenth century, ornamentation had been simultaneously tied to the exotic body and to a complex network of associations that sought to manufacture stable domestic and racial identities through the discursive regulation of female self-display. Even if Victorian middle- and upper-class women had a considerable selection of opulent, flashy jewelry at their disposal due to the explosion of styles resulting from archaeological exploration and the consolidation of empire, they were nevertheless circumscribed with restrictions regarding what they could and could not wear. Those who attempted to regulate the display of the female body universally condemned artifice and advocated simplicity. Eliza Lynn Linton, in a *Belgravia* article, blamed domestic chaos on women's love for finery. Since maids tend to imitate their mistresses, dangerously blurring class boundaries, Linton finds "the servant question . . . confessedly in a state of chaos and disorder, paralleled by none other of our social arrangements." She goes on to propose a solution; women must curb their urge to display themselves: "If the ladies of England chose that the rule of life should be one of noble simplicity . . . the false ornament and meretricious excess with which we are overweighted now would fall from us, and the servant question among others would get itself put straight."[3]

Earlier, in his *Analysis and Classification of Beauty in Women* (1846), Alexander Walker associated excess with inferior intellectual capacities, declaring that "ornamental arts" such as "landscape gardening, architecture and dress" had "chiefly bodily and sensual pleasures for their purpose" unlike the "intellectual arts," which had "a higher purpose" and were "especially dependent" on simplicity. In Walker's view, diamonds (which came initially from India and then mainly from the South African mines) signaled "love of splendor, distinction and pride" and thus "old" women, no longer sexually viable, were safely "permitted" to wear them. Walker's wife echoed his views in her own handbook, *Female Beauty:* a woman who "desires to dazzle . . . heaps ornaments upon ornaments on her person," and "*invents* new decorations every day," eventually "destroys the effect of her charms by the glare of her profuse magnificence" (my italics).[4]

Through adornment, the surface of the female body became a nightmare of inventiveness and spectacle. The author proceeded to quote Rousseau on women's manipulation of this surface, which results in masquerade: "When I see a young woman strut in her decorations, I appear uneasy to see her figure so *disguised*" (363; my italics). Jewelry could also render the ugly or deformed woman more *visible;* the bracelet is a "dangerous ornament" that, while enhancing the beauty of "a pretty arm" also threatens to expose the monstrosity of "a defective form" (365). It could be used strategically to conceal physical defects; Queen Victoria covered her fingers in a profusion of rings to hide her "ugly" hands and "stubby fingers" that often affected her table manners.[5] This playing around with, or disguising of the body's surface, which increased its resistance to ethnographic readings, must have been disquieting to men like Herbert Spencer, who believed that physiognomy and bodily characteristics were an index to "perfection of mind" and racial superiority.[6]

Women, of course, posed the most insidious threat to Spencer's textualizing of the body. To overcome women's propensities toward the spectacular artificial beauty of jewelry and cosmetics, the empire sought to incorporate the politics of adornment into its own spectacles. In imperial displays, the adorned and excessive female body could become *functional,* as long as it was subordinated to and effectively integrated into the iconographies of empire. An excessively embellished vase in the Crystal Palace exhibition catalogue was accompanied by the following description: "the group surmounting the cover represents the United Kingdom as symbolised by the figures of Britannia, Scotia and Hibernia; around the edge of the cup are four heads emblematical of the four quarters of the globe, in all of which Great Britain possesses colonies . . . while, on the lower part of the cup, as an expression of the British character, are the figures of Truth, Prudence, Industry and Fortitude" (281).[7]

In 1856, the jeweler Hancock was asked to create a magnificent suite of jewels including "a Diadem, a Coronet, a Stomacher, a jeweled Bandeau, a Necklace, a Comb and a Bracelet" that contained 88 gems for the duchess of Devonshire, the wife of the ambassador to the Russian court. The stomacher was set with cameos depicting classical scenes of male virility and military prowess. Victoria herself wore the Kohinoor diamond, symbol of imperial conquest, at the opening of the Great Exhibition and on state occasions. Ironically, she embarrassed her guests at a dinner following Lord Lytton's 1877 Delhi durbar by loading herself with "masses of jewels—large pearls and irregular uncut stones" presented to her by the Indian nobility. One of her male guests thought that the queen's display of the imperial tribute looked incongruous on her "small" body and feared that it would sow dissension and jealousy among the native princes. It is tempting to speculate that the queen's appearance on this occasion may have threatened to fissure the image of middle-class domesticity that she had worked so hard to create and that might have dispelled fears of a powerful female monarch. At the state ball after the durbar of 1903, the vicereine Mary Curzon wore her famous "peacock dress" made of gold with diamond and emerald jewelry. Logsdail's portrait of her in the dress (she had designed it herself) captures the tautness of the body and rigidity of the clasped/clenched hands. The display of Mary Curzon's body to reinforce the spectacle of her husband's power concealed her carefully suppressed illness and exhaustion; she collapsed soon after the durbar festivities.[8]

In *Sex and Suits,* Anne Hollander has suggested that the increasing level of fantasy and spectacle in women's dress countered the radicalization of men's clothing in the eighteenth and nineteenth centuries. Female fashion gradually became associated with the idea of excess. Hollander argues that "only women could wear full rigged ships and model villages on their heads in 1778," seeing the expression of "visual fantasy in dress" as "an exclusively female privilege" based on a gendered dichotomy between rational restraint and exaggerated spectacle. Hollander contends that male fantasies of extravagance, repressed in terms of dress and the body, were sublimated through "science, politics and philosophy" (and presumably, imperialism). Nevertheless, if female dress revealed a woman's innate tendencies toward excess, at the same time, its potential for creating disorderly and "unintelligible" bodies became the focus of cultural anxieties.[9]

With regard to jewelry, the male fantasy of accumulating and displaying wealth could be sanitized by blaming female greed as its cause. Mrs. Walker's recipe for domestic harmony cautioned young husbands as well as wives: "should the husband's fortune not suffice for the boundless extravagance of his wife, need we here describe the consequent embarrassments, intrigues and corruptions?"

(*Female Beauty*, 369). The most flamboyant embodiment of this greed was the courtesan, whose social position confused carefully orchestrated boundaries of class and gender. The aggressive and intelligent use of sexuality to gain social mobility (working-class women often became fashionable kept mistresses or had second careers as "clandestine" prostitutes) together with financial independence, assaulted the notion of female vulnerability.

The courtesan's lust for jewelry was a disturbing signifier of her "appetite" for both sex and food; the English courtesan Cora Pearl, whose career peaked between 1865 and 1870 in France, and who published her autobiography in 1886, apparently was said to resemble a "jeweller's window." She was described by one of her aristocratic clients in terms of her voracious appetite; if the French restaurants "served diamond omelettes, Cora would go and dine there every evening."[10] These reports of her excess were fueled by her flamboyant self-ornamentation; her love of jewelry and provocative use of elaborate and inventive makeup. On one occasion the *Illustrated London News* described her as "one blaze of diamonds."[11] The diamond necklace crunched up by Cora "Pearl" became symptomatic of cultural anxieties that strung female hunger, sexual desire, and self-adornment together on a single strand. An 1860 article in *All The Year Round,* entitled "Real Mysteries of Paris and London," presented its readers with a phantasmagoric vision of women's appetite for luxurious food and jewelry: "Who can account for the bonbon shops—those palaces almost more magnificent than the warehouses of the jewelers themselves, those huge chocolate and sweetmeat deposits, where bilious women all alike . . . sit behind counters in a state of chronic nausea horrible to think of? Do the jewelers and the bonbon vendors mutually support each other?"[12]

Cora provided her own ironic and witty commentary on these representations when she presented herself to her clients on a silver dish at the Café Anglais, wearing nothing except pearls, constructing herself as being consumed rather than consuming.[13] Other famous and powerful French and English demimondaines like Gillian Bruce, La Païva, Catherine Walters, and Lola Montez (who also published a beauty manual called *The Arts of Beauty, or Secrets of a Lady's Toilette*) amassed wealth and property. Their position was strengthened by the fact that they, unlike wives, could be property owners; as Lee Holcombe has shown, "it was not the fact of being female but the status of wife that entailed severe legal disabilities."[14]

On the operatic stage, courtesans were often tied to ornamentation and consumption through a series of more sophisticated gestures. In Jacques Offenbach's *The Tales of Hoffman* (based on individual tales by the German writer E. T. A. Hoffman and composed between 1852 and 1881) the (in)famous Venetian act involved the vampiric courtesan Giulietta bargaining with the Satanic Dapertutto to steal the soul/reflection of the poet Hoffman in exchange for a fabulous diamond. To complement Giulietta's "consumption" of the diamond and the poet's identity, another act of the opera dramatizes the fate of the transgressive daughter: the consumptive (tubercular) bourgeoise, Antonia, whose illness prevents her from singing, but who nevertheless succumbs to this desire.

Her death, in which she is literally "consumed" by her voice, also removes her from the sphere of marriage and motherhood. As a site on which competing discourses of hysteria, mesmerism, and female sexuality are played out, Giulietta's diamond comes to stand for the intractability of female desire, the power of the soprano voice, and the seductiveness of different kinds of "consumption." Furthermore, commenting on contemporary critical readings of the Venetian act, Heather Hadlock points out that "sinister, even *vampiric* qualities" are attributed to the aria in which Dapertutto tempts Giulietta with the diamond, "as if this musical representation of [his] diamond had somehow stolen the opera's authentic self. . . . The opera's *authentic* music is seen as a besieged textual body whose boundaries must be defined and policed." (123).[15]

Moreover, the courtesan's almost "barbaric" opulence, which defined her fluid sexuality, aligned her with contemporary written and visual representations of the odalisque. Diderot's 1748 novel, *Les Bijoux Indiscrets* (The Indiscreet Jewels) exploits the connections between jewelry, female sexuality, and orientalism to comment on the sexual politics of the court of Louis XV and his mistress Mme. de Pompadour. Diderot imagines a fantastic oriental seraglio where women's genitalia or "jewels" are forced to speak. For the conservative Ruskin, writing in 1859, "ornamentation of that lower kind," which included shawls and jewelry, was the provenance and "delight of the worst and cruellest nations, Moorish, Indian, Chinese," being primarily artificial and unnatural.[16]

Travel narratives alike tended to describe eastern women primarily in terms of their bodies, commenting with a hallucinatory intensity on jewelry (though in actuality, this was not always gender-specific), dress, and cosmetics. Harriet Martineau, who condemned the use of cosmetics as a "barbaric fashion" and a health hazard, the cause of "unconscious poisonings," wrote in *Eastern Life, Present and Past* of the "frightful" eyebrows of Cairene harem women, "joined and prolonged by black paint."[17] For Martineau, the oriental woman's love for irrational excess of all kinds—"gorging themselves with sweet things, smoking intemperately" as well as wearing "bundles of false hair" and "pearl bracelets on tattooed arms" (183–84)—was a sign of her moral and sexual corruption. Pardoe also noted Turkish women's "inordinate" fondness for "diamonds or emeralds" while acknowledging the flexibility and transgressive potential of Turkish dress: "no costume in the world lends itself more readily or more conveniently to the purposes of disguise" (375). Disguised in Turkish clothing, her eyebrows "stained . . . with some of the dye common in the harem," Pardoe was able to escape her gendered body as she entered a forbidden space—the mosque of Saint Sophia (19).[18]

Through their decorated bodies, the exotic woman and the courtesan participated in each other's exhibitionism, vanity, and languor. As early as 1817, in *Description of the Character, Manners, and Customs of the People of India* (1817), a popular ethnographic work reprinted several times in the nineteenth century, Abbé J. A. Dubois related the ornamented, "lascivious" bodies of dancing girls attached to Indian temples to those of European courtesans:

> Perfumes, elegant and attractive attire . . . multitudes of ornamental trinkets adapted with infinite taste to the different parts of the body . . . such are the allurements and charms which these enchanting sirens use to accomplish their seductive designs. At the same time, notwithstanding their alluring demeanour, they cannot be accused of those gross indecencies which are often publicly exhibited by women of their stamp in Europe, particularly the exposure of the person and the lascivious airs which one would think capable of inspiring the most determined libertine with disgust.

By comparing these bodies with those of European courtesans, Dubois sets up an intercorporeity between the two, defining both against bourgeois discourses of "decorum" and "virtue," attempting to manage both types of bodies by compelling each one to comment on and regulate the other's self-display. The body of the temple dancer, however (and by association that of the Western courtesan) threatens to shift from his grasp as he asserts: "these prostitutes are the only females in India who may learn to read"; their "unexpected" literacy sets up dangerous new paradigms of knowledge, power, and sexuality that cannot be subdued through ethnographic discourse.[19]

Exotic Discoveries: Archaeology and the Ornamental Aesthetic

To a very great extent, nineteenth-century Western discourses of ornamentation had their origins in the archaeological impulse. After the discovery of Nineveh, in 1869, the archeologist Sir Austen Henry Layard commissioned an elaborate parure for his wife, set with seals excavated from the ruins. Archaeological excavations in the Mediterranean and the Middle East were mirrored in the craftsmanship of jewelers such as Alessandro Castellani (1823–83), who had workshops in London, Paris, and Rome, and his successors and competitors. Although based initially in Rome, the firm of Castellani exhibited regularly in London and also had a branch in London at 13 Frith Street, Soho. British patrons in Rome and London included Robert and Elizabeth Barrett Browning, Henry, third duke of Wellington and the British Museum. Carlo Giuliano, who was believed to have been trained by Castellani, settled in London (opening a shop in Picadilly in 1874) and continued to work in the same tradition.[20]

Denon's exploration of Egyptian monuments as part of the Napoleonic expedition was followed by a series of important finds in the first half of the nineteenth century, including Giovanni Belzoni's work on Thebes (1821–22), Layard's discoveries at Nineveh, and early excavations conducted by James

Morier at Persepolis around 1810. The disinterment of Pompeii and Herculaneum had begun earlier, in the mid-eighteenth century, but continued throughout the nineteenth; the Central Baths and cemeteries coming to light in the 1880s. Egyptology, in particular, developed throughout the century both as a science/discipline and as immensely influential in aesthetic terms. The extent to which the nineteenth century architectural and ornamental aesthetic was rooted in the "uncovering" of these "buried" civilizations was evident in multiple arenas that called for close collaboration between artists and archeologists: from the design of the "Egyptian Hall" in London (1812–11) and the Egyptian Court at the Crystal Palace (1854) to costume and set designs for the performance of Verdi's opera *Aida* in 1869. Artists such as David Roberts, who had made extremely detailed sketches of the ornamental columns at the temples of Luxor and Philae during his extensive travels in Egypt in 1838–39, also contributed considerably to the creation of these hybridized interior and public spaces.

Many of the ornamental motifs that surfaced as a result of archaeological finds were reproduced in Owen Jones's *The Grammar of Ornament* (1856) (discussed in more detail below). Jones himself had traveled in Greece, Egypt, Turkey, and Spain, publishing a comprehensive survey of the Islamic architecture of the Alhambra in Granada from 1836 to 1845. The grafting of these detailed motifs—which were in essence fragments of "dead" civilizations—onto contemporary architectural designs and (in the case of archeological jewelry), onto female bodies, created an intermediate, spectralized space in which the living and the dead were brought into a peculiar relationship. The resurrection of these ornamental designs was inevitably accompanied not only by a sense of the eventual decline and fragmentation of monumental civilizations, but more disturbingly, by the *allure* of such decline.

In the *Grammar of Ornament*, Jones had laid out his "general principles" of ornamentation, which continued to be influential throughout the latter part of the century. Jones maintained that the decorative arts arts arose from, and should "properly be attendant on" architectural forms. The objective of architecture, as well as the decorative arts, should be to produce "repose," realized through "fitness, proportion, harmony." There should be no "excrescences" and "construction should be decorated"—but "decoration should never be purposely constructed "(23).[21] Yet archaeologically inspired architecture and jewelry, mimicking racial métissage, contained paradoxes and stylistic hybridities that undermined these categories. In particular, the details of archaeological jewelry, displayed on female bodies, reinforced the erotic qualities of "decoration purposely constructed" or "decoration for its own sake." Buried oriental civilizations, "rising" from their graves, *vampirized* contemporary nineteenth-century spaces and bodies by taking them over, infiltrating and altering their material textures, reproducing themselves through an obsessive juxtapostion of hybrid designs in which classical and contemporary decorative elements often competed with more "exotic" oriental ones.

As with the Sèvres Egyptian dessert service discussed in the first chapter, archaeological jewelry sought to grapple with the twin specters of elusive monumentalism and imperial decay. At the same time it represented the formulation of an aesthetic within jewelry design that separated itself from reliance on diamonds, which were intimately connected with imperial exhibitions. It also legitimized jewelry as distinct aesthetic objects rather than mere symbols of power and wealth, laying the groundwork for Lalique's radical approach at the turn of the century. In *The Art of the Jeweller* (1889), Carlo Giuliano, who had learned his craft by working with Castellani, claimed that " a piece of goldsmith's work need not necessarily be expensive; it is the style, the design, the form that will give that grace and refinement which will give one joy or pleasure."[22] Archaeological jewelry sought to replicate the materials and techniques of Greek, Roman and Etruscan jewelers, and also reflected Assyrian, Egyptian, and Indian influences. The emphasis was on gold, enameling and incorporating antique fragments such as scarabs or faience within the ornament. Of particular importance was the complex technique of granulation, which involved the fusion of minute particles of gold.

As these buried civilizations were obsessively unearthed, they were simultaneously converted into pieces of revivalist jewelry. Fragments of these civilizations were then displayed on the female body or in museums. For Alessandro Castellani, ornamentation was rooted in the decay of organic forms; he traced the inspiration for Etruscan and Phoenician jewelers as well as his own pieces to the fossilized remains of sea urchins:

> The bracelet with square compartments in the Campana Collection, the saddle-shaped earrings . . . in my collection . . . and many other jewels scattered through the various European museums, present their surface covered with hemispheres and grains of all sizes distributed in square compartments and parallel lines so strongly resembling the fossil *diademae,* as to leave no doubt about their origin. (93).[23]

In its search for origins, therefore, archaeological jewelry repeated, but also to a certain extent *reversed* natural processes of decay. It mirrored the evolutionary process, simultaneously encapsulating within its forms the threat of decomposition. The notion of the "primitive," however, was consistently undermined by the notoriously complex techniques of reproduction, as the jewelers continually grappled with the failure to surpass earlier aesthetic achievements. The "buried" designs, despite being "uncovered," remained frustratingly out of reach, resisting perfect repetition. In *Antique Jewellery and its Revival* (1861), Castellani noted this problem: "It appears that the ancient jewellers knew and used chemical and mechanical agents hardly perceptible to the naked eye; in which our modern jewelers have not yet succeeded . . . we are obliged to confess that the ancients were far superior to us in this art."[24] In his address to the Archeological Institute in 1861, Castellani explained the difficulty of recapturing the technique of granulation:

> those invisible grains, like little pearls which play so important a part in the orna-
> mentation of antique jewelry, presented difficulties nearly insurmountable. We
> made innumerable essays, employing all possible agents . . . in spite of all of our
> efforts, we have been unable to reproduce some exquisitely fine workmanship, and
> despair of being able to do so, unless aided by some new scientific discoveries.[25]

Moreover, many archaeological pieces were hybrids, combining elements from several different civilizations. For instance, a typical "Egyptianizing" parure (a chignon comb, hairpins, a necklace, brooch, and earrings) produced by the Castellani workshops around 1860–62 contained Egyptian scarabs made of steatite and faience, yet the shape of the jewels, some of the materials used, and the intaglio motifs were indebted to Greco-Roman influences. For Jones, Egyptian art was the "great parent, " the "pure original style" whose offshoots encompassed "the Greek, the Roman, the Byzantine, the Arabian, the Moresque and the Gothic"—yet Egyptian art was only visible "in a state of decline" (47), its original perfection lost in a state of obscurity.

The complex cultural resonances of these pieces, therefore, conferred a con-siderable amount of power and mystique on their owners and wearers. They were often displayed on the bodies of powerful women in Europe—female rulers as well as adventuresses—and at times, commissioned especially for them. The Comtesse Castiglione, courtesan, adventuress, and Italian revolutionary, whose portrait was painted by G. F. Watts in London in 1857, repeatedly con-structed different personas, which she had recorded by the French photogra-pher Pierre-Louis Pierson. Dripping with archaeological-style jewelry made of gilded copper, Castiglione had herself photographed in 1863 as the "Queen of Etruria" brandishing a dagger in various poses (one of which she entitled "Vengeance" and sent to her husband who had threatened to take away her son because of her sexual liaisons and "scandalous" public self-display). Elsewhere, the countess also posed as a Turkish odalisque with a dagger, titling the photo-graph "Assassin," her facial expression evoking that of "Vengeance." The exotic trappings, including the heavy antique jewelry for the Queen of Etruria poses, invested the countess's body with a certain degree of monumentality, authority, and grandeur, which she then proceeded to manipulate and adapt to her own uses. In 1890 Sarah Bernhardt, who not only had commissioned jewelry from René Lalique but whose body dramatized the sinuous forms of his designs, appeared on stage in London in Egyptian costume in Victorien Sardou's *Cléopâtre*. Earlier, in 1884, Bernhardt had taken the role of Theodora, the cour-tesan turned empress of Byzantium, in Sardou's play of the same name, order-ing a costume encrusted with thousands of semiprecious stones and positioning herself against a set in which monumental splendor vied with detailed ornamentation. Here Bernhardt used the massiveness of the oriental set and the lavish ornaments to heighten and create a performance that centered around *female* imperial power (214).[26]

Alongside the recovery of ancient civilizations, the spectral forms of female monarchs were also unearthed. In some cases, these bodies were not separable from the monument itself, as its excavation led in turn to the discovery of the traces of monumental femininity. In *A Thousand Miles Up the Nile* (1877), one of the leading British female Egyptologists of the day, Amelia Edwards, reflected on the half-buried/mutilated female forms at the Temple of Dendera:

> the famous external bas-relief of Cleopatra on the back of the Temple . . . is now banked up with rubbish for its better preservation, and can no longer be seen by travellers . . . it was however, admirably photographed some years ago by Signor Beati; which photograph is faithfully reproduced in the annexed engraving. . . . Mannerism apart, however, the face wants neither individuality or beauty. Cover the mouth, and you have an almost faultless profile. The chin and the throat are also quite lovely; while the whole face, suggestive of cruelty, subtlety, and voluptuousness, carries with it an indefinable impression not only of portraiture, but of likeness.[27]

Likeness to what? Edwards has never really seen Cleopatra, yet the archaeological impulse here works to create a spectral body that must somehow be authenticated and solidified (relegated to the realm of the familiar) yet which, at every step, resists this process. Similarly, archaeological jewelry displayed on women's bodies performed several functions: it created hybrid bodies that exhibited their affinities with the "undead," "voluptuous" forms of excavated queens; and its mixed styles announced the failure of the search for pure origins. Rather than securely consolidating the display of imperial collections, it heralded the intrusion of the adorned, exoticized woman, with all her connotations of instability and excessive display, her "excrescences," into the grand narrative of archaeological discovery. Through its very nature, by converting jewelry decisively into an art form, it challenged the separation of aesthetic purity and the extravagance of female desire. The "texts" of both Lalique and Stoker intensified and transformed these developments, bringing their own unique perspectives to bear on the hybridization of the ornamented female body, taking it further than ever before.

The Vampiric Odalisques of René Lalique

At the turn of the century only a few women—usually artists, actresses, and courtesans—"dared to ornament their toilette with jewelry by Lalique."[28] His avant-garde art nouveau designs created a new type of exotic female body, one that invited a multiplicity of readings and was often deliberately ambiguous. Rather than centralize expensive precious stones (freeing fashion from the "tyranny of the diamond"), Lalique's jewelry was based on his vision of the female form as one perpetually poised on the precipice of becoming other, continually negotiating the boundaries between the natural and the unnatural, the organic and the inorganic. Through his production of a wide variety of objects—ranging from tiaras, chokers, and corsage ornaments to looking glasses and handbags—Lalique re-created the hybrid female body as a vampiric artifact that, while simultaneously symbolizing the allure *and* terror of decay, had also somehow managed to escape the process itself.

In doing so, he moved the politics of ornamentation beyond fashion into an entirely new arena, toward an aesthetic that disturbed and unsettled the viewer/collector. Lalique's jewels destabilized the surface of women's bodies by investing them with the uncanny, layering them with "decadent," "perverse" forms. "All too many Herodiades, Cleopatras, Theodoras, too many *Flowers of Evil*" wrote Albert Thomas in *L'Art décoratif* (1900).[29] An anonymous reviewer in the British art journal *The Studio*, responding to a London exhibition of Lalique's work, wrote that although "M. Lalique is courageously Parisian in the way that he gives his great imaginative skill to the splendours of fashion, . . . he has his limitations; to our mind, too much of his talent goes to the imitation of beautiful natural forms and flowers in unnatural-looking material, which suggests sometimes an unpleasant decadence."[30] More forcefully, after viewing what could arguably be considered Lalique's most famous piece, a corsage ornament in which the body of a woman with golden claws emerges out of a dragonfly (fig. 12), a bewildered English critic commented: "Very remarkable and startling to the observer, but is it jewellery?"[31] The great French historian of jewelry design, Henri Vever, commented on the beginnings of Lalique's experimental use of the female body:

> His display at the Salon of 1895 also included a work that was curious for several reasons. It was a large brooch or clasp in the Renaissance taste. . . . In the centre stood a nude female figure chased in gold. Lalique had long dreamt of gracing one of his jewels with the harmonious and elegant contours of the female form. It was in this clasp, made between 1893 and 1894, that he first experimented with this design. . . . Naturally this departure caused great controversy. Some considered it a stroke of genius, others . . . objected to the introduction of the human form in any jewel. They found it misplaced, "unseemly" and even indecent.[32]

Lalique had begun training as a jeweler in Paris in 1876, spending two years studying the museum collections in London. Both the British Museum and the South Kensington museum contained pieces by Castellani; although Lalique was to move beyond the archaeological style, many of his pieces have links to that tradition. He created several scarab pendants with Egyptian motifs; the form of the scarab was to become crucial to several of his most phantasmagoric pieces. For Bernhardt's performance in *Cléopâtre,* he created costume jewelry that contained "sacred lotuses" in 1890. The facial features of dead Egyptian queens were replicated in several egyptianizing ornaments,[33] including a brooch made of opaque and transclucent enamel with a gold cobra springing from the forehead, and a "scarabs" corsage ornament in which three enamel scarabs are framed by two female figures at either end that are in the process of metamorphosing into *both* scarabs and dragonflies (1897–99). Lalique's art also reimagined female icons of exoticism; a pendant brooch entitled "Salammbô/Salomé" (1904–5) spectralized the central figure by casting her in transclucent blue-green glass, framed by a delicate pair of intertwined serpents. In the brooch, the frame attempts to encircle a floating body that is ephemeral and seems to elude any significant act of containment, with one foot on the edge of the frame.

As Lalique's designs in enamel and opal became more technically intricate, the hybrid bodies of his "modern" bijoux became more fantastic and transgressive. Anticipating surrealism, an elaborate necklace with interlacing motifs of insect women and black swans (designed in 1898–99) of chased gold, opal, and amethyst presented the figures of women who were metamorphosing into *both* birds and insects.[34] The womens' legs and elongated torsos connect with the beaks of the swans, becoming clawlike, while their "insect wings" encompass the bodies of the birds. Their bodies appear to have the vampiric quality of duplicating themselves by "absorbing" other species. The sense of self-duplication is intensified by the repetition of these motifs in the necklace; a single pendant would have had a different, and possibly less disturbing effect. Meanwhile, the attenuated languor of the bodies, made entirely of gold, repeats that of the odalisque and the mummy.

The vampiric possibilities of the exoticized body are more pronounced in his enigmatic masterpiece, the dragonfly corsage ornament, (see fig. 12) the creation of which coincided with the publication of Stoker's *Dracula* (1897). Two immense gold claws grow out of a winged female torso, with two small scarabs positioned on either side of its head. The torso extends itself into a tail set with chrysophrase and moonstones; blue-green transclucent enamel wings set with diamonds fan out on either side of the body. Serene, languorous, demonic—the woman's face seems to be caught in a vampiric sleep. Her eyes appear closed, yet one senses a powerful, oblique gaze beneath the green eyelids. The upper body as well as the face resemble, in some ways, the bas-relief of Cleopatra that Edwards had reproduced in her narrative, combining "subtlety and voluptuousness." Hanging suspended, the claws appear to emerge from the body and yet seem detached from it. In other ornaments, Lalique frequently used bats, frogs, and snakes, the last of which was the most prolific. His preliminary sketches for some pieces also show women transforming into bats and vice versa. The boundaries of these bodies cannot be policed or defined.

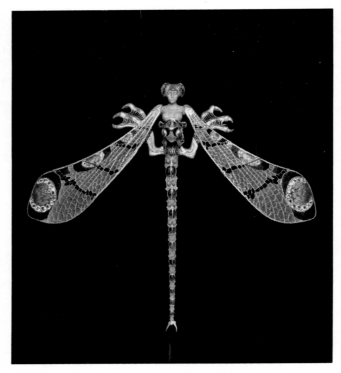

**Fig. 12. René Lalique, Dragonfly Corsage Ornament, 1897–98.
Gold, enamel, chrysophrase, moonstones, diamonds
(Museu Calouste Gulbenkian, Lisbon)**

Lalique's tantalizing version of exotic "monstrosity" in these pieces is consciously opaque and difficult to read. Rather than simply dramatizing a fear of devolution or the New Woman, his vampiric odalisques posit a complex relationship between nature and jewelry as a highly sophisticated artifact. Like vampires, their bodies are essentially those of another species, or threaten to mutate into other forms of life. They are neither "natural" nor "unnatural," "organic" nor "inorganic" but located in a hybrid, intermediate space between these two states, altering, by their very presence, the parameters of these categories. Additionally, by flooding these bodies with radiance as a result of his remarkable techniques of enameling and backlighting, Lalique suggests the transformative nature of the decadent experience rather than its regressive aspects. His exotic insect-women set in motion an "erotics of decay" in which their icy, spectral bodies highlight the pleasures/terrors of abjection and decomposition and yet remain immune to them; in this sense their fluidity becomes possibly an illusion, yet another trick played upon the imagination. Instead of decomposing/degenerating, their bodies remain perfectly preserved as exquisitely and precisely executed aesthetic objects, eternally deferring the moment of degeneration, but endlessly taunting the viewer with the threat of engulfment.

The vampiric odalisque *eroticizes* degeneration, but never succumbs to it herself. Her body remains a phantasmatic presence, always on the verge of escaping, although it is, to a certain extent, preserved *within the jewel* through Lalique's delicate techniques of "fossilization." The unsettling quality of these pieces, their haunting strangeness, arises from this paradox.[35] The performances of Lalique's most famous customer, Sarah Bernhardt "excavated" and "restored" the extravagant, ornamented bodies of oriental queens in a very different manner from that of the average archaeologist and collector. For Bernhardt in *Théodora*, Lalique's projected designs included elaborate headdresses, including the famous snake tiara that was never made, but instead adapted into a corsage ornament and displayed at the 1900 Paris exhibition (fig. 13).[36] (For another actress, Julia Bartet, in the role of another oriental queen, Bérénice, Lalique designed a tiara with figures of Isis intertwined with courtesans).[37] Rather than reduce these bodies to fragments that merely consolidated the museum culture of the late nineteenth century, Bernhardt invested them with power and a majestic presence on stage, by means of which they appeared to orchestrate their own spectacles. Similarly, in Lalique's work, the hybrid, vampire-odalisque connects the aesthetics of the avant-garde to the uneasiness engendered by archaeological acts of recovery. It is surely no accident that Bernhardt, herself an accomplished sculptor, designed an inkwell in 1880 entitled "Self-Portrait as a Sphinx" that, with its spreading clawlike wings, clearly foreshadowed the dragonfly corsage jewel.[38]

Unwrapping Stoker's Jewel: The Vengeance of Queen Tera

In Bram Stoker's 1903 novel, *The Jewel of Seven Stars,* the body of a vampiric Egyptian queen is converted into a bejeweled artifact and initially assigned its place in the archaeological exhibit. Of courses, it refuses to stay there. On some levels a savage critique of "the scramble for Egypt," the text itself reenacts the paradoxical impulses of Lalique's spectralized jewels, working out similar motifs and concerns. The Grafton exhibition of Lalique's jewelry and drawings coincided with the publication of the novel; Lalique's reputation had, however, already been consolidated prior to that moment in a successive series of major international exhibitions. Even if Stoker had not directly encountered Lalique's work, he would have come across imitations and similar motifs in the work of his followers and admirers. When it was published, the novel's front cover was adorned by a scarab.[39]

On the surface, the novel is "a guide to a century or more of British Egyptomania,"[40] informed by Stoker's personal acquaintance with amateur Egyptologists such as Sir William Wilde as well as his research into Egyptian culture.

Fig. 13. René Lalique, Snake Corsage Ornament, 1898–99. Gold, enamel
(Museu Calouste Gulbenkian, Lisbon)

In 1882, the British government established effective control over Egypt, with the nominal khedive acting under the authority of Lord Cromer. The last two decades of the nineteenth century saw the emergence of a controversy in Britain over the rapacious and unscrupulous archaeological methods used by collectors like the Egyptologist E. A. Wallis Budge, who had ransacked several tombs, citing the British Museum's superior capabilities for preservation as part of his rationale. Other British archaeologists, such as Amelia Edwards and Flinders Petrie, horrified at the violation of the monuments and crude, destructive excavation techniques, attempted to draw the attention of the British public to this problem; Edwards's efforts led to the foundation of the Egypt Exploration Fund, which applied for official permits and sought to arrest the "degeneration" of the archaeological impulse.[41] Stoker's novel provides a fascinating commentary on the Egyptological obsessions of the late nineteenth century by pitting the archaeologist against an artifact in his own collection. In *Jewel,* the ornamented, exoticized female body not only intervenes in the discourse of archaeology; it also radically dislocates it. Like Lalique's jewels, Stoker's jewel embodies the spectacular culmination of the parallel development of the discourses of archaeology, ornamentation, and exoticism. To expand Benjamin's metaphor, in this novel the jewel fuses living female bodies with dead ones and also attaches both to the "inorganic world": a fusion that not only literally reinstates the "rights of the corpse" but also initiates its return from death.

A 1650 Dutch manuscript compels British egyptologist Abel Trelawney to search out and violate the hidden tomb of Queen Tera, of the "Eleventh, or Theban Dynasty of Egyptian Kings" (111). The manuscript describes the discovery of the queen's mummified body, with her seven-fingered white hand "lying life-like above the shrouding mummy cloths" (110) guarding a hypnotically beautiful ruby in the shape of a scarab.

Unlike most mummies, although her body is "veiled" in several layers of linen, her unwrapped hand is visible, its "marble skin" recalling the flesh tones of the odalisques of Gérôme and Leighton. The monochromatic marble, however, cannot quite efface the sense of a polychromatic freshness and voluptuousness. Resembling "living flesh," the dead hand points to Tera's state of vampiric preservation: "the skin and nails were complete and whole, as though the body had been placed for burial overnight"(98). Resisting attempts to decipher the hieroglyphics of her body, Tera is the odalisque-as-corpse, the odalisque-as-vampire; her "passive" corporeal presence deliberately confusing the signs of life and death. The enigmatic jewel replaces Tera's absent gaze; as it is prized away from the hand, the Dutch narrator feels its Medusa-like power to induce a paralytic state in the viewer. After the theft of the jewel, the spectral white hand, also severed, proceeds to strangle some of the tomb robbers and then disappears.

Revisiting the tomb in the nineteenth century, when "the host of scholars" pursuing Egyptology had "wrested open the mysterious prison-house of Egyptian language," Trelawney brings back the mummy, the hand, and the jewel to his house in London, where he proceeds to install them among his other Egyptian exhibits. The seven-fingered hand, having returned to Tera's body, is itself described as a "jewel": "The end of the wrist was covered with dried blood! It was as though the body had bled after death! The jagged ends of the broken wrist were rough with the clotted blood; through this the white bone, sticking out, looked like the matrix of opal" (110). An uncanny image: as in Lalique's jewels, the exotic female body is here *fused* with the precious stone, Tera's white bones being transformed into opal (which incidentally, was also Lalique's preferred stone). Trelawney's bedroom is converted into a small museum: a room of "immense size," filled with "magnificent curios, chiefly Egyptian" (22). Here, a "phantasmatic Egypt" is arranged around Tera's sarcophagus. As his bedroom, it suggests his fetishization of Tera; yet, from the beginning, the archaeologist is never in complete control of this process. Trelawney is convinced that Tera intends to resurrect herself "in some northern land" (namely, England) and gradually becomes obsessed with the possibility of managing her resurrection (112).

When Trelawney is brutally attacked over three successive nights and slides into a coma, his daughter Margaret calls in medical specialists, detectives, and the young barrister Malcolm Ross (Stoker's narrator), who eventually becomes her lover. Trelawney's wrist is slashed with a series of "jagged tears." All those who keep watch over the body are gradually overcome by the heavy Egyptian odors of "bitumen, spices and gums," allowing Tera to evade their surveillance. Tera's penetration of Trelawney's body both mimics and reverses the narrative of archaeological violence while the excessive amount of blood in the room hints at her vampiric propensities. To extract her jewel from the safe in which Trelawney has placed it, the queen uses her "astral body" to unlock it. The ghost of this other body haunts the dismemberment of the excavated one, threatening to transform lack into plenitude. As Trelawney observes: "that hand in my room could ensure her instantaneous presence in the flesh, and its equally rapid dissolution" (152).

While Margaret appears to display all the qualities of the dutiful daughter and the perfect Victorian domestic goddess, she is always present when Trelawney is attacked. Ross confesses that there is "something about her" that has bothered him from the beginning of their relationship—an exoticism that continually impinges on her body. Like Tera's paralytic ruby scarab, the jewels worn by Margaret at their first meeting induce fear in Ross:

> The first moment when she swept across my vision at Belgrave Square. A queenly figure! . . . For ornament in her hair she wore an old Egyptian jewel, a tiny crystal disc, set between rising plumes carved in lapis. . . . On her wrist was a broad bangle or bracelet of antique work in the shape of a pair of spreading wings wrought in gold, with feathers made of coloured gems. . . . For all her gracious bearing toward me, when our hostess introduced me, I was then afraid of her." (55)

Significantly, Margaret's mother had died in childbirth during Trelawney's excavation of Tera's body. Later, Ross learns that Margaret is "unlike her mother; but in both feature and colour . . . is a marvellous resemblance to the pictures of Queen Tera" (118). The insidious and almost imperceptible hybridization of Margaret's body is at the center of the text's anxieties.

The gradual "excavation" and "unveiling" of Tera's body (presented as intersecting processes) inevitably results in an increasing sense of disorientation for both Trelawney and Ross. Relegated to being an item in Trelawney's collection that he wishes to manipulate for his own purposes, Tera is nevertheless in complete control of the exhibitionary complex. As fragments of Tera's history are revealed, pieced together from the inscriptions on the tomb, a powerful and complicated figure emerges. Defying the priests, the only child of her father, Tera had been a woman of "extraordinary character and ability," a scholar and an artist. Claiming masculine privileges, she had learned "statecraft as well as "magic" and had "won secrets from nature in strange ways" (111). In order to experiment with sleep and death, she had entombed herself for a month, mummifying herself but staying alive.

As the material symbol of Tera's desire for power, the jewel encapsulates her transgressive writing, allowing her to inhabit modernity on her own terms. Stoker is not saying here that she symbolizes an ancient, dead civilization; rather, his vision of Egypt is very "modern," making Tera a hybrid of the New Woman and Egyptian monarch. On her ruby, she had inscribed "Master Words to compel all the Gods, both of the Upper and Underworlds" (112). Despite Trelawney's struggles to interpret the inscription, the queen's purposes remain obscure. As the instrument of her resurrection, Tera's ruby scarab is not only interchangeable with her spectral or "astral" body; it also functions as a sign of her ability to undo the dichotomy between "ancient" and "modern," to preserve and textualize herself as a vampiric "undead" artifact that at every turn seduces and defeats the collector/archaeologist.

Tera's "corporeal transference," which Trelawney fears will allow "no bounds or limits" (151) to her ambition, manifests itself through her gradual takeover of Margaret's body. It is this part of her purpose, the resurrection of her own body through the hybridization of Margaret's, that remains completely unfathomed by Trelawney or Ross. At some point in the text, Margaret will become Tera/Margaret, and this moment will be veiled from the reader as well. Tera/Margaret's body, being both "dark" and "white," reinscribes racial categories as dangerously unstable and repeats, most forcefully, the intercorporeality that I have been tracing in the previous chapters. As the two bodies intersect and merge, Ross slowly becomes aware of a "mysterious veiling" of Margaret's personality. Margaret herself becomes more inaccessible and harder to read. The narrative enacts a métissage between the two women that climaxes in Margaret's reappropriation of Tera's nude body after it has been stripped by the men for the resurrection experiment. As Tera's dead body is uncovered, the erotic power of Tera-as–vampire odalisque is on view:

> the wonder of that beautiful form was something to dream of. It was not like death at all; it was like a statue carved in ivory by the hand of Praxiteles. There was nothing of that horrible shrinkage which death seems to effect in a moment. There was nothing of the wrinkled toughness which seems to be a leading characteristic of most mummies. There was not the shrunken attentuation of a body dried in the sand, as I had seen before in museums. All the pores of the body seemed to have been preserved in some wonderful way . . . the flesh was full and round,

as in a living person. . . . Margaret threw over the body a beautiful robe which lay across her arm. Only the face was then to be seen. This was more startling even than the body, for it seemed not dead but alive . . . the full, red lips though the mouth was not open, showed the . . . pearly teeth within. This woman—I could not think of her as a mummy or a corpse—was the image of Margaret as my eyes had first lit on her. The likeness was increased by the jewelled ornament which she wore on her hair, the "Disc and Plumes" such as Margaret too, had worn. It too, was a glorious jewel. (204)

Both here and throughout the novel, in literal as well as figurative terms, the ruby scarab jewel is somehow connected to Tera's own self-embodiment. Tera wills herself into being through the jewel; like Lalique's jeweled specters, she haunts the borderland between the natural and the artificial, the organic and the inorganic. The ruby resurfaces in different guises, facilitating the reentry of her body from abjection into aesthetic and archaeological discourses that she then proceeds to unravel. It is precisely this moment in the text, where the gazers obsessively read/desire Tera's preserved/decayed body and recognize it as a topos on which multiple hybridities converge, that prefigures the dissolution of their assumed control over the corpse. This dissolution is both anticipated and mediated through Ross's recollection of another jewel: "the disc and plumes" which had earlier foreshadowed Tera's desire to encroach on Margaret's body. By wearing the jewel, Margaret had unknowingly revealed her receptivity to Tera.

As Tera's influence over Margaret deepens, she demands to be left alone with the dead queen in her own bedroom, protesting against the "horrible indignity" of the unveiling. Removing the body from the orbit of male desire, Margaret can then indulge her own erotic and aesthetic gaze. Meanwhile, Trelawney and Ross set up the "Great Experiment," the main purpose of which is Trelawney's intention to convert Tera into an imperial archive. The "recovery" of Tera's body will ultimately validate the archaeological project by allowing him to penetrate the "origins" of science, thus legitimizing the "true world of human progress." By using Tera's knowledge of the "lost arts" and "lost sciences" Trelawney wishes to "restore history" (183–84), subordinating the queen's subjectivity to his own panoptical narrative of modernity.

Yet Tera controls "modernity." In the original ending of the novel, the intercorporeity between Margaret and Tera is complete, as the experiment fails, and Ross wanders in the darkness carrying the body of . . . ? Margaret or Tera? He doesn't know. Ultimately, he realizes that Margaret/Tera has "escaped" from the museum over the dead bodies of his companions. Unlike her famous fictional predecessor, the Arabian queen Ayesha in Rider Haggard's *She,* who crumbles to dust in the presence of male viewers, "degenerating" into a shriveled mummy, Stoker's text does not allow either the reader or Ross the reassurance of witnessing Tera's fate. Ultimately, her ornamented body remains unknowable, resisting all efforts to master it. Despite Ross's discovery of a body with eyes reduced to a "glassy stare" (211), "Margaret" has been completely engulfed by the Egyptian queen. As the electricity fails, the experiment of Tera's controlled resurrection ends in a real *and* metaphoric darkness, descending over the corpse of the archaeologist. The "success" of Trelawney's archaeological ambitions leads to an excavation of the hybrid vampiric odalisque-queen that not only signifies the fragility of narratives of progress but also transforms imperial history into nightmare.

❧ 6 ❧

Gothic Divas

Opera and Exoticism in Bulwer-Lytton and Vernon Lee

> . . . a voice, very low and sweet, almost a whisper, which grew and
> grew and grew, until the whole place was filled with that exquisite
> vibrating note, of a strange, exotic, unique quality.
> —Vernon Lee, "A Wicked Voice"(1890)

> For the diva-to-be, difference is power; she seeks profit in her
> deviance. For the nondiva, difference only leads to ridicule.
> —Wayne Kostenbaum, *The Queen's Throat* (1993)

Since Edward Said's critique of Verdi's *Aida* in *Culture and Imperialism* (1993),
the racial politics of nineteenth-century opera have been particularly suspect.[1]
Operas in both the French and Italian traditions (to which British audiences
had considerable exposure through performances in London) have been generally interpreted as embodying or spectacularizing the ideologies inherent in the
ethnographic discourses of the period. Recently, these views have been challenged from a variety of perspectives. With respect to Verdi, John Mackenzie
has drawn attention to the composer's hostility to imperialism and the importance of his role in the Italian independence movement (the Risorgimento). In
Opera in History (1998), Herbert Lindenberger suggests that the orientalized
heroine in works such as Meyerbeer's *L'Africaine* and Strauss's *Salomé* "becomes
a figure for women in general," providing a "voice" for European women.[2]
While such readings do call for a closer look at the complexity of operatic orientalism, they do not really investigate the way the diva has functioned in operatic history as the symptom of opera itself as "exotick and irrational."

Focusing on the figure of the "foreign" diva in this chapter, I examine the way the diva's voice, body, and performance work instead as devices that could *imperil* the formation of coherent national and sexual identities rather than bolster them. In the first part of this chapter, I argue that instead of merely reinscribing bourgeois/imperialistic agendas, operatic representations of exoticism, mediated through the diva's foreign body, may have unsettled them. After providing a brief overview of the cultural history of the diva on the London stage, I look at the way two fictional works, positioned at different cultural moments, inscribe the diva's exoticism: Edward Bulwer-Lytton's extravagantly gothic novel *Zanoni* (1842), and Vernon Lee's remarkable fin de siècle novella and a meditation on the androgynous operatic voice, "A Wicked Voice" (1890). In both works, the Italian diva's exotic body becomes a haunting, gothic presence that eludes domestication. Again, as elsewhere in this book, I define exoticism as a trope that at times includes and parallels orientalism, but is not necessarily limited to it.

Excess, Exoticism, and the Diva's Body

In the British context, opera has always occupied a somewhat equivocal space. Its connection to a specifically English identity, therefore, has always been open to question and constant shifting, from the establishment of Italian opera in London with the performance of Handel's *Rinaldo* at the King's Theatre, Haymarket, in 1711, to present-day culture wars over the fate of the Royal Opera House, Covent Garden.[3] Since Samuel Johnson (in)famously defined opera as an "exotick and irrational entertainment" in *Lives of the Poets,* there has been a tendency to view it as a "foreign," lavish, and essentially baroque form connected with social and aesthetic exclusiveness. At the same time, the operatic stage has always provided a forum for marginalized bodies and identities to make themselves visible in ways that have disrupted bourgeois constructions of the self, from the early prohibitions around the public display of female bodies to the postmodern seductiveness of the diva's "queer" identity, particularly for gay men. Operatic roles have also allowed a space in which gendered identities could unravel themselves; between 1600 and 1800, female sopranos and castrati shared both female and male roles. To a large extent then, the unstable cultural configurations of opera have prevented it from being easily appropriated by any single discourse of national identity.[4]

The forerunners of Handel's opera seria[5] in England were Sir William Davenant's *The Siege of Rhodes* (1656), which combined elements of Italian operas and French heroic poetry, and John Dryden's own work *Albion and Albanius* (1685). In his preface to this work, Dryden, who admired Italian music, defined an opera as " a poetical tale or fiction, represented by vocal and instrumental music, adorned with scenes, machines and dancing . . . the subject being extended beyond the limits of human nature, admits of that sort of marvelous and surprising conduct which is rejected in other plays"(61). For Dryden, opera's expansiveness and unpredictability are positive qualities. Interestingly, he also comments on opera as inherently androgynous in its form: "the recitative part of the opera requires a more masculine beauty of expression and sound; the other (which for want of a proper English word) I must call the *songish* part, must abound in the softness and variety of numbers" (61). The "hybridity" of opera, then, is foregrounded at the start.[6]

As Italian opera singers became more prominent in the eighteenth century, commentators such as Joseph Addison in *The Spectator* began to complain of the linguistic hybridity of operatic performances (some parts were sung in Italian and others in English), as well as the excessiveness of the staging. *Rinaldo* (sung entirely in Italian, and with a plot based on the seduction of the crusader Rinaldo in Tasso's *Gerusalemme Liberata*), was in 1711 the most spectacular opera to date. It also served to set off the regal figure of the Muslim seductress/sorceress Armida, queen of Damascus. One of the great exotic roles for sopranos in the eighteenth century, Armida kept turning up in opera after opera through the first part of the nineteenth century, as every major composer took his turn with the subject, culminating in Rossini's *Armida* (1815), which vocally centralized Armida's dazzling seductive powers by pitting her against seven tenors. Armida's erotic voice/body became a phantom double, a mirror image for opera itself, as the seduction of the English audience by Italian opera singers in *Rinaldo* was reenacted by the seduction of Rinaldo by Armida in the opera. This double seduction induced disquiet in the minds of critics such as Addison and Steele.[7]

Throughout most of the early and mid-nineteenth century, Italian opera dominated the London operatic scene, with French and German operas entering the repertoire later. As the dominance of Italian opera began to be challenged, French grand opera, with its spectacular exotic settings, was performed more regularly. Operas with exotic settings and heroines performed at Covent Garden between 1847 and 1890 included Rossini's *Semiramide* (1847) and *L'Italiana in Algeri* (The Italian Woman in Algiers) (1847); Giacomo Meyerbeer's grand opera *L'Africaine* (1865; with a hybrid Indo-African setting); Massenet's *Le Roi de Lahore* (1879; its plot centered on the priestess of a Hindu temple); a revival of Bizet's *Pearl Fishers* (1887; set in Ceylon), *Carmen* (1882), and *Djamileh* (1890; set in a harem).[8] In the staging of French grand opera, "distant" exotic settings were not intended necessarily to reproduce a "genuine" sense of place.[9] Therefore, instead of striving for ethnographic realism or authenticity, opera actually *subverted* the ethnographic impulse to classify and hierarchize by presenting a cosmopolitan, geographically indefinable spectacle in which Europe dreamed its surreal, exotic self, recasting its own politics and its own fantasies in terms of alternative landscapes. Furthermore, when French and Italian operas were performed before a British audience, the cultural layers of the operatic spectacle became even more intricate.

Although the exoticism of an opera played itself out on multiple levels—those of plot, scenery, and staging—it also provoked musical innovations, as for example, in Vincenzo Bellini's *Norma* (discussed in connection with Lydia Gwilt's visit to the opera in chapter 2). Even though the setting of the opera is not consciously oriental or exotic, the opera's most famous aria, "Casta Diva" (Chaste Goddess), sung by Norma, blended an orientalist "voluptuousness" with the Italian style. In the French repertoire, one of the most notoriously "exotic" operas of the later nineteenth century, *Carmen* (based on Prosper Mérimée's semi-ethnographic tale of a Spanish gypsy) was excoriated both for the libertinism of its heroine and the avant-garde dissonance of its music. As French reviewer Jean-Pierre Comettant wrote: "A plague on these females vomited from Hell! . . . To preserve the morale and the behaviour of the impressionable dragoons and toreadors who surround this demoiselle, she should be gagged, a stop put to the unbridled twisting of her hips. The pathological condition of this unfortunate woman, consecrated unceasingly and unpityingly to the fires of the flesh . . . is fortunately a rare case, more likely to inspire the solicitude of physicians than to interest the decent spectators who come to the Opéra-Comique accompanied by their wives and daughters" (112).[10]

Comettant's almost hysterical attack on *Carmen* clearly voiced the cultural anxieties of certain conservative sections of the French audience with regard to exoticized women and their power to inspire fear and bewilderment, to unravel the threads that held the social fabric together. Bursting onto the stage of the Opéra-Comique in 1875 from the pages of Mérimée's novella, Carmen's deliberate and carefully strategized self-display, compellingly echoed by what Comettant described as the composer's "risky dissonances," caused an uproar. "At the heart of each of the original reviews—whether pro or con, moralistic or stylistic," notes feminist critic and musicologist Susan McClary, "lies some crucial notion of difference" (115). Besides being the embodiment of difference, Carmen is also the ultimate hybrid: "half gypsy, half Andalusian; sensual, mocking, shameless; believing neither in God nor in the Devil . . . the veritable prostitute . . . of the crossroads" (112). Opera created a space these hybrid, "dissonant" bodies could inhabit and in which they could flaunt themselves vocally as well as physically.

From the late eighteenth century onward, as the fashion for castrati (male singers who were castrated before puberty to preserve the soprano voice range) declined, the female soprano gradually emerged as a central figure. Even though the rise of the tenor in the latter half of the period partially eroded that dominant position, the cultural iconography surrounding the diva continued to be associated with an increasing rhetoric of flamboyance and exhibitionism. This rhetoric was partly derived from the tradition of vocal ornamentation that had been the crucial element in operatic singing until the first half of the nineteenth century—a tradition that allowed the singer an important role in shaping the music through improvisation, embellishment, and virtuosity. Vocal ornaments included appoggiaturas (used to increase expressiveness or introduce melodic dissonance), trills (which could be of different varieties), cadenzas (virtuoso passages placed at the end of an aria), and *da capo* arias (including an ornamented, repeated section). The diva's voice, an extension of her body, could continually foreground its formidable power and technique through such ornamentation, combining seduction with vocal luxuriance. In this way, opera's excesses, manifested through the diva's vocal fireworks, were tied to a discourse of ornamentation that, as I argued in the previous chapter, was closely linked with exoticism. The "reform" of this tradition involved the consolidation of the composer's power at the expense of the soprano's; now she was expected to subordinate her self-display to the "appropriate" use of ornament and the overall "intention" of the opera. As an extension of the visibility of the female singer's "public" body, the diva's tendency toward vocal excess—"decoration purposely constructed"—was also intertwined with her eroticism, temperament, and lifestyle.

The exotic courtesan's body continued to haunt that of the diva in various ways. As John Rosselli's work on Italian singers has demonstrated, the diva's career overlapped with that of the courtesan in the seventeenth century.[11] Rosselli cites the case of Giulia (Ciulla) di Caro being described by one of her contemporaries as "actress singer musician whore" (60), and Anna Maria Sardelli, who had sung the role of Cleopatra, as "a courtesan singer if there ever was one" (60). Although Rosselli claims that the female singer moved toward greater independence as an artist as her position shifted between 1600 and 1900, he overlooks the fact that the separation of the diva's sexuality from her "technique" often served a bourgeois model of domesticity; female singers were expected to regulate their vocal ornamentation together with their sexuality, making sure that both were within the bounds of what was "appropriate." The sensuality of the diva's voice also had to be contained. Rosselli himself replicates this model when he appreciatively describes the conduct of the soprano Giuditta Pasta as "irreproachable"(69).

Yet even in the middle of the nineteenth century, the soprano's body intersected with the courtesan's as singers sought the financial backing and protection of powerful men. The wife of the composer Giuseppe Verdi, Giuseppina Strepponi (who inaugurated the roles in his early operas), was a "courtesan singer" before her marriage. In a letter, the composer defended her equivocal position: "In my house there lives a free, independent lady . . . neither she nor I owes any explanation for our actions to anyone at all; but on the other hand, who knows what relationship exists between us? What business connections? Who knows whether she is or is not my wife?"[12]

Of Verdi's sensational opera *La Traviata* (1856), which openly conflated the body of the diva with the consumptive body of the courtesan, the *Illustrated London News* reported: "Even the Parisians, lax as are their ideas of stage morality, were somewhat startled by its subject. . . . An attempt to bring it on the English stage was prevented, some time ago, we understand, by the Lord

Chamberlain's refusal of licence."[13] In *Traviata,* the diva negotiated all the tropes associated with the exotic woman—an opulent backdrop (Violetta's Paris salon), the sensuality, the alluring languor of disease—through an elaborate display of technical virtuosity, or "coloratura." While the visibility of the courtesan's body on the public stage was the immediate occasion for the controversy, the more subtle transgressiveness of the opera lay in the fact that although the courtesan "appeared" to lose strength, the fiendish coloratura technique the arias called for indicated just the opposite. The opera worked in a manner similar to Lalique's jewels; presenting an exotic body that luxuriated in decay while seeming to defer/defy it eternally.

Comparisons made between two early nineteenth-century divas, Giuditta Pasta and Maria Malibran, heightens the emerging contrast between the excessive, "exotic" diva and the more "classical," restrained singer. Malibran's brilliant and feverish career, during which she had been involved in several sexual liaisons, ended abruptly when she died of an injury from a riding accident. Both in her life and her singing, Malibran had embodied the "unmanageable" diva. The influential Victorian music critic, H. F. Chorley, contrasted Pasta and Malibran, noting the former's lack of "exaggeration" while critiquing Malibran's "vehemence too entrenched in frenzy to be true" (291). For Leigh Hunt, Pasta's physical excess, her "superfluity" of form, was effectively contained by the restraint of her singing. Malibran, on the other hand, was accused of "showing off" her voice (295).[14] Especially for the English audience, the diva's foreignness was accentuated by her exhibitionism. The soprano's display of her vocal prowess also connected her to the vanishing castrati, who had been famous for their vocal displays. After hearing another Italian soprano, Giulia Grisi (who had settled in London) sing *Norma,* Victoria compared her unfavorably with the "pure angelic voice" and "extremely quiet acting" of the more sedate Jenny Lind.[15] Many renowned Italian sopranos not only performed regularly on the London operatic stage but also chose to live in London or other parts of Britain for certain periods of time, from Caterina Gabrielli and Lucrezia Agujari (called "La Bastardina" because of her alleged illegitimacy) in the eighteenth century, to Giulia Grisi and Adelina Patti in the nineteenth.[16]

The anxieties that circulated around the foreign diva's body in English culture were only intensified by the exotic roles they performed onstage. Of the above mentioned operas performed at Covent Garden between 1847 and 1890, almost all involved some degree of defiance of religious, social, or paternal authority on the part of the exotic heroine. In *The Pearl Fishers* and *Le Roi de Lahore,* the heroines defy the priesthood by becoming involved in forbidden sexual encounters; in *Semiramide* the monumental staging serves as a background for the Babylonian queen's political and erotic ambitions; and *L'Italiana In Algeri* focuses on the disruptive collusion between Italian and Algerian odalisques in a harem setting. Verdi's early opera *Il Corsaro,* based on Byron's *The Corsair,* contained the role of Gulnara (based on the fiercely subversive odalisque Gulnare in the poem), who murders the pasha and liberates both herself and his prisoner. The librettos of these operas are driven by the articulation of desire and resistance by the exotic/exoticized woman. In comparison to operas in which the heroines are not exoticized (such as Bellini's *La Sonnambula* or Meyerbeer's *Les Huguenots*), the heroines are allowed significantly more agency. Yet, to some extent, *all* female bodies on the operatic stage were "exoticized": through its centralization of excess, display, ornamentation, public female bodies, and disorientation of the ethnographic impulse, opera itself had become exoticism's double.

Zanoni and the Spectralization of the Italian Diva

A phantasmagoric, operatic novel, Bulwer-Lytton's *Zanoni* brings the Italian diva's body within the realm of the gothic and links it to a nightmarish vision of the exotic woman's power. In *Zanoni,* the diva doubles as a phantom "veiled" female figure whose power to haunt is absolute and terrifying. In a desperate attempt to domesticate the diva, the novel's protagonist, Zanoni (who is himself orientalized), and the British artist Glyndon find themselves confronted with a gothic body that torments and pursues them relentlessly.[17] Published in 1842, *Zanoni* represents one of the strangest and most intriguing interventions in the discourse of exoticism in the early Victorian period. Because of its byzantine plot (which puts even the novels of Collins to shame), its excessively "decorated" prose, and its engagement with the occult, *Zanoni* has been dismissed or approached as an indecipherable text by Victorian critics and neglected by contemporary scholars. The few studies that attempt to grapple with the novel focus on its complex metaphysical symbolism rather than its preoccupation with the female body; my reading, therefore will centralize the latter.[18] It is also one of the few novels of this period that takes an Italian soprano as its heroine.

Situated roughly at the midpoint of Bulwer's literary career, *Zanoni* occupies an important transitional place in a novelistic output that not only covered a dizzying range of genres, but was also accompanied by his switch from liberal to conservative politics. The extensive range of Bulwer's fiction flouted generic limits as he experimented with bewildering hybrids, including Newgate/gothic/sensation novels (*Eugene Aram, Lucretia*); the historical romance (*The Last of the Barons, Harold, Rienzi;* this last, the basis for an opera by Richard Wagner); the archaeological-historical-occult novel (*The Last Days of Pompeii*); the "occult/philosophical" romances (*Zanoni, A Strange Story*); and science fiction (*The Coming Race*). Initially entering Parliament in 1831 as a member of Lord Durham's radical left-wing faction within the Whig party, Bulwer returned in 1852 as a conservative. His early attempts to construct a flamboyant, transgressive Byronic persona for himself, via clothing, lifestyle, and authorship—as well as his preoccupation with excess—are obsessively textualized in his earlier novels, several of which involve Byronic male figures who are seduced by libertinism and crime; most notably *Eugene Aram* (1831), based on an actual murder case and centering on the figure of a scholar-criminal who anticipates Dostoyevsky's Raskolnikov. *Lucretia, or the Children of the Night* (1846)—(which may have served as a source for *Armadale*) focuses on a female poisoner who uses her knowledge of toxicology, like Lydia Gwilt, to gain herself a substantial fortune.

The interlacing themes of knowledge and criminality become central to Bulwer's work from this point on, resurfacing in *Zanoni* and *A Strange Story* (1862). Furthermore, in the later novels, these concerns are linked to issues of race and mediated through exoticized female and male bodies. Even after the shift in his political beliefs, although several of his novels were written in a more domestic mode, Bulwer continued to use the sensational/gothic genre to dramatize his own investigation of the idea of the foreigner as the repository of knowledge. The excess in his own life was represented not only by his desire (and ultimate failure) to inhabit a Byronic body successfully but also by his disorderly wife, Rosina, from whom he had separated in Italy in 1833.[19]

After publishing novels herself in which she accused Bulwer of abuse, Rosina set in motion several schemes to embarrass him in public, which included a threat to disrupt the opening of his play at Devonshire House by pelting Queen Victoria with rotten eggs, and openly attacking her husband during his political campaign as a conservative MP. In order to control his unmanageable wife, Bulwer had her committed to an asylum in 1858; she was eventually released because of protests from the press. Though the Rosina affair did not erupt into open scandal until after the publication of *Zanoni*, she had posed a "problem" since their separation, that had apparently been instigated by her supposed liaison with a Neapolitan prince. Rosina's body haunts the novels as the specter of exotic feminine excess that threatens to undermine Englishness; nowhere is this more evident than in *Zanoni*.

From the beginning, both the voice and body of the Italian heroine of *Zanoni,* the soprano Viola Pisani, are located at the intersection of the gothic and the exotic. The novel also maps Italy as an intermediate topos, a point at which Western and oriental civilizations converge, as the setting shifts from the urban atmosphere of Naples and the interior of the opera house to a "savage" gothic landscape reminiscent of Ann Radcliffe's novels, inhabited by *banditti* and Italian peasants. The plot of *Zanoni* revolves around the triangular relationship between the orientalized stranger Zanoni (whose racial origins are obscure), the Italian Viola, and the English artist Glyndon. Zanoni, having fallen in love with Viola, removes her from the public arena of the opera house and attempts to domesticate her as a wife and mother. Glyndon, who also desires Viola, but cannot bring himself to marry an Italian singer, makes a deal with Zanoni to give up his pursuit of her in exchange for knowledge of the "elixir of life," putting himself under the tutelage of Zanoni's Arab teacher, the sorcerer Mejnour. When Glyndon disobeys Mejnour's instructions about entering his laboratory and performing certain forbidden actions, he unleashes a veiled female specter called the "Dweller of the Threshold" who pursues him relentlessly and causes the death of his sister. In this chapter I read *Zanoni* as a text that exoticizes, doubles, and spectralizes the diva's body: both the "dweller" and Viola bear traces of each other's bodies; ultimately, neither can be "managed."

The story opens in Naples in the second half of the eighteenth century, a period that coincided with the rise of the soprano as a dominant figure on the operatic scene. Viola is the daughter of the violinist and composer Gaetano Pisani, whose "arias and symphonies . . . excited a kind of terror" in his audience" (1). Obsessed with his art and isolated from others, Pisani is described as "worn and haggard, with black, careless locks . . . he and his art . . . both quaint, primitive, irregular" (3). Pisani is clearly based on the legendary eighteenth-century violinist and composer, Giuseppe Tartini, who was said to have composed his most famous sonata, "The Devil's Trill" after having been visited by the devil in a dream:

> One night I dreamed that I had made a bargain with the devil for my soul . . .
> then the idea suggested itself to hand him my violin to see what he would do with
> it. Great was my astonishment when I heard him play, with consummate skill, a
> sonata of such exquisite beauty as surpassed the boldest flights of my imagination. . . . Seizing my violin I tried to reproduce the sounds I had heard. But in
> vain . . .[20]

Like Tartini, Pisani's compositions are inspired by "harpies and witches" who "had clawed hold of his instrument" (2); perpetually emerging from a dream, he is constantly wrestling with the inaccessibility of his own music.

Viola's mother, however, is English: "fair and gentle, with a sweet English face," one of those Englishwomen in Victorian fiction who are exiled and deracinated through their sexual relationships with foreigners; for instance, in Elizabeth Gaskell's gothic tale "The Old Nurse's Story," a woman is expelled from the family after being seduced by a foreign musician.[21]

Pisani is tormented and consumed by his masterpiece, an opera called "The Siren." It is "unpublished, unpublishable and imperishable" and haunts him continuously. His two children are his demonic violin and its "twin": his daughter, Viola (named after another musical instrument) whose body traverses the iconography of the hybrid odalisque. Raised to be "the prima donna" of the Teatro San Carlo (one of the most significant opera houses in Italy) Viola is a "combination, a harmony of opposite attributes," blending the golden hair of the North with an eye "almost of oriental splendour" and a complexion that constantly changes, "vivid in one moment, pale the next"(6). She also has a tendency toward "superstition," a gothic appetite for Greek and Etrurian legends of vampires, which allows her to understand and interpret her father's music more effectively. Having become the toast of Naples by virtue of her voice and beauty, Viola arranges to stage her father's opera, *The Siren,* at San Carlo.

In classical mythology, sirens were hybrid bird-women who had mesmeric vocal powers. The siren/enchantress was a popular figure in baroque opera; a symbol of opera's self-reflexiveness as a genre. It is possible that Bulwer was thinking of Handel's opera *Alcina,* a popular success in London in 1735, in which the siren/sorceress Alcina inhabits an island where she seduces men and transforms them, Circe-like, into rocks, streams, trees, and beasts. Although there is no record of *Alcina* having been revived in London in the 1830s, Bulwer's notes to *Zanoni* reveal his knowledge of opera history. The setting for Pisani's *The Siren* in the novel includes an ocean cave; Handel's *opera seria* was staged with an enchanted garden, rocks/grottoes and a subterranean cavern. Besides, it included several bravura arias for Alcina herself, along with arias in the "Neapolitan style" for the castrato roles. In a famous aria at the end of act 2, "Ombre Pallide," Alcina calls on the "pale shadows," the "daughters of the night," to help restore her waning powers. This invocation also resonates with my reading of *Zanoni,* as we shall see. Another version of *Alcina* was composed in 1625 by the pioneering Italian female composer Francesca Caccini, who used tonal contrasts to highlight the instabilities of gender. Caccini's opera, acclaimed for the beauty of its siren aria, was based on a feminist libretto that contained an androgynous sorceress.

Playing the role of the "regal Siren" herself, Viola enthralls the Neapolitan audience. While on stage, she is momentarily paralyzed by anxiety, but regains her composure when she locks gazes with Zanoni, who is in the audience. Zanoni's mesmeric gaze acts as Viola's muse, inspiring her "Siren's voice" to "pour forth its entrancing music," his "brilliant eyes . . . inspiring her with powers never known before" (16). With his past shrouded in obscurity, Zanoni is suspected of either being a European gone native or of mixed blood, believed to have spent years in "the interior of India" (23). Possessed of great wealth and powers reputedly comparable to Cagliostro's, Zanoni has learned the secret of the "elixir of life" from his teacher, the oriental sorcerer-philosopher Mejnour. But Zanoni is also an orientalist scholar; having "mastered all the languages of the East," his knowledge allows him a disturbing mastery, enabling him to decode a variety of cultural scripts easily: "all manners, all nations, all grades of men seemed familiar to him" (87).

As Zanoni struggles with his erotic attraction to Viola, he becomes increasingly apprehensive about the effect their relationship might have on his intellectual powers. Mejnour warns him that he must reject the passions in order to achieve "happiness . . . the last stage of being" (195). Yet like Alcina's, Viola's passionate, erotic voice threatens to deplete Zanoni's knowledge and emasculate him. His orientalist scholarship cannot withstand the onslaught of the diva's hybridized body and her ornate vocal embellishments. The only way that Zanoni can achieve control over the "sorcery" of Viola's sirenlike voice is to remove her from the opera house and silence her. Although Mejnour is "orien-tal," in *Zanoni* it is the Italian soprano who is perceived as a threat to the male philosopher and to Glyndon's English identity; it is through *her* body rather than Mejnour's that the subversiveness of exoticism is articulated.

Viola's visibility on the operatic stage also invests her with an ambiguous sex-ual presence that aligns her with the courtesan; desperate to prevent her from becoming one, Zanoni rescues her from the clutches of a libertine (shades of Rosina?) and isolates her on a remote Grecian island. The novel pointedly com-ments on the equivocal nature of the diva's social position as overlapping with that of the demimondaine through the reluctance of her English suitor, Glyn-don to propose marriage. Although trying to cultivate a Byronic artistic persona (like Bulwer himself), Glyndon allows himself to be persuaded by his friend Mervale's arguments regarding Viola's lack of respectability: " in England no one would believe that a young Englishman, of good fortune and respectable birth, who marries a singer from the Theatre of Naples, has not been lamenta-bly taken in. I would save you from a fall of position so irretrievable. Think how many mortifications you will be subjected to; how many young men will visit at your house, and how many young women will as carefully avoid it" (97). While the text appears to critique Glyndon's and Mervale's narrow bourgeois ideol-ogy, it simultaneously sanctions the removal of Viola's "contagious" sexuality from the public sphere. Of course, by 1842, English society had already been "invaded" by Italian sopranos.

Escaping Viola, Glyndon soon finds himself confronting her doppelgänger, the demonic "dweller of the threshold," in a gothic castle situated in the "wild-ness" of the Italian countryside, peopled by "savage" peasants (200). Having exchanged places with Mejnour's former pupil, Zanoni, Glyndon seeks entry into their brotherhood of philosopher-scientists. Entering Mejnour's labora-tory, Glyndon sees "dim, spectre-like, but gigantic forms floating through the mist." Mejnour tells him that they are the "intermediate tribes," "some of sur-passing wisdom, some of horrible malignity" that stand between him and the elixir (knowledge of and control over Nature), the "barrier" that can only be "penetrated . . . through a higher chemistry" (225). Bulwer's language here repli-cates that of the travel narrative, the penetration of an unexplored interior, the word *tribe* evoking an ethnological gaze:

> He who would establish intercourse with these varying beings resembles the traveller who would penetrate into unknown lands. He is exposed to strange dangers and unconjectured terrors . . . amidst the dwellers of the threshold is one, surpassing in malignity and hatred all her tribe . . . whose eyes have para-lyzed the bravest. (226)

Despite Mejnour's warnings, Glyndon prematurely performs the ritual that releases the "phantom" by opening a crystal vial and inhaling its odors:

By degrees, this object shaped itself to his sight. It was as that of a human head, covered with a dark veil, through which glared with livid and demoniac fire eyes that froze the marrow of his bones. Nothing else of the face was distinguishable—nothing but those intolerable eyes; but his terror, that even at the first seemed beyond nature to endure, was increased a thousandfold, when after a pause, the Phantom glided slowly into the chamber. . . . Its form was veiled as the face, but the outline was that of a female . . . that burning glare so intense, so livid, yet so living, had in it something that was almost *human* . . . something to show that the shadowy Horror was not all a spirit, but partook of matter enough. . . . As, clinging with the grasp of agony to the wall, his hair erect, his eyeballs starting, he still gazed back upon that appalling gaze—the Image spoke to him: "Thou hast entered the immeasurable region. I am the Dweller of the Threshold. What wouldst thou with me? Silent? Dost thou fear me? Am I not thy beloved? Is it not for me that thou hast rendered up the delights of thy race? Wouldst thou be wise? Mine is the wisdom of countless ages. Kiss me, my mortal lover." (243)

Intercourse with the dweller, then is an *erotic* communion that separates Glyndon from the "delights" of his *race* and deracinates him, just as he had feared his marriage to Viola would. The dweller also *embodies* the knowledge, the oriental archive that Glyndon desires access to and yet cannot manage to penetrate. Instead, he is penetrated by the specter's eyes and her "kiss" threatens to emasculate him still further, depriving him of speech and sanity. Yet *Zanoni* goes beyond this, constructing the dweller through a greater degree of complexity. This demonic succubus, who is also a veiled woman—a terrifying odalisque with an unbearably searing, hypnotic gaze—is intertwined with Viola on several levels. Like the voice of Pisani's Siren, her gaze has the power to paralyze. Just before the appearance of the demon, Glyndon hears music, "the ghost as it were of voice" (242). In some ways, the phantom is literally the ghost of Viola's voice, the revenant/remnant that refuses to stay buried, recalling the female demons—the harpies, witches, and furies—who had pushed the limits of representation and inspired her father's music. The narrator tells us at the start of the novel that compositions entitled "The Feast of the Harpies," "The Witches at Benevento," and "The Eumenides" had been discovered amongst Pisani's manuscripts (2).

When Viola becomes pregnant and falls ill, Zanoni is obliged to ask the demon's help in saving her life, as his appeal to masculine spirits fail. The demon presides over Viola's labor and crouches over the child, asserting her claim over both. Later, Viola finds herself in Zanoni's laboratory (a mirror image of Mejnour's), and inhales the same fragrance that Glyndon had used to conjure the dweller. She then sees herself transformed into a "phantom": "This double phantom—here herself a phantom—gazing upon her phantom self, had in it a horror which no words can tell, no length of life forego" (315). Bulwer's use of the word "horror" here is interesting. What is it about her phantasmatic self that horrifies Viola? If we read the dweller as the "ghost" of her voice, the figuration of a rage the silenced diva cannot acknowledge, this "recognition" on Viola's part also involves a recognition of her own complicity in abandoning that voice.

An extension of her father's demonic violin and opera (*The Siren*), the demon is also the diva's exotic voice and gaze, neither of which can be exorcised. As she pursues Glyndon, she invades the "respectable" English home of the Mervales (Mrs Mervale is described as someone who prefers reading Johnson to concerts and operas!) and destroys Glyndon's sister Adela, whose "enthusiasm" is of a "far purer order" than that of her brother, "restrained within proper bounds ... partly by the sweetness of a very feminine nature, and partly by a strict and methodical education" (282). Gliding to Adela's bedside, the vampiric specter pervades her body and mind.

In the final section of the novel, which takes place in revolutionary France, the "haunter" comes to symbolize the incendiary and uncontrolled spirit of revolution itself, which eventually claims the lives of Viola and Zanoni. The silenced voice of the soprano/siren is transformed into the spectral gaze of an exotic succubus who also reverses the orientalist gaze of the male scholar/scientist. Like Alcina's "ombre pallide," the dweller of the threshold carries out Viola's vengeance, exacting a terrible price for the suppression of the diva's voice. While Zanoni and Glyndon compel the "spectralization" of Viola through the erasure of her public body, in order to further and preserve their own intellectual projects, they get more than they bargained for. The appearance of the spectral Viola signals the failure of the "brotherhood" of masculine knowledge. Haunted by the double, they are tortured by the dweller's exotic liminality (the threshold) and driven almost to madness by the phantasmatic echo of Viola's displaced, yet still revolutionary and sirenic voice.[22]

Wicked Voices: Vernon Lee's Late Victorian Gothic Divas

Having traveled through Italy extensively as a child and an adult, and having produced a considerable amount of scholarship on music and opera, Vernon Lee (Violet Paget) was uniquely positioned among female writers of the later Victorian period. In Lee's superbly uncanny gothic fictions we have compelling interventions that engage not only with constructions of operatic exoticism and the diva's virtuosity, but also with the sexual politics of the androgynous woman at the turn of the century. Like Bulwer, Lee looks back to the eighteenth-century operatic tradition of the voice with ambivalence, anxiety, and admiration. She goes much further, however, in celebrating the exotic and "wicked voice" of the opera singer as a powerful interruption of the colonizing discourses of late nineteenth-century national identity. Her work also transforms the metaphor of the "buried voice" in ways that connect with the archaeological concerns discussed in chapter 5. Two of Lee's interlinked gothic tales,

"Winthrop's Adventure" (1881) and "A Wicked Voice" (1890), which I shall examine here, are intensely preoccupied with the resurrection of "dead"voices of extreme virtuosity, capable of the most intricate and fascinating ornamentation, that return, like vampires, to possess and haunt the listener.[23]

Born Violet Paget in 1856 near Boulogne, her mother's second child by her second marriage, Lee was later to adopt her half-brother's name in her pseudonym. Descended from a French émigré on her father's side and a colonial family on her mother's, Lee's childhood and adolescence were spent on the Continent. Her brilliant mother, Matilda Adams-Paget (described by Lee's biographer Peter Gunn as a "*philosophe*" who "would have been more at home in the salons of Pre-Revolutionary France than in the drawing rooms of mid-Victorian England" combined a love for music and intellectual pursuits with radical views on religion.[24]The bohemian/cosmopolitan influences of Lee's early life were cemented by her European education; she visited England for the first time in 1881. Displaying a highly cultivated mind, Lee's fictional works are embedded in her scholarship on aesthetics, music, and culture; in order to understand their significance, it is necessary to approach them in conjunction. Also, as Kathy Psomiades has shown, Lee's interest in androgyny and the erotic female gaze are present in her work as manifestations of a lesbian identity that she was never able to acknowledge or embrace fully. Most apparent in her gothic tales focusing on opera, her ambivalent negotiation of lesbian desire inevitably intertwines with her investigation of the exoticized, androgynous body and voice of the castrato.[25]

In an 1880 essay, "The Art of Singing: Past and Present," published shortly before "Winthrop's Adventure," Lee had critiqued the decline of the centrality of the singer in vocal music, arguing that the great singers of the eighteenth century had been "composers" in the way they had used "extensive and entirely original passages of ornamentation." Instead of merely functioning as a "perfectly constructed machine," the voice had a sheer physicality, a sensuality that was enhanced through artistic license. Through "a free fancy" and a "power of invention," it modulated into brilliance of interpretation accompanied by the exuberance of an individual vocal personality. The beauties, defects, and excesses of the voice—the appoggiaturas, trills, and cadenzas—were not "excrescences" that had to be controlled or subordinated to a greater design, but allowed to reinvent themselves continually through the free play of imagination and fantasy.[26]

In particular, Lee associated this brilliant flexibility with famous castrati or "male sopranos" such as Farinelli or Senesino. Of Farinelli, Lee had written in her most acclaimed critical work, *Studies of the Eighteenth Century in Italy* (1880) that he had a voice "infinitely more voluminous, extensive and beautiful than any other that had ever been heard before or since; his musical talent more versatile and astonishing than any other."[27] The legendary talents of Farinelli had included curing Philip V of Spain of "melancholy madness by the magic of his voice" (112). While the androgynous vocal and erotic powers of the castrati had attained almost mythical dimensions in eighteenth-century Europe, at the same time this androgyny was artificially produced by a process that involved bodily mutilation. The castrato was both empowered and powerless. Both "Winthrop's Adventure" and "A Wicked Voice" turn the castrato into a gothic diva, a new kind of exotic "female" body; a hybrid that borrows from the tropes of both male and female odalisques and moves beyond them.[28] In both narratives, and especially in "A Wicked Voice," Italy is a gothic, tropicalized landscape containing traces of buried voices that must be recovered by narrators who are either English or firmly committed to an Anglo-German cultural tradition. Once recovered, these voices refuse to be silenced. Lee's construction of the Italian castrato is brilliantly nuanced: while she celebrates the aesthetic power of a voice and body freed from the imperatives of gender, she also allows the castrato to revenge the colonization and violence visited on his body.

In the earlier tale, "Winthrop's Adventure," the English narrator, the artist Julian Winthrop, visits a collector, Maestro Fa Diesis (Master F-sharp) in Lombardy, who has assembled a "perfect museum" of "things musical" (155). The old man's passion, however, is not for music, but for arranging his exhibits: "not a chord, not a note was ever heard in the house . . . he would have died rather than spend a soldino on going to the opera"(156). Among his musical antiquities, Winthrop discovers a portrait of the eighteenth-century singer Rinaldi, who had been murdered by his mistress's jealous husband, the Marchese Negri. The face in the portrait is dark, feminine and voluptuous: "with intensely red lips and a crimson flush beneath the transparent bronzed skin . . . it had something at once sullen and effeminate, something odd and not entirely agreeable; yet it attracted and riveted your attention with its dark, warm color. . . . I became gradually aware that the portrait was haunting me" (160–62). Although Winthrop mentions the portrait being done in the style of Greuze, the voluptuous red lips and the "sullen effeminacy" anticipate the glamor of fin de siècle portraits of exotic women, such as Dicksee's *Leila*. Its orientalist flavor is accentuated as, mesmerized by it, Winthrop wanders dazedly around the town of M—— surrounded by its "Oriental-like cupolas and minarets" (162). Returning to M—— several years later, he again feels an urge to view the portrait, only this time he is overcome by a "giddiness and sickness, as if of long desired, unexpected pleasure." Unable to get Rinaldi's "soft, downy gaze" and perverse, vampiric lips out of his mind, Winthrop decides to spend a night in the abandoned Villa Negri, the site of the singer's murder. Lee invests the Villa Negri with a gothic presence; it is a "gaunt, grey villa" in ruins, with a touch of Egyptomania: "broken obelisks on its triangular front"(181).

In this gothic pile Winthrop encounters the ghost of Rinaldi and hears the dazzling virtuosity of the castrato voice as it glides "dexterously through complicated mazes of song," effortlessly rounding off "ornament after ornament" (198). As the murder is reenacted, the cascades of sound are abruptly cut off, and turn into a "long, agonizing cry." Winthrop suddenly finds himself in darkness, trapped in a moment in which the listener/voyeur/collector is left alone with the "modulation broken off unfinished" (198), caught between desire and its fulfillment. Lee arrests the narrative at the precise moment at which the voice and its ornamentations are themselves arrested; from that point on, Winthrop, along with the reader, will be haunted by that dissonance: the lack of a melodic resolution and the perpetual postponement of pleasure. From this point onward, Winthrop's own art becomes increasingly more "arabesque," his "thoughts and images growing into inextricable tangles" (144). The singer's body floats uneasily between masculinity and femininity, between absence and presence, as Winthrop's desire to know and "possess" the history of the portrait fails. Instead, he becomes "possessed" by the sense of being pursued by "something indefinable."

In a preface to a collection of stories that included "Winthrop's Adventure," Lee stated that she had recast it as "A Wicked Voice," transforming the singer from victim into aggressor, "a voice seeking fresh victims even in its posthumous existence." The later novella develops the voice of the androgynous, exoticized "diva" more self-consciously as a response to Wagnerian opera, which was deeply connected to German nationalism and developed the role of the helden-tenor (heroic tenor), a male voice category that further diffused the dominance of the soprano voice. Throughout her literary career, Lee opposed aggressive nationalism, criticizing England's involvement in the Boer War and writing against Italy's expansionist foreign policy in Tripoli in 1911 in Italian and English journals. In 1908, in *The Sentimental Traveller*, she wrote: "I maintain that we are all of us the better, of whatever nationality (and most, perhaps, we rather too-too solid Anglo-Saxons) for some transfusion of a foreign element."[29]

Set in a sensual and indulgent Venice toward the end of the nineteenth century, "A Wicked Voice" is narrated by a young composer, Magnus, who is attempting to compose a heroic, nationalistic opera based on Nordic mythology, in the Wagnerian style. Magnus describes himself as suffering from the "strangest of maladies" and begins by cursing its cause, the demonic voice of the title:

> O cursed human voice, violin of flesh and blood, fashioned with the subtle tools, the cunning hands, of Satan! O execrable art of singing, have you not wrought mischief enough in the past, degrading so much noble genius, corrupting the purity of Mozart, reducing Handel to a writer of high-class singing exercises . . . ? Is it not enough to have dishonoured a whole century in idolatry of that wicked and contemptible wretch the singer, without persecuting an obscure young composer . . . ? (229)

For Magnus, the singer *is* the voice made flesh. Both are impure, yet he cannot escape from it, there can be no opera *without* the voice. Both are also framed by the exoticism of Venice, a location orientalized here in a manner similar to that in Dacre's *Zofloya*. Lee constructs Venice through Magnus's eyes in terms of luxurious decadence and tropical disease, evoking a hothouse atmosphere that threatens to melt his musical/nationalistic aspirations. Venice becomes an incarnation of the voice, seeming to "swelter in the midst of the waters, exhaling, like some great lily, mysterious influences which make the brain swim and the heart faint—a moral malaria, distilled, as I thought, from those languishing melodies" (230). Tropes of sinuousness, languor, and tropical exhaustion abound: the heat is "stifling" and the air clogged with the scent "of all manner of white flowers, faint and heavy in their intolerable sweetness: tuberoses, gardenias, and jasmines." The city dissolves the composer's aesthetic ideas "into hopeless confusion" (235) through the "contagious" melodies that arise out of its waters like "miasmas," "sickening" and "intoxicating" his soul.

A Venetian nobleman, Count Alvise, tells Magnus about the castrato Zaffirino, the legendary possessor of a hypnotic voice that had caused the death of a woman known for her virtue. As the earlier figure of Rinaldi metamorphoses into Zaffirino, the murdered voice returns to claim its own victims. Zaffirino is an androgynous libertine who seduces *and* kills women with his voice, but also a more explicitly exoticized and feminine figure than Rinaldi in "Winthrop's Adventure." Zaffirino's voice has a "strange, exotic, unique quality" (236), and Magnus repeatedly visualizes the castrato as possessing a woman's face: "That effeminate, fat face of his is almost beautiful, with an odd smile, brazen and cruel. I have seen faces like this, if not in real life, at least in my boyish romantic dreams, when I read Swinburne and Baudelaire, the faces of wicked, vindictive women."

Obsessed with the singer, Magnus follows a trajectory similar to Winthrop's as he journeys to the Villa Mistra, where he witnesses the specter of Zaffirino, in an extravagant saloon, with eight chandeliers revolving like "huge spiders," murder a woman with an "exquisite vibrating note" which goes on "swelling and swelling" until it is interrupted by the victim's cry. The death here clearly signifies a sexual climax, a state of arousal brought on by the voice itself: a voice that defies classification because it cannot be assigned a gender. Zaffirino's baroque voice pursues Magnus, who begins to hear it in his head and all over Venice, where rumors grow of a mysterious singer haunting the city whose singing leads people "to dispute whether the voice belonged to a man or woman" (240). The voice also appears to be "veiled," in a "soft, downy, wrapper" (238). Tearing its own veil, it "pierces" the composer's breast, enacting a reversal of the historical violation of the castrato's body and also invoking the image of a woman rending her veil. As Magnus becomes possessed, Zaffirino's ornamentations continue to echo endlessly in his head, invading and destroying his ability to compose his Wagnerian opera.

Lee's text refuses to gender the exotic/gothic diva's voice or body; the figure of Zaffirino is not only based on the vanished castrati, but also acts as a transgressive "mask" for the soprano, who continued to haunt opera as a reminder of its own excessive and exotic past. "A Wicked Voice" proposes to reclaim the exotic voice as a powerful force that can postpone the nationalist project indefinitely. Through its elaborate roulades and glamorous, cascading trills, the gothic diva's voice deliberately flaunts its decadent "impurity," perpetually inaccessible, yet perpetually exhibiting itself. By the end of the narrative, its intense corporeality grips Magnus all the more tenaciously because it cannot be tied to a specific bodily presence. Like the libertine, the exotic voice in Lee's novella seeks complete mastery through seduction and detachment.

As the size of the orchestra increased, in late nineteenth-century operas (especially those of Wagner) the operatic voice had to cut through dense orchestration that continually threatened to overwhelm it. Despite Magnus's efforts to control the voice through the Wagnerian orchestration of his opera *Ogier the Dane,* the difference of the "wicked voice" remains persistent, making him compose music that he says, "is certainly by me, since I have never heard it before, but which is still not my own, which I despise and abhor: little tripping flourishes and languishing phrases." In Lee's operatic texts, the moment at which the voice is arrested or lost also engenders its reemergence. The spectral voices continue to haunt the protagonists because they frustrate all expectations of a harmonic resolution.[30] In this remarkable novella, Vernon Lee allows the "wicked" operatic *voice* to resurface from silence, providing a radical twist on the exotic *body*—and through Magnus's dissolution, ensures the triumph of both.

Coda: That Obscure Object of Desire

In his 1977 surrealist masterpiece *That Obscure Object of Desire*, based on Pierre Louys's 1898 novel, *La Femme et Le Pantin* (The Woman and the Puppet), the Spanish director Luis Buñuel conceived the brilliant and innovative plan of using two different actresses, Carole Bouquet and Angela Molina, to play *simultaneously* the role of a Spanish dancer, Conchita, pursued by the aging libertine Mathieu.[1] The switching back and forth between the two women, sometimes in the course of the same sequence, creates a deep sense of unease in the viewer, undermining any attempt to "grasp" Conchita's identity. As their bodies repeatedly merge and separate, Bouquet provides a more "classical" look, while Molina's dark sensuality evokes the odalisque-courtesans of Leighton, Gérôme, and Manet. In a famous shot where Mathieu watches Conchita dancing for other men, the lines of her body echo those of the odalisque while capturing the surrealist moment. Conchita, Bouquet, and Molina frustrate Mathieu's desire and fracture his gaze by playing a series of intellectual and erotic games, and continually deferring his possession of their bodies (body?). Buñuel's sleight of hand allows the presence of one to evoke the absence of the other, and vice versa. Inviting his desire, they (she) block(s) it at the precise moment of penetration.

At the core of Buñuel's film is the inevitably inaccessible body of the exotic woman, which, while masquerading as the "object of desire," reveals itself instead as the embodiment of a radical "modern" subjectivity. Conchita claims: "I belong to no one but myself, and I'll stay my own." Conchita's shifting body is offset by random terrorist attacks throughout the film; anxiety about her elusiveness is connected to wider insecurities on a national and social level. Behind Buñuel's surreal vision of intercorporeity lies the hybrid body of the odalisque; a body that defies ownership and colonization, that absorbs desire while undermining the stability and the gaze of those who attempt to master it.

By following certain strands within the "labyrinth of incarnations"[2] generated by the exotic female body in nineteenth-century British (and European) culture, I have argued that Western cultural/aesthetic discourses created nuanced spaces for the exotic woman that allowed her to move beyond passivity and access considerable agency and power. In so doing, I offer a provocative theoretical reading of both exotic and domestic "female" bodies. Expanding the limits of the term *odalisque* both literally and figuratively, we can experience this body, like the heroine of Buñuel's film, as a composite: a hybrid in terms of race, gender, and sexuality, a gothic body that is at times transgendered.

Until now, most studies of exoticism within the British context have focused heavily on Britain's encounter with India. Moving away from this exclusive focus demonstrates that the idea of the exotic within British culture in the nineteenth century was richer and more multilayered, including oriental as well as continental influences. It is this layering that deepens its complexity. Moreover, because inventions of the exotic feminine had more to do with the construction of the Western self than with the Eastern, by reading this trope primarily as a symbol of Western hegemony over the Orient, some postcolonial theorists have offered too narrow or too limited a view. Rather, as is evident from an interdisciplinary reading of the cultural and fictional texts examined in this book, particular manifestations of exoticism had a destabilizing effect on constructions of domesticity, imperialism, and nationalism.

Several of my readings also demonstrate a unique relationship between the hybridized exotic body and modernity. A close look at its position within the emerging disciplines of medicine, ethnocriminology, and archaeology, together with changing discourses of gender and sexuality, reinforces the way the idea of modernity and the idea of the exotic impinged on and infiltrated each other. As Said, speaking of Mann's *Death in Venice,* comments in a "Note on Modernism": "the combination of dread and promise, of degeneration and desire . . . is Mann's way of suggesting, I believe, that Europe, its art, mind, monuments is no longer invulnerable, no longer able to ignore its ties to its overseas domains."[3] As I have shown, this vulnerability was to a large extent mediated through transgressive visions of the exotic female body, a process that began much earlier than the cultural moment Said locates here. It also functioned as a means of interrogating narratives of modernity built on national and imperial discourses.

As a final note, I would like to point to an intriguing moment in postcolonial literature that engages with the idea of the exotic woman as generated by a European consciousness. In Egyptian novelist Ahdaf Soueif's 1999 novel set in the later Victorian period, *The Map of Love,* the English heroine, Anna Winterbourne, eventually travels to Egypt, marries an Egyptian intellectual, and embraces Egyptian culture.[4] While in England, she nurses her first husband, an imperialist who has returned from the Sudan ill with "an infection of the tropics" (of course!) and disillusioned with empire. While her husband recuperates, Anna goes to the South Kensington Museum to view the odalisques of John Frederick Lewis. Anna says in her diary: "they are possessed of such luminous beauty that I feel in their presence as though a gentle hand had caressed my very soul" (27). The paintings pave the way for Anna's resistance to colonialism, her love and appreciation for Egypt, and her own hybridization.

Here we have a complex sequence of layers: an Egyptian postcolonial woman novelist writing about an Englishwoman viewing images of "Egyptian" women by an expatriate English artist who had "gone native" and settled in Cairo! Soueif attempts to inhabit these paintings as a way of opening a cultural dialogue that moves beyond the boundaries of national/imperial identities. The possibility of these conversations has, from the beginning, haunted my pursuit of the exotic woman, that obscure object and defiant, desiring subject.

Notes

Notes to Prelude: Hauntings

1. For the genesis of *The Giaour*, see Susan Wolfson and Peter Manning, eds., *Lord Byron: Selected Poems* (London: Penguin, 1996), 790–91.

2. Byron's spectralization of the exotic was not restricted to his *Oriental Tales*. This motif surfaces in a key episode in *Don Juan* where Juan's androgynous presence in a Turkish seraglio leads to one of the harem women having a nightmare in which her desire is actualized in a spectral form. Juan's masculinity becomes phantasmatic in this instance. Furthermore, the poem ends with Juan's obsession with a specter who turns out be a voluptuous, orientalized Englishwoman. For Byron, the idea of spectralization was crucial to the interplay among race, nation, and history. See *Don Juan*, ed. T. G. Steffan (London: Penguin, 1996), cantos 6 and 17.

3. Throughout this book I am using "uncanny" (and by extension, "spectral") in the sense of one of the definitions suggested by Nicholas Royle in his study of Freud's "The Uncanny": "the uncanny has to do with a strangeness of framing and borders . . . a foreign body within oneself, even the experience of oneself *as* a foreign body"; See Nicholas Royle, *The Uncanny* (New York: Routledge, 2003), 2–26. Royle points out that the uncanny resists definitions; a trap Freud falls into when attempting to define it in his essay on the topic.

4. Judith Thurman, *Secrets of the Flesh: A Life of Colette* (New York: Ballantine, 1999), 171.

5. Bram Stoker, *The Jewel of Seven Stars* (New York: Oxford, 1996), 81, 98, 112.

6. Edward Said, *Orientalism* (New York: Random House, 1979), 187–88.

7. In a later interview, Said has acknowledged that certain works in the Western literary tradition "remain interesting and powerful because they are interesting and powerful works," and are not mere "ideological cartoons." He claims that to miss this would amount to a "distortion" of his argument. See Gauri Viswanathan, ed., *Power, Politics and Culture: Interviews with Edward Said* (New York: Vintage, 2001), 151. Although Said's argument in *Orientalism*, if followed closely, does allow for considerably more ambiguity than the work of some postcolonial critics who claim to have been influenced by him, he often hesitates to work through such ambiguity (as in the case of Kuchuk).

8. See Matthew Sweet, *Inventing the Victorians* (London: Faber and Faber, 2001), 189; and Michael Mason, *The Making of Victorian Sexuality* (Oxford: Oxford University

Press, 1995), 178. See also Jill Matus, *Unstable Bodies: Victorian Representations of Sexuality and Maternity* (Manchester: Manchester University Press, 1995).

9. John Mackenzie, *Orientalism: History, Theory and the Arts* (Manchester: Manchester University Press, 1995), 10.

10. Lisa Lowe, *Critical Terrains: French and British Orientalisms* (Ithaca: Cornell University Press, 1991), 87.

11. Hollis Clayson, "Henri Regnault's Wartime Orientalism," in *Orientalism's Interlocutors*, ed. Jill Beaulieu and Mary Roberts (Durham: Duke University Press, 2002), 144–49.

12. For recent reconsiderations of orientalism and gender, see Reina Lewis, *Gendering Orientalism* (London: Routledge, 1996); Meyda Yegenoglu, *Colonial Fantasies: Towards a Feminist Reading of Orientalism* (Cambridge: Cambridge University press, 1998); and Mohja Kahf, *Western Representations of the Muslim Woman: From Termagant to Odalisque* (Austin: University of Texas Press, 1999). Of these, Kahf's reading perpetuates the idea of the nineteenth-century odalisque as a submissive, fetishized object.

13. See Roger Benjamin, "Ingres Chez Les Fauves," *Art History* 23 (2000): 743–771; quotation on 766.

14. For instance, see Firdous Azim, *The Colonial Rise of the Novel* (London: Routledge, 1993) and also Gayatri Spivak's celebrated "Three Women's Texts and a Critique of Imperialism," *Critical Enquiry* 12 (1985): 243–61.

15. See Marcel Hénaff, *Sade: The Invention of the Libertine Body* (Minneapolis: University of Minnesota Press, 1999), 259. Hénaff characterizes the debate effectively: "On one team were the enemies of the novel, for whom it was one and the same thing to denounce the dangers of amorous passion, the seductions of women, and the novel as a genre. On the other hand were the friends of the novel, for whom it was one and the same thing to defend them."

16. See Homi Bhabha, "DissemiNation: time, narrative and the margins of the Modern Nation," in *Nation and Narration*, ed. Homi Bhabha (London: Routledge, 1990), 298. Bhabha speaks of the "splitting" of the national subject in terms of a "movement of signification" that simultaneously constitutes the exorbitant image of power and deprives it of the certainty or stability of centre or closure." In a sense, Bhabha also sees ideologies of power as "vacillating," "sliding from one enunciatory position to another."

17. See Judith Walkowitz, *City of Dreadful Delight: Narratives of Sexual Danger in Late-Victorian London* (Chicago: University of Chicago Press, 1992) 21; and *Prostitution in Victorian Society* (Cambridge: Cambridge University Press, 1980).

18. Bhabha, "DissemiNation," 308.

Notes to Chapter One

1. This term was first used by Mary Louise Pratt in *Imperial Eyes: Travel Writing and Transculturation* (New York: Routledge, 1992), 6–7. For the reference to Richardson's *Clarissa*, see Samuel Johnson, *A Dictionary of the English Language*, printed by W. Strahan, 1755 (New York: AMS Press, 1967).

2. Bram Stoker, *Dracula*, ed. Nina Auerbach (New York: Norton, 1997).

3. See Joseph Sheridan LeFanu, "Carmilla," in *The Penguin Book of Vampire Stories* (New York: Penguin, 1988), 134.

4. Théophile Gautier, "Arria Marcella," in *Demons of the Night: An Anthology*, ed. Joan Kessler (Chicago: University of Chicago Press, 1995), 118–144.

5. Aileen Ribeiro, *Ingres in Fashion: Representations of Dress and Appearance in Ingres' Images of Women* (New Haven: Yale University Press, 1999), 201. Ribeiro comments on the "self-containment" of Ingres' odalisques.

6. Analyzing Montagu's experience of the harem, Billie Melman claims that she "offers her readers a refined sensuality" rather than a voyeuristic or blatantly erotic representation. See Billie Melman, *Women's Orients: English Women and the Middle East, 1718–1918: Sexuality, Religion and Work* (Ann Arbor: University of Michigan Press, 1992), 92. Montagu herself refers to the turkish bath as the women's "coffee house." See Isobel Grundy, ed. *Lady Mary Wortley Montagu: Selected Letters* (London: Penguin, 1997), 149.

7. See Lisa Lowe, *Critical Terrains: French and British Orientalisms* (Ithaca and London: Cornell University Press, 1991), 107; Edward Fitgerald, *The Rubaiyat of Omar Khayyam* (London: Hodder and Stoughton, 1909).

8. See "Denon and the Discovery of Egypt," in *Egyptomania: Egypt in Western Art, 1730–1930*, ed. Jean-Marcel Humbert, Michael Pantazzi, and Christiane Ziegler (Ottawa: National Gallery of Canada, 1995), 201–224; quotation on 202.

9. Immanuel Kant, *Critique of the Power of Judgement* (Cambridge: Cambridge University Press, 2000), 142–145.

10. Humbert, Pantazzi, and Zeigler, "Denon and the Discovery of Egypt," 220–24.

11. For a forceful argument in this regard, see Linda Nochlin, *The Politics of Vision: Essays on Nineteenth-Century Art and Society* (New York: Harper and Row, 1989).

12. See Griselda Pollock's discussion of the other woman in Manet's *Olympia* in *Differencing the Canon: Feminist Desire and the Writing of Art's Histories* (New York: Routledge, 1999). See also Carol Ockman, Ingres' *Eroticized Bodies: Retracing the Serpentine Line* (New Haven: Yale University Press, 1989); and Alison Smith, "Nature Transformed: Leighton, the Nude and the Model," in *Frederic Leighton: Antiquity, Renaissance, Modernity*, ed. Tim Barringer and Elizabeth Prettejohn (New Haven: Yale University Press, 1999), 19–48.

13. Ockman, *Ingres's Eroticized Bodies*, 33–48.

14. Ibid., 85.

15. Smith, "Nature Transformed," 43. Smith also discusses the controversy around Leighton's *Phryne:* "Phryne confused critics: while they believed Leighton was respecting classical conventions, he was also contravening classical standards by presenting Phryne as a curious racial mixture, a blend of what they considered to be oriental and reposeful Greek" (43).

16. See Joseph Kestner, "The Male Gaze in the Art of Frank Dicksee," *Annals of Scholarship* 7 (1990): 181–202; quotation on 194. And see Marcel Hénaff, *Sade and the Invention of the Libertine Body* (Minneapolis: University of Minnesota Press, 1999), 275.

17. Quoted in Mildred Archer, *Early Views of India: The Picturesque Journeys of Thomas and William Daniell 17876–1794: The Complete Aquatints* (London: Thames and Hudson, 1980), 71.

18. As argued by Sara Suleri in *The Rhetoric of English India* (Chicago: University of Chicago Press, 1992), 83–110.

19. For an analysis of diverse European reactions to Indian temple architecture, see Partha Mitter, *Much Maligned Monsters* (Chicago: University of Chicago Press, 1992).

20. Geneviève Lacambre, *Gustave Moreau: Between Epic and Dream* (Princeton: Princeton University Press, 1999), 162.

21. Charlotte Brontë, *Villette* (Oxford: Clarendon Press), 1984.

22. Julia Pardoe, *The City of the Sultan, and Domestic Manners of the Turks in 1836* (London: Henry Colburn, 1837), 19 and 104.

23. Alison Smith conjectures that the dangerous impact of the courtesan's exposed body undermined the Kantian aesthetic that linked physical beauty to a detached gaze; instead, the unveiling of Phryne signifies "loss of composure." See Alison Smith, ed., *Exposed: The Victorian Nude* (London: Tate Publishing, 2001), 91. Smith also comments that the elevation of Phryne on a platform may have intensified anxieties that were circulating around the issue of female artist being allowed access to the nude.

24. Homi Bhabha, "Signs Taken for Wonders," in *Race, Writing and Difference*, ed. Henry Louis Gates (Chicago: University of Chicago Press, 1985), 114.

25. See Robert Young, *Colonial Desire: Hybridity in Theory, Culture and Race* (New York: Routledge, 1995), for a detailed discussion of the ambivalence in Victorian race theory. Young argues that "the naming of human mixture as 'degeneracy' both asserts the norm and subverts it, undoing its terms of distinction, and opening up the prospect of the evanescence of 'race' as such. Here, therefore, at the heart of racial theory, in its most sinister, offensive move, hybridity also maps out its most anxious, vulnerable site: a fulcrum at its edge and centre where its dialectics of injustice, hatred and oppression can find themselves effaced and expunged" (19).

26. See R. Radhakrishnan, "Adjudicating Hybridity, Co-ordinating Betweenness" *Jouvert* 5, no. 1 (2000): 1–5. Bhabha also highlights the idea of the nation disrupted from within in "DissemiNation."

27. Maurice Merleau-Ponty, *The Visible and the Invisible* (Evanston: Northwestern University Press, 1968), 141.

28. Daniel Defoe, *Roxana or the Fortunate Mistress* (Oxford: Oxford University Press, 1964).

29. Bruce Seymour, *Lola Montez: A Life* (New Haven: Yale University Press, 1996), 18.

30. Alexandre Dumas, *La Dame aux camélias* (Oxford: Oxford University Press, 1986). For descriptions of La Païva's bathroom, see Joanna Richardson, *The Courtesans* (Cleveland, Ohio: World Publishing, 1967), 91.

31. Honoré de Balzac, *A Harlot High and Low* (*Splendeurs et miseres des courtisanes*) (Harmondsworth, Middlesex, Eng.: Penguin, 1970), 72–73.

32. Henry Mayhew, *London Labour and the London Poor* (New York: Dover, 1968), 4:36.

33. Anne McClintock, *Imperial Leather: Race, Gender and Sexuality in the Colonial Contest* (New York: Routledge, 1995), 37.

34. See Paul Broca, *On the Phenomena of Hybridity in the Genus Homo* (London: Longman, Green, Longman and Roberts, 1864), 1–24.

35. G. J. Barker-Benfield, *The Culture of Sensibility: Sex and Society in Eighteenth-Century Britain* (Chicago: University of Chicago Press, 1992).

36. Ann Radcliffe, *The Mysteries of Udolpho*, ed. Bonamy Dobrée (Oxford: Oxford University Press, 1966).

37. Jean Baudrillard, *Seduction*, trans. Brian Singer (New York: St. Martin's, 1990), 39.

38. Eliza Lynn Linton, "The Girl of the Period," in *Criminals, Idiots, Women and Minors: Victorian Writing by Women on Women*, ed. Susan Hamilton (Peterborough, Ontario: Broadview, 1995), 172.

39. Isabella Beeton, *The Book of Household Management* (London: Ward, Lock and Tyler, 1869).

40. Michael Ryan, *The Philosophy of Marriage in its Social, Moral and Physical Relations . . . being part of a course of obstetric lectures delivered at North London School of Medicine* (London: H Bailliere, 1839), 262 and 266. Victor Hugo, "Les Orientales," in *Poems* (Boston: Dana Estes, 1919), 193 and 196.

41. See Bram Dijkstra, *Idols of Perversity* (New York: Oxford University Press, 1986).

42. Charles Bernheimer, *Figures of Ill Repute: Prostitution in Nineteenth-Century France* (Cambridge, Mass.: Harvard University Press, 1989), 17–23.

43. Charlotte Dacre, *Zofloya, or The Moor* (New York: Oxford University Press, 1997). For an important critical reading of this novel, see Adriana Craciun's introductory essay in her edition of *Zofloya* (Peterboroug, Ontario: Broadview, 1997).

44. In her recent work on Regnault, Hollis Clayson sees Regnault's representation of the male odalisque in "Hassan et Namouna" as posing a complex connection to the militarization of the artist's own masculine identity during the War of 1870 in France. See "Henri Regnault's Wartime Orientalism," *in Orientalism's Interlocutors*, ed. Jill Beaulie and Mary Roberts (Durham: Duke University Press, 2003), 165.

45. For a survey of British artists and the Islamic Orient in the eighteenth and nineteenth centuries, see John Sweetman, *The Oriental Obsession* (Cambridge: Cambridge University Press, 1988).

46. Philip Meadows Taylor, *Confessions of a Thug* (New York: Oxford University Press, 1998).

47. Gayatri Spivak, *A Critique of Postcolonial Reason* (Cambridge, Mass.: Harvard University Press, 1999), 49.

48. Edward Thornton, *Illustrations of the History and Practices of the Thugs* (London: Nattali and Bond, 1851).

49. James Johnson, *The Influence of Tropical Climates on European Constitutions* (New York: Wood, 1846).

Notes to Chapter Two

1. Irene Gedalof, *Against Purity: Rethinking Identity with Indian and Western Feminisms* (New York: Routledge, 1999), 12–13.

2. For general accounts of these trials, see Mary Hartman, *Victorian Murderesses* (New York: Schocken Books, 1977), Donald Thomas, *The Victorian Underworld* (New York: New York University Press, 1998), and Thomas Boyle, *Black Swine in the Sewers of Hampstead: Beneath the Surface of Victorian Sensationalism* (New York: Viking, 1989).

3. Alexandre Dumas, *The Count of Monte Cristo* (London: Penguin, 1996).

4. See Ann Laura Stoler, "Sexual affronts and racial frontiers: European identities and the cultural politics of exclusion in colonial Southeast Asia" in *Hybridity and Its Discontents: Politics, Science, Culture,* eds. Avtar Brah and Annie E. Coombs (London and New York: Routledge, 2000), 20.

5. See Charlotte Brontë, *Shirley* (Harmondsworth: Penguin, 1985), 399.

6. In the appendix to *Armadale,* Collins claimed: "Wherever the story touches on questions connected with Law, Medicine or Chemistry, it has been submitted, before publication to the experience of professional men. The kindness of a friend

supplied me with a plan of the Doctor's Apparatus—and I saw the chemical ingredients at work, before I ventured on describing the action of them in the closing scenes of this book." See *Armadale*, ed. John Sutherland (London: Penguin, 1995), 679.

7. William Baker, *Wilkie Collins's Library: A Reconstruction* (Westport, Conn: Greenwood, 2002), 155.

8. Alfred Taylor, *On Poisons In Relation to Medical Jurisprudence and Medicine* (Philadelphia: Lea & Blanchard, 1848), 2. For an excellent survey of the development of toxicology in Victorian England, see Thomas Forbes, *Surgeons at the Bailey: English Forensic Medicine to 1878* (New Haven: Yale University Press, 1985).

9. Ian Burney, "A Poisoning of No Substance: The Trials of Medico-legal Proof in Mid-Victorian England," *Journal of British Studies* 38 (January 1999): 59–92.

10. Orfila's role in the Lafarge case is discussed in detail in Jürgen Thorwald, *The Century of the Detective* (New York: Harcourt Brace, 1965).

11. Marie Lafarge, *The Memoirs of Madame Lafarge; written by herself* (Philadelphia: Carey & Hart, 1841). After finding herself trapped in a provincial marriage with the petty bourgeois Lafarge, the semi-aristocratic Parisienne apparently became desperate after she found he was embroiled in debt and refused to release her from the contract. In her memoir, Marie described her extreme anxiety as she warded off episodes of near rape in her sexual relationship with her husband. In December 1839, she sent him a poisoned cake while he was in Paris. After he developed cholera-related symptoms and returned home, she continued to hover over his sickbed, lacing his food liberally with arsenic.

12. The Marsh test involved a delicate and complex procedure whereby fluid containing arsenic was mixed with zinc and acid, producing arsine gas, which, once ignited, left a metallic deposit of arsenic on a porcelain bowl. The chemicals themselves, however, had to be tested for traces of arsenic in order to ensure accurate results. Traces of graveyard earth tested with the Marsh apparatus also produced arsenic, intensifying the possibility of contamination. In 1842, the German chemist Hugo Reinsch devised another method: that of mixing the arsenic solution with hydrochloric acid, and boiling it to produce a coating on a copper mesh. For a detailed description of these two tests in their historical context, see Thorwald, *The Century of the Detective*, 277–81 and 340–41.

13. See Forbes, *Surgeons at the Bailey*, 139.

14. For statistics on poisoning, see Forbes, *Surgeons at the Bailey;* and Taylor, *On Poisons* (Philadelphia: Henry Lea, 1875), 178–79.

15. The Pharmacy Act of 1868 included "opium and all preparations of opium or of poppies" in the list of poisons, restricted its sale to professional pharmacists, and also initiated labeling restrictions. Because of the variety of opium preparations, however, there were several loopholes, such as the exclusion of opium-based patent medicines. For a detailed discussion of the complexities of the act, see Virginia Berridge and Griffith Edwards, *Opium and the People: Opiate Use in Nineteenth-Century England* (London: Allen Lane; New York: St. Martin's Press, 1981), 113–22. As Berridge and Edwards point out, "the way the 1868 Act operated in practice was rather different from original legislative intentions" (122).

16. For Christison's classification, see Robert Christison, *A Treatise on Poisons* (New York: AMS Press, 1973), 510–30.

17. *Lancet* 1(1839): 597–99; for the *Medical Gazette* statistics, see Taylor, *On Poisons,* 176.

18. According to Alison Smith, "the impact of French salon painting on the formation of the English nude was such that by the 1870's audiences had become accustomed to viewing the works of Gérôme and Cabanel at important venues in both London and the provinces." See Alison Smith, *The Victorian Nude: Sexuality, Morality and Art* (Manchester: Manchester University Press, 1996), 168.

19. The gaze of Delacroix's odalisques is described as "bitter" by Algerian feminist Assia Djebar in *Women of Algiers* (Charlottesville: University of Virginia Press, 1992), 140. Djebar implies that this bitterness can be connected to resistance. Also see Lynne Thornton, *Women As Portrayed in Orientalist Painting* (Paris: ACR, 1985), 40–41. As Thornton has pointed out, the use of the narghile became linked to the French artistic community; users included Gautier, Baudelaire, and Sand.

20. See John Sweetman, *The Oriental Obsession: Islamic Inspiration in British and American Art and Architecture, 1500–1920* (New York: Cambridge University Press, 1988), 196. The association of hybridity and opium use turns up in Collins's *The Moonstone* (1868), in which the racially mixed Anglo-Indian Ezra Jennings is not only an opium addict himself, but also reveals the crucial role played by opium in the narrative of the Indian diamond.

21. Tamar Heller points out the resemblance between Collins and Ezra Jennings, arguing that "Jennings becomes the novel's most important mirror of its author. Collins and his creation have obvious similarities: both are opium addicts who live on the margins of respectability." See Tamar Heller, "Blank Spaces: Ideological Tensions and the Detective Work of *The Moonstone,*" in *Wilkie Collins,* ed. Lynn Pykett (New York: St. Martin's Press, 1998), 262.

22. All references to Collins's letters are from William Baker and William M. Clarke, eds., *The Letters of Wilkie Collins,* 2 vols. (New York: St. Martin's Press, 1999).

23. See Madeleine Smith's statement in Alexander Forbes Irvine, *Report of the Trial of Madeleine Smith* (Edinburgh: T. T. Clark, 1857), 73. For analyses of the Maybrick trial, see Hartman, *Victorian Murderesses,* 247; and George Robb, "The English Dreyfus Case: Florence Maybrick and the Sexual Double Standard" in *Disorder in the Court: Trials and Sexual Conflict at the Turn of the Century,* ed. George Robb and Nancy Edner (New York: New York University Press, 1999) 57–77.

24. Collins, *The Woman in White,* ed. Matthew Sweet (New York: Penguin 1999), 567.

25. Ferdinand Gregorovius, *Lucrezia Borgia, According to Original Documents and Correspondence of Her Day* (New York: B. Blom, 1968), 361. For a brief account of Donizetti's opera, see Charles Osborne, *The Bel Canto Operas of Rossini, Donizetti, and Bellini* (Portland, Oreg.: Amadeus, 1994), 224–27.

26. George Eliot, *The Lifted Veil* (Oxford: Oxford University Press, 1999), 19.

27. For an eyewitness account of the death of Madame Brinvilliers, see Madame de Sévigné, *Selected Letters* (London: Penguin, 1982), 296.

28. See Luce Irigaray, *Speculum de L'Autre Femme* (Ithaca: Cornell University Press, 1974), 227–40.

29. For the cases of Marie Brinvilliers and La Voisin, see Frances Mossiker, *The Affair of the Poisons* (New York: Knopf, 1969); Frantz Funck-Brentano, *Princes and Poisoners: Studies of the Court of Louis XIV* (London: Duckworth, 1901); and Albert Smith, *The Marchioness of Brinvilliers* (London: Bentley, 1846).

30. Théophile Gautier, *One of Cleopatra's Nights* (New York: Walter Black, 1928), 25.

31. For Victorian critics' reactions to Lydia, see Catherine Peters, *The King of Inventors: A Life of Wilkie Collins* (Princeton: Princeton University Press, 1993), 272.

32. Poison is an important motif in several of Collins's lesser-known novels. Some of these have been completely neglected by critics, and are only beginning to be "rediscovered." See Wilkie Collins, *Jezebel's Daughter* (Gloucestershire, Eng.: Alan Sutton, 1995), in which the would-be chemist, Madame Fontaine, experiments with the poisons of the Borgias and *The Law and The Lady* (London: Penguin, 1999), based on the Madeleine Smith poisoning case.

33. All references to *Armadale* are from John Sutherland, ed., *Armadale, by Wilkie Collins* (London: Penguin, 1995).

34. See James Tod, *Annals and Antiquities of Rajasthan, or the Central and Western Rajpoot States of India* (London: Routledge and Kegan Paul, 1972).

35. For a discussion of oriental poison myths, see N. M. Penzer, *Poison Damsels and Other Essays in Folklore and Anthropology* (London: Privately printed for Chas. J. Sawyer Ltd., 1952), 3–71.

36. In both Sanskrit and Arabic sources, imperialists such as Alexander or the Indian king Chandragupta Maurya are saved from poison-women by the advice of their ministers. Several of these sources were translated into different European languages. The ninth-century Sanskrit play *The Signet Ring of Rakshasha* by the dramatist Visakadatta, in which the poison-woman is frequently mentioned, but is never actually seen onstage, was translated into English by the Orientalist scholar H. H. Wilson at the beginning of the nineteenth century.

37. The ritual of presiding over tea is ironically presented as erotic fetish in another popular Victorian sensation novel involving a murderess. See Mary Elizabeth Braddon, *Lady Audley's Secret* (New York: Viking Penguin, 1985). Braddon describes her heroine, the "fair demon" Lucy Audley seated amidst "floating mists from the boiling liquid" that envelop her in "a cloud of scented vapour" (190). Here the ritual of tea is also linked to discourses of empire and civilization.

38. Cesare Lombroso and William Ferrero, *The Female Offender* (London: T. Fisher Unwin, 1895).

39. Osborne, *Bel Canto Operas*, 338.

40. Catherine Clément, *Opera, or The Undoing of Women* (Minneapolis: University of Minnesota Press, 1999), 103. Iconographically, the poisoner and the sorceress were often connected. In his famous work on medieval witchcraft hysteria, *La Sorcière* (1862) the French sociologist and historian Jules Michelet, referred to the use of the healing properties of poisons by "sorceresses" or female medical practioners: "All the plants which were confounded together under the name of *Witches' herbs* were supposed ministers of death. Found in a woman's hands, they would have led to her being adjudged a poisoner or fabricator of accursed spells." Analysing the radical *La Sorcière* and other texts (including those by Freud), Cixous and Clément see the sorceress and hysteric as existing along the same continuum, using their spectacular and pathological bodily symptoms to instill a sense of dis-ease into "the public, the group, the men, the others to whom they are exhibited." Situated at the margins, these figures create spaces for themselves in which they encounter " a relationship with the other that is not yet stable but metastable—uneasy, such that one can pass without fixed identity from body to body: from woman into beast, from woman into woman." By exhibiting their "pathological symptoms," they rupture the terms of the

discourse that marks them as pathological. For the sorceress, see "The Guilty One," in Hélène Cixous and Catherine Clément, *The Newly Born Woman* (Minneapolis: University of Minnesota Press, 1996), 91; and Jules Michelet, *Satanism and Witch-craft (La Sorcière)* (New York: Citadel, 1939), 83.

41. *The Extraordinary Life and Trial of Madame Rachel* (London: Diprose and Bateman, 1868).

42. Richard Corson, *Fashions in Makeup* (London: Peter Owen, 1981), 376.

43. Ibid., 344–50.

44. For their reactions to Lydia's death, see *The Letters of Wilkie Collins*, 2:275–76. Collins's own response: "My own idea is that I have never written such a good end to a book . . . at any rate I never was so excited myself, while finishing a story. . . . Miss Gwilt's death quite upset me." See *Letters*, 2:275.

45. See Nicholas Royle, *The Uncanny* (New York: Routledge, 2003), 2. Analyzing Freud's concept of the uncanny, Royle defines it as a feeling of experience oneself as alien, as a "foreign" body.

46. Vincenzo Bellini, *Norma* (London: EMI: Callas Edition, 1997), 59.

47. Although I have not been able to find evidence that Collins was familiar with this work, it is very likely that he would have known it, because of his interest in issues of heredity and degeneration, not only in *Legacy*, but in previous novels such as *The Law and The Lady*, where the links among madness, degeneration, and genius are explored through the character of Misserimus Dexter.

48. Francis Galton, *Hereditary Genius* (New York: St. Martin's Press, 1978), 1.

49. Wilkie Collins, *The Legacy of Cain* (Gloucestershire, Eng.: Alan Sutton, 1998.) All references are to this edition.

50. Hélène Cixous, "Bathsheba," in *Stigmata: Escaping Texts* (London: Routledge, 1998), 8.

Notes to Chapter Three

1. Michel Foucault, *The Birth of the Clinic: An Archaeology of Medical Perception* (New York: Pantheon, 1973). Foucault maintains that in the nineteenth century, "the prestige of the sciences of life" were "linked originally not with the transferable character of biological concepts, but rather, with the fact that these concepts were arranged in a space whose profound structure responded to the healthy/morbid opposition. When one spoke of the life of the race, or even of the 'psychological life,' one did not think at first of the internal structure of the organized being, but of the medical bipolarity of the normal and the pathological" (35).

2. See Philip Curtin, *Death By Migration: Europe's Encounter with the Tropical World in the Nineteenth Century* (New York: Cambridge University Press, 1989).

3. Charlotte Brontë, *Shirley* (Harmondsworth: Penguin, 1985), 399.

4. For a discussion of the miasma theory of disease and the spread of cholera in the nineteenth century, see W. F. Bynum, *Science and the Practice of Victorian Medicine* (Cambridge: Cambridge University Press, 1994).

5. For a more comprehensive list of works, see David Arnold, *Colonizing the Body: State Medicine and Epidemic Disease in Nineteenth-Century India* (Berkeley and Los Angeles: University of California Press, 1993), 24.

6. Flora Annie Steel, *The Garden of Fidelity: Being the Autobiography of Flora Annie Steel, 1847–1929* (London: Macmillan, 1930), 33.

7. Ibid., 69–70. See also Philippa Levine "Rereading the 1890s: Venereal Disease as 'Constitutional Crisis' in Britain and British India, *Journal of Asian Studies* 55 (1996): 586–612. Levine stresses that "the topic tearing apart the smooth running of colonial India and the processes of Whitehall, was venereal disease . . . long after the domestic Contagious Diseases Acts had been laid to rest" (586). She argues that this issue was key both to the "policing of the binaries of rule and the maintenance of a critical moral-imperial universe" (603). Imperial stability was founded on military stability, which could be seriously eroded through contact with Indian women and contagion.

8. For an account of the debate over colonial prostitution, see Kenneth Ballhatchet, *Race, Sex and Class Under the Raj: Imperial Attitudes and Policies and Their Critics, 1793–1905* (New York: St. Martin's, 1980), 10–67.

9. In fact, colonial women's encounters with disease and medicine have only recently begun to receive attention through the work of historians of empire such as Arnold, Dane Kennedy in *The Magic Mountains: Hill Stations and the British Raj* (Berkeley and Los Angeles: University of California Press, 1996), and Nupur Chaudhuri "Memsahibs and Motherhood in Nineteenth-Century Colonial India" *Victorian Studies* 31, no. 4 (1988): 517–35. Such work calls for careful scrutiny of the discursive practices of colonial medicine, suggesting that furtherance of (as well as the rationale for) the imperial project may well have been dependent on the construction of "docile," sanitized bodies. Ann Stoler has enriched this Foucauldian context further in her extended critique of *The History of Sexuality*, arguing that nineteenth-century European bourgeois "cultivations of self" and sexual identity were not only refracted through, but actually *produced* by racial/imperial configurations of "healthy" and "contaminated" bodies; see Ann Laura Stoler, *Race and the Education of Desire* (Durham: Duke University Press, 1995), 194–95.

10. R. M. Coopland, *A Lady's Escape From Gwalior, and Life in the Fort of Agra During the Mutinies of 1857* (London: Smith, Elder, 1859), 79–80.

11. Flora Annie Steel, *The Complete Indian Housekeeper and Cook* (London: Heinemann, 1909), 216.

12. See John Bradley, ed., *Lady Curzon's India: Letters of a Vicereine* (New York: Beaufort Books, 1985), 37.

13. Edward Tilt, *Health in India for British Women and on the Prevention of Diseases in Tropical Climates*, 4th ed. (London: Churchill, 1875), 55. Subsequent references to this source will be made parenthetically in the text.

14. See Janaki Nair, "Uncovering the Zenana," in *Expanding the Boundaries of Women's History*, ed. Cheryl Johnson-Odim and Margaret Strobel (Bloomington: Indiana University Press, 1992), 38–43.

15. For analyses of the zenana in transition, especially in nineteenth-century Bengal, see Malavika Karlekar, *Voices from Within* (New York: Oxford University Press, 1991); and Meredith Borthwick, *The Changing Role of Women in Bengal, 1849–1905* (Princeton: Princeton University Press, 1984).

16. Edward Storrow, *The Eastern Lily Gathered* (London: John Snow, 1856), 35.

17. See Mary Weitbrecht, *The Women of India and Christian Work in the Zenana* (London: James Nisbet, 1875). Quoted in Karlekar, *Voices from Within*, 123–25.

18. Quoted in Karlekar, *Voices from Within*, 49.

19. For a survey and analysis of the work of the Dufferin Fund, see Arnold, *Colonizing the Body*, 260–68.

20. For work on the material practices governing the lives of European women in the colonies, especially on India, see Pat Barr, *The Memsahibs* (London: Secker and Warburg, 1976); Margaret Macmillan, *Women of the Raj* (New York: Thames and Hudson, 1988); Antoinette Burton, *Burdens of History: British Feminists, Indian Women, and Imperial Culture* (Chapel Hill: University of North Carolina Press, 1994) and Margaret Strobel, *European Women and the Second British Empire* (Bloomington: Indiana University Press, 1991).

21. See Violet Powell, *Flora Annie Steel: Novelist of India* (London: Heinemann, 1981), 44. Powell comments that "inevitably her writing was often compared with Rudyard Kipling's, a standard against which the veracity of her material was measured."

22. Steel, *The Complete Indian Housekeeper and Cook* (London: Heinemann, 1909), 178.

23. "Tropical Lands and White Races," *Transactions of the Society for Tropical Medicine and Hygiene* (1907–8): 201–228. See also Kennedy, *Magic Mountains*, 32–33.

24. Rebecca Saunders, in "Gender, Colonialism, and Exile: Flora Annie Steel and Sara Jeanette Duncan in India," in *Women's Writing in Exile*, ed. Mary Lynn Broe and Angela Ingram (Chapel Hill: University of North Carolina Press, 1989), 303–24 provides a reading of the role of "fallen memsahib" in *On the Face of the Waters*. There is very little published criticism of Steel's novels, and almost all assessments focus on her Mutiny novel. See, for instance, Jenny Sharpe, *Allegories of Empire* (Minneapolis: University of Minnesota Press, 1993), 85–110; Benita Parry, *Delusions and Discoveries* (London: Allen Lane, 1972), 100–130; and Nancy Paxton's "Mobilizing Chivalry: Rape in British Novels About the Indian Uprising of 1857," *Victorian Studies* 36, no. 1(1992): 5–30. In "The Construction of Woman in Three Popular Texts of Empire: Towards a Critique of Materialist Feminism," *Textual Practice* 3, no. 3 (1989): 323–59, Rosemary Hennessy and Rajeswari Mohan look at the short story "Mussumat Kirpo's Doll," (the subject of which is child marriage), to situate Steel within the "liberal colonial tradition of outrage in the face of indigenous practices" (which, ironically, at the same time "necessitated" imperial rule and the civilizing mission).

25. Stoler uses this term to describe "bourgeois white identities" in flux. She concludes that although these identities were unstable, stereotypes of the racial other continued to be fixed and unchanging. It seems to me that such a sharp dichotomy undermines her earlier contention: images of the racial other, as I show here, were by no means so "fixed" as has been assumed; instead, they existed in a peculiarly ambivalent reciprocal relationship with those of whiteness, and especially of white women. See *Race and the Education of Desire*, 163.

26. Flora Annie Steel, *Voices in the Night: A Chromatic Fantasia* (London: Macmillan, 1900).

27. The connection between the bazaars and colonial prostitution is traced in Ballhatchet, *Race, Sex and Class*, 10–39.

28. W. J. Simpson, "Recrudescence of Plague in the East," *The Lancet* (September 9, 1899).

29. See Arnold, *Colonizing the Body*, 210–11.

30. See Veena Oldenburg, "Lifestyle as Resistance: The Case of the Courtesans of Lucknow," in *Contesting Power: Resistance and Everyday Social Relations in South Asia*,

ed. Douglas Haynes and Gyan Prakash (Berkeley and Los Angeles: University of California Press, 1992), 23–61.Oldenburg's brilliant essay on nineteenth-century and present-day Indian courtesans provides an excellent starting point for reevaluating the courtesan's role in patriarchal cultures. Jyotsna Singh also comments on the subversive staging of identity by nautch girls in *Colonial Narratives*, 104–14.

31. For a detailed account of the Indian Contagious Diseases Acts and the controversy surrounding the licensing system, see Ballhatchet, *Race, Sex and Class*, 40–67.

32. See Levine, "Rereading the 1890s,"591.

33. Roberts's comments and other accounts of the nautch are excerpted in K. K. Dyson, ed., *A Various Universe: A Study of the Journals and Memoirs of British Men and Women in the Indian Subcontinent, 1765–1856* (New York: Oxford University Press, 1978).

34. Public dancers in North Africa are discussed in Wendy Buonaventura, *Serpent of the Nile* (New York: Interlink Books), 1990. Buonaventura defines the ghawazee as "invaders" or "outsiders," explaining that the term was originally associated with gypsy tribes.

35. See Mary Anne Stevens, ed. *The Orientalists: Delacroix to Matisse* (London: Weidenfield and Nicolson, 1984), 140.

36. Edward Lane, *Manners and Customs of the Modern Egyptians* (New York: Dutton, 1954).

37. See Francis Steegmuller, *Flaubert in Egypt: A Sensibility on Tour* (Boston: Little, Brown, 1972); and Lucy Duff Gordon, *Letters From Egypt, 1862–1869* (New York: Praeger, 1969).

38. Dyson, *A Various Universe*, 354. After conducting a series of interviews with present-day courtesans in Lucknow, Veena Oldenburg has drawn the conclusion that many of these performances continue to parody/subvert marriage and socially sanctioned heterosexual relationships. "These routines, studded with subversive and irreverent jokes and obscene gestures, are performed like secret anti-rites"; Oldenburg, "Lifestyle as Resistance," 41–42.

39. See Jean Baudrillard, *Seduction* (New York: St. Martin's, 1979) 39–41 and 69–71, for a theoretical approach to the distinction between "seductive" and "productive" bodies.

40. Levine, "Rereading the 1890s," 601.

41. Powell, *Flora Annie Steel*, 72. Steel, *The Potter's Thumb* (London: Heinemann, 1894).

42. Steel, *Potter's Thumb*, 42. The term "purdahnishin" means "woman in purdah" (seclusion).

43. Homi Bhabha, *The Location of Culture* (London: Routledge, 1994), 86. Bhabha sees the "partial presence" of the colonial subject emerging from "a discursive process by which the excess or slippage produced by the ambivalence of mimicry . . . does not merely rupture the discourse, but becomes transformed into an uncertainty." In Steel's fiction, mimicry cuts both ways, as colonizers and colonized constantly mimic each other.

44. Saunders, "Gender, Colonialism, and Exile," 314.

Notes to Chapter Four

1. See Dane Kennedy, *The Magic Mountains* (Berkeley and Los Angeles: University of California Press, 1996), 19–38. See also Edward Tilt, *Health in India for British Women*

and on the Prevention of Diseases in Tropical Climates, 4th ed. (London: Churchill, 1875).

2. See D. L. Macdonald and Kathleen Scherf, eds., Frankenstein: The Original 1818 Text (Ontario, Canada: Broadview, 1999), 358.

3. Kennedy, Magic Mountains, 19–38.

4. Ann Ardis, New Women, New Novels: Feminism and Early Modernism (New Brunswick: Rutgers University Press, 1990), 12–28.

5. Sally Ledger, "The New Woman and the Crisis of Victorianism," in Cultural Politics at the Fin-de-Siècle, ed. Sally Ledger and Scott McCracken (Cambridge: Cambridge University Press, 1995), 22–44; Lisa Hamilton, "New Women and Old Men: Gendering Degeneration," in Women and British Aestheticism, ed. Talia Schaffer and Kathy Psomiades (Charlottesville: University of Virginia Press, 1999), 62–80; and Nancy Paxton, Writing Under the Raj (New Brunswick: Rutgers University Press, 1999), 196–99.

6. Mary Louise Pratt, Imperial Eyes: Travel Writing and Transculturation (New York: Routledge, 1992), 6–7.

7. See Carol Senf, ed., The Critical Response to Bram Stoker (Westport, Conn.: Greenwood, 1993), 173–83; and David Seed, "Eruptions of the Primitive into the Present," in William Hughes and Andrew Smith, eds. Bram Stoker: history, psychoanalysis and the Gothic (New York: St. Martin's, 1998), 201.

8. Barbara Belford, Bram Stoker: A Biography of the Author of Dracula (New York: Knopf, 1996), 319–21. The suggestion of syphilis comes from Daniel Farson, who allows this conviction to color his interpretation of Lair; see The Man Who Wrote Dracula: A Biography of Bram Stoker (London: Michael Joseph, 1975), 223. Even when the diagnosis of syphilis is questioned, the psychosis remains. H. P. Malchow, in Gothic Images of Race in Nineteenth-Century Britain (Stanford: Stanford University Press, 1996), claims that "Stoker's life ended with the wild dissolution of personal identity in dementia praecox (schizophrenia) a condition that may or may not have been the result of the terminal stage of syphilis" (131). For a different view, see Belford, Bram Stoker, 320.

9. Nancy Stepan, "Biology and Degeneration: Races and Proper Places," in Degeneration: The Dark Side of Progress, ed. J. Edward Chamberlin and Sander (New York: Columbia University Press, 1985), 97–120.

10. In his recent study of Stoker's fiction, David Glover argues that "the forays into cultural criticism or the conjectures on history or religion in Stoker's novels frequently draw upon medicine or science." He documents Stoker's preoccupation with ethnology, criminal anthropology, phrenology, mesmerism, and psychiatry—concerns that are evident in Dracula (1897). See David Glover, Vampires, Mummies and Liberals: Bram Stoker and the Politics of Popular Fiction (Durham: Duke University Press, 1996), 10–11.

11. See Leslie Shepard, "The Library of Bram Stoker," in Bram Stoker's Dracula: Sucking through the Century 1897–1997, ed. Carol Margaret Davison (Toronto: Dundurn, 1997), 413. Shepard mentions that Stoker's library contained the reports of the Wellcome Research Laboratories at the Gordon Memorial College, Khartoum, published in three volumes from 1906 to 1911.

12. See Havelock R. Charles, "Neurasthenia and Its Bearing on the Decay of Northern Peoples of India," Transactions of the Society of Tropical Medicine and Hygiene 7 (1913): 2–31.

13. Anna Davin, "Imperialism and Motherhood," *History Workshop* 5 (1978): 9–65; quotations on 49 and 20.

14. Stephen Arata, *Fictions of Loss in the Victorian Fin-de-Siècle* (Cambridge: Cambridge University Press, 1996), 117. For other recent discussions of Stoker and race, see Cannon Schmidt, *Alien Nation: Nineteenth-Century Gothic Fictions and English Nationality* (Philadelphia: University of Pennsylvania Press, 1997); H. P. Malchow, *Gothic Images of Race* (Stanford: Stanford University Press, 1996); Glover, *Vampires, Mummies and Liberals;* and Rebecca Stott, *The Fabrication of the Late Victorian Femme Fatale: The Kiss of Death* (Houndmills: Macmillan, 1992). Most of these (except for Glover and Stott) focus on *Dracula.*

15. For the construction of whiteness as an ongoing process prior to, during, and after colonial encounters, see Robert Young's rereading of Victorian ethnological texts in *Colonial Desire: Hybridity in Theory, Culture and Race* (New York: Routledge, 1995). For the history of degeneration as "scientific" discourse, see Daniel Pick, *Faces of Degeneration: A European Disorder, 1848–1918* (Cambridge: Cambridge University Press, 1989). Pick argues that "degeneration was never successfully reduced to a fixed idiom or theory . . . rather it was a shifting term produced, inflected, refined and reconstituted in the movement between human sciences, fictional narratives and socio-political commentaries" (7).

16. All textual references are to the American reprint of the original 1911 version of *The Lair of the White Worm,* which was published in the United States under the title *The Garden of Evil* (New York: Paperback Library, 1966), 11. Subsequent references will be made parenthetically in the text.

17. For a discussion of stigmata in degeneration theory, see Eric Carlson, "Medicine and Degeneration: Theory and Praxis," in Chamberlin and Gilman, *Degeneration,* 127–36. The founder of French degeneration theory, Benedict-Augustin Morel, had emphasized the existence of "stigmata" as evidence of decline over the course of several generations. Later degenerationists came up with elaborate lists of stigmata, ranging from lack of resistance to disease to sexual perversion and insanity. In his classic treatise *Degeneration,* Max Nordau listed six different types of mental stigmata: moral insanity, emotionalism, mysticism, melancholia, hysteria, and lack of will; see *Degeneration* (London: William Heinemann, 1895), 15–33. In contrast, Stoker's degenerate Caswalls are noted for their willpower, through which they channel their mesmeric capabilities.

18. Patrick Bade, *Femme Fatale: Images of Evil and Fascinating Women* (London: Ash and Grant, 1979), 36.

19. See Bram Dijkstra, *Idols of Perversity: Fantasies of Feminine Evil in Fin-de-Siècle Culture* (New York: Oxford University Press, 1986).

20. See Jane Abdy, "Sarah Bernhardt and Lalique: A Confusion of Evidence," *Apollo* 125 (1987): 325–30.

21. Gustave Flaubert, *Salammbô* (Harmondsworth, Middlesex, Eng.: Penguin, 1977), 174.

22. Joseph Fayrer, "On Serpent Worship and on the Venomous Snakes of India," *Journal of the Transactions of the Victoria Institute* 26 (1892): 88, 86, 107. The serpent has a complex significance in Hinduism, a context that Fayrer more or less ignores here.

23. As Belford puts it: "The hole is repeatedly described in vaginal terms. . . . Salton delubricates it and destroys it with dynamite." Belford, *Bram Stoker,* 318.

24. Julia Kristeva's work on abjection is relevant here; in *Powers of Horror,* she meditates that "a wound with blood and pus, or the sickly acrid smell of sweat, of decay does not *signify* death" but instead represents the "border" between life and death, from which the body has to "extricate" itself in order to live: "something rejected from which one does not part," and that "beckons to us and ends up engulfing us." A more compelling case for a Kristevan reading can be made if we consider the classification of the physical stigmata thought to be symptoms of the degenerative process, which often included the production of an excess of bodily fluids. Julia Kristeva, *Powers of Horror: An Essay on Abjection* (New York: Columbia University Press, 1982), 3–4. For the importance of bodily fluids as an index to the degenerative process, see Cesare Lombroso's classification of the criteria for examination of "insane and criminal patients" in Gina Lombroso-Ferrero, *Criminal Man* (Montclair, N.J.: Patterson Smith, 1972), 256 and Carlson, "Medicine and Degeneration," 128.

25. Edward Tilt, *A Handbook of Uterine Therapeutics* (New York: William Wood, 1881), 289, 292–93.

26. Nupur Chaudhuri, "Memsahibs and Motherhood in Nineteenth-Century Colonial India," *Victorian Studies,* 31, no. 4 (Summer 1988): 517–35.

27. Bram Stoker, *Dracula,* ed. Nina Auerbach (New York: Norton, 1997), 247. See also Joan Copjec, "Vampires, Breast Feeding and Anxiety," *October* 58 (Fall 1991): 25–43.

28. Alice Perrin, "The Centipede," in *Stories From the Raj: From Kipling to Independence,* ed. Saros Cowasjee (New Delhi: HarperCollins, 1992), 124–25.

29. Copjec, "Vampires, Breast Feeding and Anxiety."

30. Ruth Perry, "Colonizing the Breast; Sexuality and Maternity in Eighteenth-Century England," *Eighteenth-Century Life,* 16, no. 1 (February 1992): 185–213. See also *The Lair of The White Worm* (London: W. Foulsham, 1925).

31. Excerpted in Nicholas John, ed., *Violetta and her Sisters: The Lady of the Camellias: Responses to the Myth* (London: Faber, 1994), 44–48. For Parent-Duchâtelet's influence, see Alain Corbin, *Women For Hire: Prostitution and Sexuality in France after 1850* (Cambridge: Harvard University Press, 1990), 3–4.

32. See Elizabeth Wilson, "Bohemians, Grisettes and Demi-Mondaines," in John, ed., *Violetta and her Sisters,* 24.

33. Bade, *Femme Fatale,* 9. Bade quotes the poet Emile Bergerat's vision of La Païva at a concert: "You either believe in vampires or you don't, I believed in them at that concert." La Païva's career is traced in Joanna Richardson, *The Courtesans: The Demi-Monde in Nineteenth-Century France* (London: Weidenfield and Nicolson, 1967). For a more recent account of La Païva's career, see Virginia Rounding, *Grandes Horizontales: The lives and legends of Marie Duplessis, Cora Pearl, La Païva and La Présidente* (New York and London: Bloomsbury, 2003), 75–96.

34. Havelock Ellis, *Studies in the Psychology of Sex* (New York: Random House, 1936), 2:305–11.

35. Marcel Hénaff, *Sade: The Invention of the Libertine Body* (Minneapolis: University of Minnesota Press, 1999), 273–74.

36. Giuseppe Verdi, *La Traviata* (New York: Sony Music Entertainment, 1993), 68. For *Traviata's* reception in London see John ed., *Violetta and Her Sisters,* 249.

37. Max Nordau, *Degeneration* (London: William Heinemann, 1895), 8.

38. Cesare Lombroso and William Ferrero, *The Female Offender* (London: T. Fisher Unwin, 1895), 101, 128–29.

39. See *Dracula*, 295–96. Salli Kline comments on Nordau's favorable reception and popularity in Britain in *The Degeneration of Women* (Rheinbach-Merzbach: CMZ Verlag, 1992), 160–61.

40. See Bibliothèque Nationale (France), *Albert Besnard: L'Oeuvre Grave* (Paris: Bibliothèque Nationale, 1949).

41. Lombroso and Ferrero, *The Female Offender*, 102.

42. Edward Tilt, *The Change of Life in Health and Disease* (New York: Bermingham, 1882), 167–69. "On analyzing Esquirol's article on demonomania, I am struck by the fact that all his cases occurred at this epoch. One patient, aged forty-six, thought the devil had placed a cord from the pubis to the sternum; another, aged forty-nine, had been troubled by cerebral symptoms ever since cessation (of menstruation) . . . and thought the devil lodged in her womb" (168).

43. Lisa Tickner, *The Spectacle of Women: Imagery of the Suffrage Campaign 1907–14* (Chicago: University of Chicago Press, 1988).

43. "Women's Suffrage and National Danger," in *The Opponents: The Anti-Suffragists*, ed. Marie Mulvey Roberts (London: Thoemmes, 1995), 71–72; see also Thomas Watts Eden and Cuthbert Lockyer, eds., *The New System of Gynecology* (London: Macmillan, 1917), 402.

44. Christabel Pankhurst, *The Great Scourge and How to End It* (London: E Pankhurst, 1913), 17.

45. Jennifer DeVere Brody, *Impossible Purities: Blackness, Femininity, and Victorian Culture* (Durham, Duke University Press, 1998), 172.

46. See Emily Apter, "Female Trouble in the Colonial Harem," *Differences: A Journal of Feminist Cultural Studies*, 4 no. 1 (Spring 1992): 203–24. For a conventional account of this painting as a sadomasochistic fantasy, see Ruth Yeazell, *Harems of the Mind* (New Haven: Yale University Press, 2000), 185. Emily Apter defines this "jouissance of claustration" or "feminocentric libidinal economy" as the "haremization effect": "the harem genre . . . has also been the haven of sapphic fantasies, themselves rooted in the dream of an alternative, feminocentric libidinal economy. In colonial fiction sapphism is often so prevalent that one might begin to interpret it in terms of a "haremization effect." . . . In the harem, new forms of love . . . incubate and multiply . . . an 'other' female eroticism is seemingly put into place combining the *jouissance* of claustration with the pleasure of sexual secrets privately discovered and shared among women" (208–19).

48. Quoted in Alison Smith, *The Victorian Nude: Sexuality, Morality and Art* (Manchester: Manchester University Press, 1996), 168. If this motif crops up less frequently in British than in French orientalist art, it is probably due to the motif's being less easily representable in visual terms; instead, it resurfaces in late Victorian fiction, especially that of Stoker. Because most Middle Eastern harems were more racially diverse than Indian zenanas, and the British colonial experience was mostly in India, it might be argued that this is one reason for the prevalence of this motif in French vis-à-vis British art. However, as Smith notes, the French influence did become more pronounced toward the end of the century. For the French influence, see Smith, 172–73.

49. Paul Broca, *On the Phenomena of Hybridity in the Genus Homo* (London: Longman, Green, Longman and Roberts, 1864), 22.

50. For an exploration of the ethnological term "Caucasian," see J. C. Nott and George Gliddon, *Types of Mankind* (Philadelphia: Lippincott, 1854), 88–110; quotation on 409.
51. Ibid., 450.

Notes to Chapter Five

1. See Clare Phillips, "Jewellery and the Art of the Goldsmith," in *Art Nouveau 1890–1914*, ed. Paul Greenlagh (London: Victoria and Albert Museum, 2000), 237.
2. Bram Stoker, *The Jewel of Seven Stars*, ed. David Glover (New York: Oxford University Press, 1996). For the reception of the novel, see Glover's introduction. All references to *The Jewel of Seven Stars* henceforth will be from this edition.
3. Eliza Lynn Linton, "Woman's Place in Nature and Society," *Belgravia* 29 (1876): 349–63; quotation on 357.
4. Alexander Walker, *Beauty: Illustrated Chiefly by an Analysis and Classification of Beauty in Women* (London: Henry G. Bohn, 1846), 111–17; and Mrs. Alexander Walker, *Female Beauty* (New York: Scofield and Voorhies, 1840), 365.
5. The coronation ring was forced onto Victoria's fourth finger, which had to be bathed in ice water to get it off. See Charlotte Gere, *Victorian Jewellery Design*, (Chicago: H. Regnery Co., 1973), 17.
6. Herbert Spencer, "Personal Beauty" in *Essays Moral, Political and Aesthetic* (New York: D. Appleton, 1868), 149–62.
7. *Illustrated London News*, exhibition supplement 19 (1851): 511.
8. For a discussion of Hancock's jewelry, see A. Kenneth Snowman, ed., *The Master Jewelers* (New York: Harry Abrams, 1990) 46–60. Victoria's self-display and her domesticity are discussed respectively in Stanley Weintraub, *Victoria: An Intimate Biography* (New York: Dutton, 1987), 423; and Margaret Homans, "'To the Queen's Private Apartments': Royal Family Portraiture and the Construction of Victoria's Sovereign Obedience," *Victorian Studies* (Autumn 1993): 1–41. For an account of Mary Curzon's life in India, see Marian Fowler, *Below the Peacock Fan: First Ladies of the Raj* (New York: Viking, 1987).
9. Anne Hollander, *Sex and Suits* (New York: Knopf, 1994), 74 and 76.
10. Quoted in Joanna Richardson, *The Courtesans* (London: Weidenfield and Nicolson, 1967), 56.
11. For a recent biographical study of Cora Pearl, see Virginia Rounding, *Grandes Horizontales: The Lives and Legends of Four Nineteenth-Century Courtesans* (New York: Bloomsbury, 2003), 243.
12. "Real Mysteries of Paris and London," *All The Year Round* 4 (1860): 69–72.
13. See Rounding, *Grandes Horizontales*, 237.
14. Lee Holcolmbe, *Wives and Property: Reform of the Married Woman's Property Law in Nineteenth-Century England* (Toronto: University of Toronto Press, 1983), 4.
15. See the libretto of *The Tales of Hoffmann*, ed. Michael Kaye (Paris: Erato, 1996). For a perceptive analysis of the positioning of the courtesan Giulietta within the Venetian act, see Heather Hadlock, *Mad Loves: Women and Music in Offenbach's Les Contes D'Hoffmann* (Princeton: Princeton University Press, 2000), 121–133. Hadlock,

however, does not specifically provide a reading of the courtesan's connection to the diamond.

16. See Partha Mitter, *Much Maligned Monsters: A History of European Reactions to Indian Art (Oxford: Clarendon Press, 1977)*, 241–48, for an analysis of Ruskin's response to oriental decorative art forms.

17. See Harriet Martineau, *Eastern Life: Present and Past* (Philadelphia: Lea and Blanchard, 1848), 267. Apparently the courtesan La Païva also used kohl to blacken her eyelids, creating a "fierce and hawklike" look. See Rounding, *Grandes Horizontales*, 234.

18. See Gayle Graham Yates, *Harriet Martineau on Women* (New Brunswick, N.J.: Rutgers University Press, 1985), 181–84, 230.

19. Dubois's comments on Indian temple dancers are quoted in Frederique Apffel Marglin, *Wives of the God-King: The Rituals of the Devadasis of Puri* (New York: Oxford University Press, 1985), 4–5.

20. For an overview of the history of the firms of Castellani and Giuliano, see Geoffrey Munn, *Castellani and Guiliano: Revivalist Jewellers of the 19th Century* (New York: Rizzoli, 1984).

21. Owen Jones, *The Grammar of Ornament* (New York: DK Publishing, 2001). The first edition was published by Day & Son, Lincoln's Inn Fields, London in 1856.

22. Carlo Giuliano, "The Art of the Jeweller," in *The Journal of the Society of the Arts* (1889): 391–410; quoted in Munn, 149.

23. Quoted in Munn, *Castellani and Giuliano*.

24. Ibid., 131.

25. Quoted in Judy Rudoe, "Alessandro Castellani's Letters to Henry Layard," *Jewellery Studies* 5 (1991): 107–19.

26. For descriptions of the Comtesse Castiglione's photographs, see Pierre Apraxine and Xavier Demange, *La Divine Comtesse: Photographs of the Countess de Castiglione,* (New Haven: Yale University Press, 1999), 171. For an account of Bernhardt's performance in *Théodora,* see Arthur Gold and Robert Fitzdale, *The Divine Sarah: A Life of Sarah Bernhardt* (New York: Knopf, 1991), 213–15.

27. Amelia Edwards, *A Thousand Miles Up the Nile* (London: George Routledge, 1889), 123.

28. Florence Muller, "Lalique and Fashion," in *The Jewels of Lalique,* ed. Yvonne Brunhammer (Paris: Flammarion, 1998), 105.

29. Quoted in Brunhammer, *Jewels of Lalique,* 218.

30. "The Exhibition of Jewellery by Rene Lalique," in *The Studio* 35 (July 1905) 127–34.

31. See Phillips, "Jewellery and the Art of the Goldsmith," 244.

32. Henri Vever, *French Jewelry of the 19th Century* (London: Thames and Hudson, 2001): 1233–34.

33. For a descriptive catalog of Lalique's Egyptian style jewels, see Jean Marcel Humbert, Michael Pantazzi and Christiane Zielger, *Egyptomania: Egypt in Western Art 1730–1930* (Ottawa: National Gallery of Canada, 1994), 483–84.

34. See Brunhammer, *Jewels of Lalique,* 36.

35. It is difficult to find theoretical readings of Lalique's jewelry, but Brunhammer's *The Jewels of Lalique* offers a range of perspectives as well as biographical information. Although I am indebted to these essays for a discussion of Lalique's techniques and his location within the art nouveau movement, the "theorization" of the jewelry offered in this chapter is entirely my own.

36. For Bernhardt's performance in *Izeyl*, a story set in India, Lalique designed a huge lotus as a corsage ornament. The snake tiara projected for Théodora was adapted into a corsage; according to Jane Abdy, "it would have been agonizing to wear" as a tiara. See Jane Abdy, "Sarah Bernhardt and Lalique: A Confusion of Evidence," *Apollo* 125 (1987): 325–30; quotation on 326.

37. Vever, *French Jewelry*, 1227.

38. See Ghislaine Wood and Paul Greenhalgh, "Symbols of the Sacred and Profane" in *Art Nouveau 1890–1914* ed. Paul Greenhalgh (London: Victoria and Albert Museum, 2000), 85.

39. The few critical readings of *Jewel* tend to focus more on the culture of the mummy than the implications of the jewel itself. For a provocative psychoanalytic reading that posits *Jewel* as vampire fiction, see Lawrence Rickels, *The Vampire Lectures* (Minneapolis: University of Minnesota Press, 1999), 234–39. Because the Freudian implications of the term "jewel" are obvious, I have resisted pursuing such a reading here.

40. See Glover's introduction to Stoker, *Jewel of Seven Stars*.

41. For a survey of the rise of Egyptology during the latter half of the nineteenth century, see Brian Fagan, *The Rape of The Nile: Tomb Robbers, Tourists and Archaeologists in Egypt* (London: Moyer Bell, 1975).

Notes to Chapter Six

1. For Said's reading of *Aida*, see Edward Said, *Culture and Imperialism* (New York: Random House, 1994), 111–32. This view has been challenged initially by John Mackenzie in *Orientalism: History, Theory, and the Arts*, 155–56, and by Bart Moore-Gilbert in *Postcolonial Theory: Contexts, Practices, Politics* (London: Verso, 1997), 68–69.

2. Herbert Lindenberger, *Opera in History: From Monteverdi to Cage* (Stanford: Stanford University Press, 1998), 160–91.

3. For the status of the Covent Garden opera house within British culture after 1945, and its relationship to British national identity see Norman Lebrecht, *Covent Garden: The Untold Story* (Boston: Northeastern University Press, 2000).

4. For a provocative, "operatic" analysis of the diva's body and queer identity, see Wayne Kostenbaum, *The Queen's Throat: Opera, Homosexuality and the Mystery of Desire* (New York: Vintage, 1993).

5. A term applied to "serious" opera, with a heroic or tragic subject.

6. For Dryden's preface to *Albion and Albanius*, see Piero Weiss, ed., *Opera: A History in Documents* (New York: Oxford University Press, 2002).

7. For Addison and Steele's comments, see Weiss, *Opera*, 68–72.

8. This list is provided in Harold Rosenthal: *Opera at Covent Garden: A Short History* (London: Victor Gollancz, 1967), 176–92.

9. For an exhaustive analysis of the staging of French grand opera, including "exotic" ones, see Hervé Lacombe, *The Keys to French Opera in the Nineteenth Century* (Berkeley and Los Angeles: University of California Press, 2001).

10. For contemporary critical responses (including Comettant's), to *Carmen* as well as a critical reading of the opera, see Susan McClary, *Georges Bizet: Carmen* (Cambridge: Cambridge University Press, 1992); page references are to this text. Also see

Prosper Mérimée, "Carmen," in *Carmen and Other Stories* (Oxford: Oxford University Press, 1993). For the libretto of the opera, see Henri Meilhac and Ludovic Halévy, *Carmen* (New York: Dover, 1972).

11. John Rosselli, *Singers of Italian Opera: The History of a Profession* (Cambridge: Cambridge University Press, 1992).

12. See Mary Jane Phillips-Matz, *Verdi: A Biography* (New York: Oxford University Press, 1996), 225.

13. Quoted in. Nicholas John, ed., *The Lady of the Camellias: Responses to the Myth* (London: Faber, 1994), 231.

14. For a discussion of the Pasta-Malibran comparison, see Stelios Galatopoulos, *Bellini: Life, Times, Music, 1801–1835* (London: Sanctuary, 2002); quotations on 291 and 295.

15. Mary Burgan, "Heroines at the Piano: Women and Music in Nineteenth-Century Fiction" in *The Lost Chord: Essays on Victorian Music*, ed. Nicholas Temperley (Bloomington: Indiana University Press, 1989), 42–67. Burgan's essay also provides a study of the way music emerges as a central motif in major Victorian novels.

16. For eyewitness accounts of the London performances of Agujari and Gabrielli, see Frances Burney, *Journals and Letters: A New Selection*, ed. Peter Sabor and Lars E. Troide (London: Penguin, 2001), 60–61.

17. Edward Bulwer-Lytton, *A Strange Story/Zanoni* (Boston: Aldine,1900).

18. For studies of the Rosicrucian motifs in *Zanoni*, see Marie Mulvey-Roberts, *Gothic Immortals: The Fiction of the Brotherhood of the Rosy Cross* (London: Routledge, 1990); and Robert Lee Wolff, *Strange Stories and Other Explorations in Victorian Fiction* (Boston: Gambit, 1971). For Victorian responses to *Zanoni*, see Wolff. Also see Mulvey-Roberts, "Edward Bulwer-Lytton," in *Gothic Writers: A Critical and Bibliographical Guide*, ed. Douglass H. Thomson (Westport, Conn: Greenwood, 2002).

19. For biographical studies of Bulwer-Lytton, see James Campbell, *Edward Bulwer-Lytton* (Boston: Twayne, 1986); and Wolff, *Strange Stories.* Wolff provides an important reading of the occult symbolism in *Zanoni*.

20. Tartini's account of his dream is reproduced in Eric Blom, ed., *The Grove Dictionary of Music and Musicians* (London: Macmillan, 1954), 313.

21. Elizabeth Gaskell, "The Old Nurse's Story," in *Gothic Tales*, ed. Laura Krantzer (London: Penguin, 2000), 26.

22. In a "key" to Zanoni, Bulwer attempted to explain that Mejnour and Zanoni symbolized "Science" and "Idealism" respectively; Viola represented "Instinct," and the dweller, "Fear," from "whose ghastliness men are protected . . . by Prescription and Custom." See *Zanoni*, 424.

23. Vernon Lee, "A Wicked Voice" in *Ninteenth Century Short Stories by Women*, ed. Harriet Devine Jump (London: Routledge, 1998); and "Winthrop's Adventure," in *For Maurice: Five Unlikely Stories* (New York: Arno, 1976), 143–205.

24. Peter Gunn, *Vernon Lee: Violet Paget, 1856–1935* (London: Oxford University Press, 1964), 16.

25. Lee remains one of the most fascinating and most neglected writers of the late Victorian period, although her work has begun to receive critical attention lately. On Lee, see Gunn, *Vernon Lee*; and Burdett Gardner, *The Lesbian Imagination (Victorian Style): A Psychological and Critical Study of Vernon Lee* (New York: Garland, 1987).

For an excellent reading of the connection between Lee's aesthetic theories and lesbian desire, see Kathy Psomiades, "Still Burning from This Strangling Embrace: Vernon Lee on Desire and Aesthetics," in *Victorian Sexual Dissidence*, ed. Richard Dellamora (Chicago: University of Chicago Press, 1999), 21–41. For alternative readings of "A Wicked Voice," see Angela Leighton, "Ghosts, Aestheticism and Vernon Lee," *Victorian Literature and Culture* (2000): 1–14; and Carlo Caballero, "A Wicked Voice: On Vernon Lee, Wagner and the Effects of Music," *Victorian Studies* 35 (1992): 386–408.

26. Vernon Lee, "The Art of Singing: Past and Present," *Quarterly Review* 72 (October 1880): 172 and 164–67.

27. Vernon Lee, *Studies of the Eighteenth Century in Italy* (New York: Da Capo, 1978), 111.

28. Roland Barthes, in *S/Z: An Essay*, reads the figure of the castrato in Balzac's novella "Sarrasine" as a "copy" of femininity that radically alters the "original": "in copying woman, in assuming her position on the other side of the sexual barrier, the castrato will transgress morphology, grammar, discourse" (66). For the male lover of the castrato in "Sarrasine," this dislocation ultimately leads to death; in "A Wicked Voice" it leads to madness. Barthes does not, however, explore the castrato's elaborate vocal abilities and their connection to this dislocation. See Barthes, *S/Z* (New York: Hill and Wang, 1974).

29. Quoted in Gunn, *Vernon Lee*, 28. For Lee's anti-imperialist views, see Gunn, *Vernon Lee*, 164–65.

30. See Slavoj Žižek and Mladen Dolar, *Opera's Second Death* (New York: Routledge, 2002), for Žižek's contention that "we find speech only by finding it again, after being reduced to muteness" (194). In the introduction, Dolar and Žižek argue for a more rigorously psychoanalytic approach to opera, contending that "what we usually get in readings of opera is a deconstructionist reading of the libretto, or, perhaps even worse, a rather primitive Freudian denunciation of its (patriarchal, anti-Semitic, and/or anti-feminist) biases. The contention of this book is that opera deserves something better." This feeling has also informed my reading of the diva in this chapter.

Notes to Coda

1. *That Obscure Object of Desire*, dir. Luis Buñuel, 104 min., Rialto Pictures, 1977, motion picture.

2. A phrase used by Merleau-Ponty and quoted by Edward Said in *Reflections on Exile* (Cambridge, Mass.: Harvard University Press, 2002), 12.

3. Edward Said, *Culture and Imperialism* (New York: Random House, 1994), 188.

4. Ahdaf Soueif, *The Map of Love* (New York: Anchor Books, 2000).

Index

courtesans, xx, 7; in Buñuel, 127; Castiglione as, 96; in colonial India, 33, 59, 61, 65–68, 70–72, 142n30; hybridization of, 17, 18, 26, 82; as odalisques, 19, 20; and ornamentation, 87, 91–93, 97, 101; and public space, 80; Moreau's Salomé as, 15; and singers, 112, 118; and suffragettes, 83; in *Zofloya*, 28

Cowper, Frank Cadogan, *Vanity*, 11, 12

Dacre, Charlotte, *Zofloya or The Moor*, 2, 13, 27–30

Daniell, Thomas and William, 13

Darwin, Charles, 4

Defoe, Daniel, 20

degeneration, 128; as a term, 144n15; climatic, 33, 62, 66; and the courtesan, 81; as defined by Nordau, 83; in French degeneration theory, 144n17; and female poisoners, 50, 55–58; and Lalique, 100–101; and opium use, 48; and gynecology 71, 74–75, 77, 86

Delacroix, Eugène, xiii; *Death of Sardanapalus* 4; *Women of Algiers*, 41

Denon, Dominique-Vivant, 5, 6, 93

Dickens, Charles, 55

Dicksee, Frank, *Leila*, 8, 10–11, 11, 41, 122

Diderot, Denis, 92

Djebar, Assia, 137n19

Donizetti, Gaetano, *Lucrezia Borgia*, 43

Dryden, John, 109, 110

Dubois, Abbé J. A., 93

Dumas, Alexandre: *The Count of Monte Cristo*, 35–36

Dumas, *fils*, Alexandre, *La Dame Aux Camélias*, 20, 81

Edwards, Amelia, 97, 102

Egypt, xx, 6, 15, 21, 67, 69, 94; in *The Jewel of Seven Stars*, 105; in *The Map of Love*, 129; Napoleonic invasion of, 5; as phantasmatic, 104

Egyptology, 94, 101, 103

Eliot, George, 43–44

Ellis, Havelock, 81

Farinelli, 121

fetishization, xiv, 32, 44, 49, 104, 138n37

Fitzgerald, Edward, *Rubáiyát of Omar Khayyám*, 4

Flaubert, Gustave, xv, 69; *Salammbô*, 6, 78, 99

Foucault, Michel, 59, 60, 139n1, 140n9

Freud, Sigmund, "The Uncanny," 131n3; and opera, 151n30

Galton, Francis, 55, 56

Gaskell, Elizabeth, 116

Gautier, Théophile, *Une Nuit de Cléopâtre*, 44–45

Gérôme, Jean-Léon, 7, 25, 103; and Buñuel, 127; *Almeh Performing the Sword Dance*, 8, 9; *Dance of the Almeh*, 8, 9, 69; and English nude, 137n18; *Phryne Before the Tribunal*, 17–18, 18; and Turkish Bath 41, 84

Girodet-Trioson, Anne-Louis, *Revolt of Cairo*, 31, 33

Giuliano, Carlo, 93, 95

Gliddon, George, 85

Gobineau, J. A., Comte de, 22

Great Exhibition, 89–90, 94

Greece, xiii, 2, 21, 94

Grisi, Giulia, 113

Grimshaw, John Atkinson, *Dulce Domum*, 41, 42

Gros, Antoine-Jean, *General Bonaparte Visiting the Pesthouse at Jaffa*, 31, 33

Haggard, Henry Rider, 106

Handel, George Frideric, *Rinaldo* 109, 110, *Alcina*, 117

harem: in Byron, xiii, 131n2; in *Confessions of a Thug*, 32; and cosmetics, 92; and domesticity, 15–17; and "haremization effect," 146n46; in opera, 110; as orientalist trope, xv, xvi, xvii, xix, 3; and lesbianism, 30; in *The Potter's Thumb*, 71; and reform, 64

Hemyng, Bracebridge, 20–22

Hénaff, Marcel, 10, 81, 132n15

Hoffman, E. T. A., 91

Hugo, Victor, 25, 43

hybridity: in Bulwer-Lytton, 114; and courtesan, 17, 20; and decadence, 87; as defined by Bhabha, 19; and the diva, 117; "eugenesic," 22, 84, 85; and female body, 59, 72, 122; and female poisoner, 46, 48, 51, 52, 54; and interiors, 94, 42; in jewelry, 96, 99, 97; in *The Jewel of Seven Stars*,